No Para

The World's Women Face the New Century

edited by

Judith Mirsky and Marty Radlett

PANOS/Zed

(c) The Panos Institute, 2000
All rights reserved

Published by The Panos Institute and Zed Books

The Panos Institute
9 White Lion Street
London N1 9PD, UK
Tel: +44 (0) 20 7278 1111
E-mail: panos@panoslondon.org.uk
Web site: http://www.panos.org.uk/

Zed Books Ltd
7 Cynthia Street
London N1 9JF, UK
Tel: + 44 (0) 20 7837 4014
E-mail: sales@zedbooks.demon.co.uk
Web site: http://zedbooks.demon.co.uk

Distributed exclusively in the USA by
St Martin's Press Inc
175 Fifth Avenue, New York
NY 10010, USA

British Library Cataloguing in Publication Data
A catalogue record for this book is available from the British Library
ISBN 1 85649 922 7 pb
      1 85649 921 9 hb

Extracts may be freely reproduced by the press or non-profit organisations, with acknowledgement. Panos would appreciate clippings of published material based on No Paradise Yet: The world's women face the new century.

Funding for this publication was provided by Sida, Danida, DFID, UNFPA, Misereor and NORAD. The Commonwealth Foundation, the Simon Population Trust, and User Perspectives of Fertility Regulation, Technologies and Services supported Suzanne Francis Brown, Swati Bhattacharjee and Pat Made, respectively. No opinions expressed in this document should be taken to represent the views of any funding agency or reviewer. Signed articles do not necessarily reflect the views of Panos or any of its funding agencies.

Commissioning editors: Judith Mirsky, Marty Radlett
Text editors: Wendy Davies, Judith Mirsky, Marty Radlett, Lezak Shallat
Design and production: Sally O'Leary
Printers: Cambrian Printers, Aberystwyth
Front cover picture: Joth Shakerley/Panos Pictures

Contents

Acknowledgements	iv
Preface	v
Introduction	vii
Sexuality under Wraps	1
Acknowledging adolescence in India	
Tested to their Limit	19
Sexual harassment in schools and educational institutions in Kenya	
Sacred Knots and Unholy Deals	39
The road towards pro-women legal reform in Egypt	
No Paradise Yet	61
Women and child custody laws in Bangladesh	
A Field of her Own	81
Women and land rights in Zimbabwe	
Women no Cry	101
Female-headed households in the Caribbean	
Legalised Cruelty	119
Anti-women laws in Pakistan	
Democracy in the Nation, but not at Home	137
Domestic violence and women's reproductive health in Chile	
File under "Hurt"	157
Domestic violence in Sri Lanka	
Less than Human Treatment	175
Maternity protection in Kenya	
'Business Orphans'	193
Maternity rights and child care in the Philippines	
No Mother's Day for Women Workers	213
Sex discrimination in Mexico	
Notes	233
Contributors	258

Acknowledgements

The Panos London Reproductive Health and Gender Programme wishes to acknowledge the help given by many individuals and organisations across the world in preparing this publication.

The following expert readers provided invaluable advice on individual chapters: Dr Junice Lirza Demeterio-Melgar, executive director, Linangan ng Kababihan Inc, The Philippines; Dr Sylvia Estrada-Claudio, Women and Development Program, University of the Philippines; Sandra Kabir, founder, Bangladesh Women's Health Coalition; Marie Assaad, coordinator, FGM Task Force, Egypt; Susana Vidales journalist and campaigner for working women, Mexico; Lynda Yanz, Maquila Solidarity Network, Mexico; Shahla Zia, Aurat Foundation, Pakistan; Dr Susie Jacobs, lecturer, Manchester Metropolitan University, UK; Sheila Stuart, coordinator, Caribbean Rights; Audrey Ingram Roberts, consultant, Unifem; Soledad Larrain, researcher, Chile; Teresa Valdes, Facultad Latinoamericano de Ciencias Sociales, Chile; Vimala Ramachandran, Indian Institute of Health Management Research; Sunila Abeyesekera, INFORM/Women and Media Collective, Sri Lanka; Dr Radhika Coomaraswamy, UN Special Rapporteur on Violence against Women; Mary Makoffu, gender coordinator, ICFTU–AFRO, Kenya; Abigail Kidero, formerly of Support Kenyan Women Against Sexual Harassment (SKWASH), Kenya.

Additional research for the chapter, 'A Field of Her Own', was undertaken by Susan Matetakufa.

The editors are grateful to Alexandra Fischer for careful proofreading and Rebecca Shaw for administrative assistance.

Preface

Two major conferences in the 1990s – the International Conference on Population and Development (ICPD) in Cairo in 1994 and the Fourth World Conference on Women in Beijing in 1995 – established firm international standards for the rights and health of the world's women. Central to both international agreements was the recognition that a sustainable and equitable society, free from all forms of violence and oppression, can be achieved only if women are fully empowered to take control of their lives, including their productive and reproductive roles.

Women's rights were a key issue at the 1999 United Nations General Assembly special session, which reviewed implementation of the ICPD Programme of Action. The 'ICPD + 5' review showed that although significant gains had been made in many countries in the five years since Cairo, particularly in the provision of reproductive health and family planning services, women's reproductive rights and sexual health remained severely compromised. Why?

Essential as health, information and other services are, UNFPA has learnt that the wider legal and social context is equally crucial to women's enjoyment of reproductive rights and health. The Beijing Platform for Action and the ICPD Programme of Action incorporate new and related objectives for addressing women's needs and rights in a holistic and integrated way.

This book examines some of the areas (many coinciding with Beijing's 'critical areas' of action) where legal and social reform is urgently needed. It highlights campaigns led by courageous women striving to liberate their own and other women's lives, some of which are beginning, against substantial odds, to make a difference. These efforts are wide-ranging: they include struggles to change the unequal basis of marriage, divorce and child custody; to legislate against domestic violence; to give women access to land in their own right; to combat sex discrimination in the workplace; to end sexual harassment in educational institutions; to raise awareness of the needs of adolescents; and to raise men's awareness of the responsibility involved in marriage and parenthood.

UNFPA believes that until such reforms are enshrined in law and accompanied by attitudinal and behavioural change at the individual, family and community level, the human rights of women – girls, young women, mothers, married women, never-married women, widows, divorcees and elderly women – will remain curtailed. Moreover, their reproductive rights and health, over which law and custom exercise such extensive control, will continue to be threatened. To take two examples from this book: a woman in rural Zimbabwe with no independent access to land will be much more likely to stay in an abusive marriage, which puts her health at risk, than if she had the economic resources to support herself; similarly, an adolescent girl in India who is denied information about sex and reproduction will be much more likely to fall pregnant inadvertently than if these subjects were openly acknowledged and discussed.

All the case studies in this book were researched and written by women journalists in the South and will also be disseminated through national print and electronic media; thus, the book contributes to another 'critical area' of action identified in Beijing, that of 'women and the media' – allowing women to speak for themselves. The personal stories they tell are often intensely painful; often, too, they are inspirational, demonstrating potently the determination of individuals and organisations to strive for women's human rights and fundamental freedoms.

Nafis Sadik
Executive Director, United Nations Population Fund (UNFPA)
April 2000

Introduction

Kenya:

"...women students have virtually retreated into their hostels.... They cook and eat from their rooms, use the library sparingly, attend class only when it is an absolute necessity and avoid social functions on campus. Even common rooms in their hostels have become no-go areas because it is no longer safe for them to use these facilities.... a lot of women cope with the harassment by walking in large groups, especially at night."

Egypt:

"After the formal ceremony Dalia and Ahmed sign the wedding contract.... 'I know we could have included things like my own right to divorce or to insist that if he takes another wife I could get my divorce automatically; but we agreed [not to],' says Dalia. 'It's not that we're against the idea, but it's not socially acceptable.'.... Ahmed adds, however: 'Had the new marriage contract that requests the man and woman to detail their stances on these issues been passed...it would have been all right – but we could not take the initiative.'"

Bangladesh:

"In Bangladesh, to be referred to as '*Josna-r Ma*' or '*Alamin-er Ma*' ('so-and-so's mother') is a sign of respect for the status that only motherhood can confer on women. Children are taught: '*Ma-er pa-er tolai beheste*' ('Paradise lies at your mother's feet').... Ironically, the same society that subsumes a woman's identity within motherhood routinely denies her the right to keep her children if her marriage breaks down."

Pakistan:

"In rape cases (*zina-bil-jabar*), a woman, if unable to prove she has not given her consent to sexual intercourse, may find herself convicted instead [for engaging in sex outside marriage].... If she conceives as a result of rape, the courts can interpret the pregnancy as proof of consent to sex and she may be liable to punishment.... Some of the falsely accused and imprisoned are children."

Mexico:
"Pregnancy testing as a condition of employment is routine; forced resignation if the worker becomes pregnant is commonplace. 'In this respect...employers have proved to be faithful believers in the Holy Spirit, since no one has yet to hear of a man being required, on asking for a job, to show proof of not having got anyone pregnant'."

The social straightjacket

Women facing the new century – as students, wives, mothers or workers – still find themselves up against walls of prejudice and discrimination that deny them basic social, legal and reproductive rights. The reports in this book describe, through the lives of ordinary women and men, some of the human costs that result and the determination of individuals and communities to achieve change.

The book was produced by the Panos Institute's Reproductive Health and Gender Programme, which works to raise awareness of progress and contradictions in policy, law, culture and economics that affect people's reproductive health and rights, particularly in developing countries. All the reports were commissioned from journalists in the South and each has been published in a major daily paper in their country of origin in one or more languages.

The purpose of *No Paradise Yet* is to help advance understanding of 'reproductive health' and 'reproductive rights' – new international development goals agreed at the United Nations International Conference on Population and

Development (ICPD) held in Cairo in 1994 and to encourage a holistic interpretation of the ambitions of the Cairo Conference. In particular, the reports in this book reveal the pressing need to address the wider social context of women's reproductive health and rights and to identify the policy and legal changes that will determine how much society as a whole is willing to allow women the freedom to determine the course of their own reproductive and sexual lives. The reports show that the realities of women's daily lives are still a very long way from the prospects held out to them at Cairo.

Increasingly there is evidence of the need to define women's reproductive rights more broadly – in a way that includes security, equal rights within the family and an appropriate environment for raising children, among other freedoms. Imagine, for example, a woman who has access through well-funded health care systems to a complete package of reproductive health services including the provision of contraceptives, infertility services, ante- and post-natal services, treatment for reproductive tract infections, and access to safe, legal abortion. Does she attain reproductive health and exercise reproductive rights?

In spite of the excellent services available to her, the answer could very easily still be 'no'. There are other questions that need to be asked. Is she sexually harassed as a student or at work? Is she one of the estimated 20 percent of women worldwide who have been physically or sexually abused at some point in their lives?[1] If she is raped, does her attacker escape the law if he marries her? Is she expected to marry young and bear her first child quickly? Has her community already subjected her to female genital mutilation (FGM)?[2] Once married, is her husband's right to conjugal relations enshrined in the law and does she have legal redress in the case of marital rape? Is she pressurised to abort her foetus if it proves female? Is she pressurised to continue bearing children until she produces enough sons? Does she have the same recourse to divorce as her husband? If divorced, is she granted a fair share of marital property? If divorced, does she have a fair claim to custody of her children? Is she required to prove that she is not pregnant in order to get a job? If she has a child, do laws and policies in her country enable her to breastfeed for at least the minimum length of time advocated by the World Health Organization (WHO) – if she is also struggling to stay in a job?

These are questions that millions of women face every day and the answers to them are critical to determining whether women can enjoy sexual and reproductive health and exercise their sexual and reproductive rights. They also have crucial implications for women's wider social and economic rights and freedoms.

From Cairo to a new century

Reproductive health and rights gained legitimacy and prominence as development goals as a result of a 20-year policy agenda adopted in 1994 – the 16-chapter Programme of Action of the UN International Conference on Population and Development. Such conferences act as fora for hammering out internationally-agreed development priorities, help shape the goals each country sets for its own development, and inform the strategies of international donors.

Throughout the preparations for the conference, the terms 'reproductive health' and 'reproductive rights' aroused intense opposition from a small group of states.[3] Their concerns centred on how much freedom adolescents should have to access information and services, and whether or not the conference would pave the way to more liberal policies on abortion. Nonetheless, after unprecedented rounds of negotiation involving thousands of government representatives, non-government organisations, activists and academics and a final nine days of deliberation, the Programme of Action was unanimously adopted by 179 nations.[4]

Introduction

The third international conference on population in as many decades, Cairo is spoken of as a 'paradigm shift' because it initiated a move away from a prevailing and narrow focus on family planning as a means to reduce rapid population growth rates. It formally pushed a wider range of health and rights concerns up the policy agenda. Of fundamental importance, Cairo recognised that women's empowerment is inextricably linked to their ability to shape their reproductive lives, and stressed the centrality of women's rights to fair population and development policies. Grounded in the principles of existing international human rights treaties, it declared in its guiding principles:

> Advancing gender equality and equity and the empowerment of women, and the elimination of all kinds of violence against women, and ensuring women's ability to control their own fertility, are cornerstones of population and development-related programmes.... [5]

From the perspective of women's groups and non-government organisations from all over the world, which had spent years advocating for a new policy consensus, the conference was a watershed.

The days of coercive policies to limit family size and slow population growth would, in theory, be gone. A new era would dawn where women's own perceptions of what constituted control over their sexual and reproductive lives would begin to be more fully realised. Henceforth not only women would be calling for change; governments, too, were putting their signatures to a new set of goals.

Extracts from the Cairo Programme of Action (emphasis added):

Reproductive health is a state of *complete physical, mental and social well-being* and not merely the absence of disease or infirmity, *in all matters relating to the reproductive system and to its functions and processes.* Reproductive health therefore implies that people are able to have *a satisfying and safe sex life* and that they have *the capability to reproduce and the freedom to decide if, when and how often to do so....* [6]

Reproductive rights embrace certain human rights that are already recognized in national laws, international human rights documents and other consensus documents... [and include the] *right to make decisions concerning reproduction free of discrimination, coercion and violence,* as expressed in human rights documents.... *full attention should be given to the promotion of mutually respectful and equitable gender relations* and particularly to meeting the educational and service needs of adolescents to enable them to deal in a positive and responsible way with their sexuality. Reproductive health eludes many of the world's people because of such factors as: inadequate levels of knowledge about human sexuality and inappropriate or poor-quality reproductive health information and services; the prevalence of high-risk sexual behaviour; *discriminatory social practices; negative attitudes towards women and girls; and the limited power many women and girls have over their sexual and reproductive lives....*[7]

A year later, the UN Fourth World Conference on Women, held in Beijing, re-endorsed Cairo's policy mandate, elements of which appeared in almost every one of the twelve areas of critical concern identified by Beijing as priority areas for action.

Though not a legally binding document for governments, the Programme of Action has set important international precedents and provides a valuable tool for advocating policy change in the fields of health and rights, especially in conjunction with other instruments to protect and promote women's human rights.

The closing decade of the last millennium saw a number of related steps towards the goal of recognising women's human rights. In 1993, the Declaration and Programme of Action of the World Conference on Human Rights declared that women's human rights must be protected not only in courts, prisons and other areas of public life – traditionally the domain where attempts have been made to uphold people's human rights – but also in the privacy of the home, a landmark step forward in attempts to protect women from domestic and sexual violence. The same year, a newly-created international human rights instrument, the Declaration on the Elimination of Violence against Women, cites such violence as "one of the crucial mechanisms by which women are forced into a subordinate position compared with men". The UN appointed a Special Rapporteur on Violence against Women to collect data and recommend measures to eliminate the violence and its causes.

In 1995, the World Summit for Social Development and the Fourth World Conference on Women each laid out further policy platforms emphasising the indivisibility of the human rights of women and the need for holistic approaches to ensure women's full participation in development.

Finally, in the last weeks of the century and 20 years after it came into being, the 1979 Convention on the Elimination of All Forms of Discrimination against Women (the Women's Convention), a legally-binding human rights treaty that has been ratified by 165 countries,[8] was given more teeth. Described as the international bill of rights for women, the Convention defines what constitutes discrimination against women and sets up an agenda for national action to end it. An "optional protocol" to the Convention was adopted in October 1999 – a mechanism that allows individual women or groups of women to take complaints of discrimination directly to the UN treaty monitoring body and have them considered, if they are unable to achieve redress in their own countries. Once operational, it will put the Women's Convention on an equal footing with other international human rights treaties that already have individual complaints procedures – for example, the International Covenant on Civil and Political Rights, the Convention on the Elimination of All Forms of Racial Discrimination, and the Convention against Torture and other Forms of Cruel, Inhuman or Degrading Treatment or Punishment.

Women's empowerment was the defining spirit of Cairo. Yet, in June 1999, at the five-year review of progress on implementation (ICPD+5), experts concluded that between 1994 and 1999, with notable exceptions, policies and programmes "tended to be shaped primarily by the health sector to the exclusion of other sectors which have an important role to play in this area".[9]

Conceptualising reproductive health and rights as issues of people's, primarily women's, empowerment, has different policy – and financial – implications from seeing them only as health concerns. Discussions about resource allocation at Cairo failed to put a price on the funds required to address empowerment issues. While ICPD+5 also failed to remedy this problem, it did urge donor countries:

> ...to increase significantly official development assistance for other elements of the Programme of Action as contained in Chapter 13 [National Action], in particular, improvement in the status and empowerment of women.[10]

Also agreed at ICPD+5 was the need to include sexual and reproductive health indicators in future when UN bodies monitor the human rights of women.[11]

Penalties, "protection" or power?

Useful as international deliberations are, for most women they are taking place on a different planet. Poverty combined with a lack of information, political and religious turbulence all combine with discrimination against women to generate deeply entrenched opposition to change. Today women still bear the brunt of reproductive health problems. They also face far greater restrictions on their lives than men because of society's perceptions of their reproductive roles. In the face of these constraints they make decisions and reorder priorities in a constant series of adjustments, compromises and agreements within partnerships characterised by harmony or conflict, in societies that offer greater or lesser room for manoeuvre.

Gender inequities that affect reproductive and sexual wellbeing not only exist within relationships but are embedded in social, legal, political and economic structures that can have a direct or an indirect, knock-on effect on women's reproductive wellbeing. Even the right to vote – the most basic prerequisite of citizenship - has not been granted to women in all states.[12] Across the world, women make up an average of just under 14 percent of parliamentarians.[13] This lack of political representation severely restricts the influence women can have over the laws that affect their reproductive lives.

Education and employment were championed by Cairo as two main engines of women's empowerment that would benefit their reproductive health and wellbeing, reduce fertility rates and improve child health.

Yet there are brakes on these twin engines of empowerment that are having a direct and damaging effect on women's reproductive wellbeing. One of the reports from Kenya in this book shows how crippling the effects of sexual harassment, including coercion and violence, can be, by denying girls and women access to education and employment. Many girls and women choose not to pursue – or are prevented by their families from pursuing – educational or career paths where they could face this kind of discrimination and violence. The various forms of violence against girls by their male peers serve to heighten parental fear, and that of girls themselves, of attending school. Harassment and coercion are also experienced at the hands of teachers, lecturers and other education professionals. Even where girls and women are not deflected personally or by their families from accessing education, encountering harassment compromises their ability to benefit from their schooling.

Employment policies, like those described in the reports from Mexico, the Philippines and Kenya, that discriminate against women who are married, pregnant or have young infants also compromise women's reproductive wellbeing as well as directly reducing their access to jobs and – in some cases – endangering their children's prospects of survival.

These issues, like most addressed in this book, are social or legal constraints that have an immediate and direct impact on women's and girls' reproductive and sexual lives. Policy changes at this level fall well within the ambit of Cairo and could be hastened by alliances between Cairo advocates and actors outside the health sector – educationalists and trade unionists, for example.

The book identifies five main areas where interventions outside the health sector would have an immediate and direct benefit for women's and girls' reproductive and sexual wellbeing: education (combating sexual harassment in schools and educational institutions); employment and income generation (ending discrimination against women who are married, pregnant or have a young infant, and discrimination against women in access to land); family policy (formulating and implementing fairer marriage, divorce and child custody laws); gender violence (in particular, campaigns against domestic violence); and programmes for youth (creating more openness about the realities of adolescence).

The list is not exhaustive and the issues are not neatly divided but each report in the book lays a particular emphasis on one or other of these five concerns; each shows how reproductive wellbeing is inextricably linked to social, economic, legal and political circumstances; each represents an area where there is a policy vacuum in the country concerned or an ongoing effort to achieve policy change; each was chosen because of its international relevance – every country in the world has its own story to tell on the issues raised here.

As many of the reports make clear, women are all too often penalised for transgressions against society's norms of sexual and reproductive behaviour in a way that men are not. In this collection we hear how Caribbean women, expected to be 'strong' at all costs, can be censored for not having a child or bear all the responsibility for contraceptive use and childrearing, while men are largely free to have children in or outside marriage without necessarily providing for their economic survival. In Bangladesh, divorced women frequently lose custody of their children. In Pakistan, false accusations of adultery against individuals who choose their own marital partner, can result in severe punishment and loss of liberty. We hear in other reports of women being offered various kinds of protection – for example, through laws providing for maternity leave – though, in reality, what is offered is often inadequate, even derisory, and women still pay unjustified penalties in the workplace for being mothers. What the women in these stories are seeking is an end to the penalties and a move beyond inadequate protection towards gaining power to implement change. If we too readily confine ourselves to health initiatives in the wake of Cairo, we are betraying the women whose lives are so vividly described in these reports.

Judith Mirsky
Marty Radlett

[1] *Violence Against Women*, World Health Organization, Fact Sheet WHO/FRH/WHD/97.8, 1997

[2] Genital mutilation involves cutting the genitals of girls and women, ranging from cutting the tip of the clitoris to removing the entire clitoris and the outer folds of the vagina. The practice is carried out in the belief that it will assure a woman's marriageability. Approximately 130 million women worldwide have undergone FGM

[3] Seventeen nations expressed reservations to specific chapters or paragraphs in the final text, while still endorsing the document

[4] For an examination of selected issues of reproductive health raised by the policy agenda set out at ICPD – including safe motherhood, unnecessary caesarian sections, prenatal sex selection, female genital mutilation and sexually transmitted infections, see the award-winning Panos book, *Private Decisions, Public Debate: Women, Reproduction and Population*

[5] Report of the International Conference on Population and Development, Cairo, 5–13 September 1994, A/CONF.171/13, 18 October 1994 (preliminary version)

[6] Para 7.2, Cairo Programme of Action

[7] Para 7.3, Cairo Programme of Action

[8] Although the Convention has been widely ratified, many countries have lodged substantive reservations to it. For example, several states have lodged reservations against Article 16, a core provision that guarantees equality between men and women in family life.

[9] Para 69, report of the International Forum for the Operational Review and Appraisal of the Implementation of the Programme of Action of the International Conference on Population and Development, which was held at The Hague from 8 to 12 February 1999, note by the Secretary-General, 7 February 1999, E/CN.9/1999/PC/3. One of two documents before the March preparatory committee for the ICPD+5 review for information.

[10] Para 95, Report of the Ad Hoc Committee of the Whole of the 21st Special Session of the General Assembly, Addendum, Key actions for the further implementation of the Programme of Action of the International Conference on Population and Development, 1 July 1999, A/S-21/5/Add.1

[11] Para 40, Report of the Ad Hoc Committee of the Whole of the 21st Special Session of the General Assembly, Addendum, Key actions for the further implementation of the Programme of Action of the International Conference on Population and Development, 1 July 1999, A/S-21/5/Add.1

[12] These rights remain elusive for women in at least two countries with a national legislature (Kuwait and the United Arab Emirates), women's rights to vote and to stand for election are not yet recognised, Women's Suffrage Chronology, Inter-Parliamentary Union (IPU), the World Organisation of Parliaments of Sovereign States. http://www.ipu.org/wmn-e/suffrage.htm

[13] Women in National Parliaments, situation as of 15 April 2000, IPU, http://www.ipu.org/wmn-e/world.htm

Sexuality under Wraps
Acknowledging adolescence in India

Swati Bhattacharjee

At an exclusive residential school near Calcutta, authorities have segregated deer living on the grounds into male and female enclosures, convinced that watching them copulate will be a bad influence on the schoolboy inmates. Some days male deer can be seen butting their heads against the female compound, trying to get in. Yet, at the very same school, the bathroom walls have to be whitewashed every few days to blot out students' explicit graffiti depicting oversized male organs and sexual acts.

Meanwhile at a Calcutta branch of Parivar Sewa Sanstha, the India chapter of the family planning organisation Marie Stopes, at least 20 petrified young girls line up for abortions every month. "Girls in school uniforms come to our clinic. Their fear of being found out is so extreme that they do not hesitate to take hazardous steps. Many girls deliberately leave behind their prescriptions for medicines to be taken after the operation, as they fear that their parents may find out and ask questions," says Indrani Mukherjee, a member of the organisation's Reproductive Health Education and Training unit.

While premarital sex among adolescents in India might not be so prevalent as it is in the West, existing research suggests that it is not so uncommon as widely perceived. According to adolescent health expert Shireen Jejeebhoy, roughly one in four to one in five adolescent boys and one in 10 adolescent girls are sexually active before marriage.[1] More recent data confirm this. In August 1998, the United Nations Population Fund (UNFPA) published figures based on eight independent studies conducted across India indicating that one out of 10 boys below 16 years of age has had sexual experiences.[2] In Chandigarth, the Commonwealth Youth Programme polled 100 teenagers between 14 and 16 years to find that 38 percent of boys and 27 percent of girls had experimented with sex.[3]

India also has 3.3 million adolescent mothers, an unsurprising number, given the prevalence of early marriage. Yet adolescent sexuality is a subject most Indians prefer to keep under wraps.

Cultural norms place a high premium on chastity with the result that adolescent sexuality is conveniently brushed under the carpet. Few Indian mothers speak to their daughters about sexuality. Parents' fear and distrust of their daughters' sexuality often prompts them to stop girls going to school once they reach puberty, especially in rural areas. The same parents would, however, send an adolescent daughter twice the distance to collect water or firewood. Boys and girls spend their early youth ignorant of, and deeply anxious about, masturbation, pregnancy, abortion and sexually transmitted diseases.

"The consequences of this ignorance are dire," says Jejeebhoy. For unmarried girls, "as many as 88 percent..., most from the rural areas, who sought abortion were unaware of the link [between] sexual relations and pregnancy".[4]

But the fear of AIDS, and a steadily increasing population, are forcing more and more people to acknowledge adolescent sexuality. Even politicians are beginning to brave the wrath of the electorate to address the issue. "We breed like rabbits yet shy away at the mention of sex education," remarked health minister Renuka Chowdhury contentiously in 1997, becoming the first high-ranking federal official to make a strong public statement in favour of sex education for adolescents.

Although extreme right-wing groups like the Rashtriya Swayamsevak Sangh, an ideological ally of the 1999 Hindu nationalist Bhartiya Janata Party government, have taken a public stand against sex education in schools, most sectors now concede that adolescents can no longer be kept in the dark about their reproductive faculties. From being an anathema, sex education is today the latest entrant into the realm of the 'politically correct'.

After remaining invisible for nearly 50 years, a fifth of the country's population of 900 million, officially defined as boys and girls between 10 and 19 years of age, have finally found a place in the national health policy. Earlier, health policies provided services only for pregnancy, childbirth and infant care, hygiene and nutrition. Post-Cairo 1994 (International Conference on Population and Development) and Beijing 1995 (Fourth World Conference on Women), the concept of reproductive health has finally widened – at least on paper.

The Reproductive and Child Health Care (RCH) programme, a new package introduced in India in 1996, includes several new components over previous policies. The adolescent health component is one of them.

While the government machinery – like a huge, sluggish pachyderm – is slowly creaking into motion to tackle the issue, it is non-government organisations (NGOs) and the media that have been taking the lead. Newspapers are running columns answering questions from adolescents on sex. Various channels of the state-run All India Radio, as well as private FM channels, broadcast call-in programmes where comperes punctuate their answers to queries on sex with pop music. Telephone hotlines in several cities are advising and reassuring callers on AIDS and sex-related questions. The average caller is a nervous school student, fumbling with a coin at the public booth or whispering urgently into the phone at home when no one else can overhear.

In response to the specific needs of their constituents, NGOs are shaping their own programmes. Some, like the Lucknow chapter of the Family Planning Association of India (FPAI) in northern India and Parivar Seva Sanstha, Calcutta, target school and college students. Others, like the Centre for Health Education, Training and Nutrition Awareness (CHETNA) in the western city of Ahmedabad, and the Children in Need Institute (CINI) in Calcutta, work among illiterate young people and school drop-outs in rural or semi-urban areas.

Disturbing trends

Such efforts, though belated, are very welcome because several disturbing trends are becoming apparent in the realm of adolescent sexual health. A module planned for medical officers in primary health centres, the smallest unit in the hierarchy of state health care, states that adolescents have sexual relations more frequently and at an earlier age than a decade ago, that the incidence of pregnancies among unmarried teenage girls is rising, and that sexually transmitted diseases (STDs) among adolescents are becoming more common.[5] Although studies of STDs among adolescents are few, data from studies among the general population and from treatment facilities suggest that STDs in the age group 15-25 years may have doubled since the 1980s, and the typical patient at an STD clinic is a young man aged between 20-25.[6]

Studies have also discovered that a large proportion of unmarried male adolescents and university students have had relations with a sex worker at one time; one multicentre study found that 19 percent of sexually active young men were clients of sex workers; as were 25 percent of unmarried male college students in Hyderabad, according to another study.[7]

At a November 1998 UNAIDS-sponsored conference, Young People's Voices on AIDS, college student Gunjan

Shah, a peer educator on family life education with the NGO Sevedham Trust, observed: "Pune...has a number of universities and institutes. There are sex workers whose major clientele is students." At the end of 1997, UNAIDS estimated 4.1 million Indians were infected with HIV, and both sex workers and their clients are at risk.[8]

By only touching upon teenage pregnancies, however, the module glosses over a more troublesome issue: the high rate of abortion among adolescents, especially unmarried girls. No national-level studies on abortions among unmarried adolescent girls have been done; however, hospital-based studies in various areas during the 1970s and 1980s point to a large number of unmarried adolescent abortion seekers.[9]

Estimates of their number by health officials and medical practitioners vary. Studies indicate that 27-30 percent of all abortion seekers in rural and urban hospitals, respectively, are adolescents.[10] But many adolescents prefer private, often illegal clinics for reasons of secrecy.

According to Dr Arati Basu Sengupta, a senior gynaecologist practising in Calcutta, 50 percent of the clientele seeking abortions from private practitioners in Calcutta are unmarried adolescents.

The rural scenario is even worse. Says Dr B.R Satpathy of the health and family welfare ministry, West Bengal, "My experience shows that at least 60 percent of the clientele of illegal abortionists in rural West Bengal are unmarried adolescents." Still another danger is that adolescents, especially unmarried girls, are likely to delay abortion to the second trimester – partly due to ignorance about pregnancy and availability of services, and partly due to social stigma. This increases health risks. A hospital study in Mumbai shows that one in four adolescents suffer complications after undergoing unsafe abortions.[11]

Early marriage, early motherhood

Although there are signs of declining adolescent fertility rates, the rate of decline among adolescents appears to be more gradual than among older women. And the absolute number of adolescent mothers in India continues to increase as a result of population growth.[12]

In 1992-93, 40 percent of Indian girls aged between 15 and 18 were found to be married. In some states, such as Bihar, Madhya Pradesh, Uttar Pradesh and Rajasthan, 60 percent of the adolescent girls are married.[13]

According to Jejeebhoy, who published a 1998 overview of existing studies on Indian adolescent reproductive and sexual behaviour, as many as 36 percent of married adolescents between 13 and 16 years of age and 64 percent of those between the ages of 17 and 19 years are mothers or pregnant with their first child.[14] Available data confirm that maternal deaths are much higher among adolescents than older women. Estimates from a community-based study in rural Andhra Pradesh suggest that adolescent maternal mortality ratios are nearly twice as high as those found among women aged 25 (1,484 and 736 per 100,000 live births, respectively).[15]

Nationally, only seven percent of married adolescents use contraceptives, and this is largely due to family and social pressures on a young bride to prove her fertility.[16] "I had my child eight years after my marriage," says Sukriti Chakraborty, a middle-class housewife in Jaipur village of Hoogly district, West Bengal. "In the last few years, I had stopped going to social functions and family gatherings. Women offered all kinds of advice. Even small children would question me on why I did not have babies. My relatives made me take magic potions, observe fasts and worship certain deities. I was relieved when my daughter was born."

Women bear the consequences of childlessness – or not bearing a son – despite the fact that sperm determines the sex of the child. These range from violent abuse, desertion or divorce to straightforward condescension and a resulting lack of self-esteem. Perhaps in deference to popular sentiment, family planning policies tend to avoid interfering before the birth of the first child and instead aim primarily at birth spacing and limiting family size to two children.

Says Dr D.K Ghorai, Joint Director, Health and Family Welfare, West Bengal, "Though our guideline is to discourage motherhood before 21, this is not a part of the policy." Consequently, say researchers, it is difficult for an average adolescent to utilise the contraceptive method most suitable for him or her. The oral pill is rarely promoted in the family planning programme while the condom is grossly underutilised. According to one study, 30 percent of married adolescents desire to delay the next birth or limit childbearing, but do not use any contraceptives.[17]

Skewed gender relations

Aggravating these disturbing trends is the complex web of gender relations. The overwhelmingly patriarchal value system robs most young women of control over their own bodies.

"We often get the impression that girls are emotionally pressurised into sex," admits Indrani Mukherjee from Marie Stopes. "Boyfriends often accompany girls seeking abortion to our clinics, sometimes pretending to be brothers. Instead of being worried about the welfare of the girl, they tend to bargain on the costs of the operation. We try to convince them of the dangers of taking the girls to cheaper clinics, where equipment is often not sterilised. But they are not easily persuaded."

Indian society, including most adolescents, holds a double standard regarding premarital chastity, particularly for young women. A 1992 magazine survey of readers of both sexes found that half of both men and women believed that it is imperative that a woman – but not a man – be a virgin at marriage.[18] A 1993 survey of urban educated youth aged up to 24 from 16 cities showed that 63 percent of females and 38 percent of males disapproved of couples having sexual relations before marriage, even if in love.[19]

Even so, young men and women are experimenting with sex, but without knowledge. When given the opportunity, both sexes seek answers to questions about sex, although the concerns of boys and girls vary. Arindam Sengupta, who is in charge of Friday Happening, says on a programme (now finished) on sexual queries on HMV FM, a private radio channel, "Boys mostly exhibit curiosity about a girl's sexual functions. Does she have orgasm? Can she ejaculate? Girls, on the other hand, show a great deal of anxiety over virginity. If she has premarital sex, can her husband find it out on the wedding night? Can a single [act of] intercourse destroy virginity/cause AIDS/cause pregnancy?"

Vina Lakhumalani, senior project officer at the British Council, Calcutta, agrees. Lakhumalani has conducted AIDS awareness programmes in several schools in and around Calcutta. "I find boys asking questions on different ways of intercourse, such as oral or anal sex. 'Is kissing safe?' 'Are condoms reliable?' Girls tend to ask about ruptured hymens and pregnancy. They also worry a lot about the first night of sex."

The connotations of 'sex education' also differ between boys and girls. At a workshop organised by the Indian Institute of Young Inspirers (IIYI), an NGO for youth, and the Family Planning Association of India (FPAI), Lucknow, in December 1996, college students were asked why they considered sex education essential. Boys stressed the dangers of myths and misinformation about sex, and the need for correct information. Girls, on the other hand, said that lack of information left them vulnerable to sexual abuse, and their family's grip over their sexuality, and through it their lives, curtailed their independence and career options. Demographer Margaret Greene regards society's views on sexuality as "a limiting factor in girls' lives".[20] Sex education could reduce such limitations.

More experimentation, less information

Both boys and girls, however, are far less inhibited about their sexuality and more prone to sexual experimentation than previous generations, say doctors and counsellors. But their ignorance about their bodies remains where it was years ago.

While there is a deluge of pornographic books, magazines and films on the market in India, there is very little in the way of simple, accurate information about sex for young readers. In schools, biology books either illustrate chapters on reproduction with the love life of toads, or teachers daintily skip chapters on human sex organs.

"Our biology teacher asked us to read the chapter on reproduction at home," says Papia Bhattacharjee, 17, a student at an elite school in Calcutta. Paromita Sen, 18, a student of psychology at a college in Calcutta, says that their teacher refused to explain a chapter on sexual abuse. He only dictated notes and left. "We hated him for that," says Sen. "Why can't teachers talk about it openly?"

Even higher education does not equip students with basic information about their bodies. "University students rush to us asking for an abortion the day after their first intercourse," says Indrani Mukherjee.

The letters written to newspaper columns and radio programmes betray the extent of this ignorance – and the stranglehold of old myths on young minds. Numerous boys complain of feeling weak and looking pale after masturbation. Does a drop of semen really equal a thousand drops of blood, they ask. Some other common queries are:

Does masturbation make one impotent? Do big breasts indicate more sexual prowess in women? Should girls stop taking certain foods during their period?

Adolescent girls know next to nothing of common afflictions of the reproductive system. "Every time I have periods, I thrash around like a fish brought upon land," complains a 14-year-old girl from Polian, a village near Calcutta, at a workshop for adolescents organised by the Children in Need Institute (CINI). Other teenage participants at the workshop for rural girls from lower income groups complain of fever on the first day of their period, and irregular and heavy bleeding. None of them have any information about what they see as 'shameful' diseases.

Learning body basics

A national workshop on Expanding Adolescent Relationships organised by UNFPA and Prerna, a Delhi-based health NGO, in 1996 showed that severe abdominal pain during periods and heavy discharge were two of the most common reproductive health problems suffered by adolescent girls in India. "Ignorance and shame force these girls to suffer in silence," says Sonal Mehta of CHETNA, which has begun projects to enlighten young girls about reproductive health.

Its programme of weekly health fairs targets mainly rural girls in the western states of Gujarat and Rajasthan. An innovative method used by CHETNA is making the girls wear an apron on which the major organs of the body are painted so they become familiar with their own anatomy. Organisations targeting school and college students run workshops or lecture sessions with audio-visual aids. To make these more socially acceptable, NGOs' programmes are usually packaged not as 'sex education' but 'health education' or 'AIDS awareness'. CHETNA calls its programme 'life-useful education', in which 'personality development' is part of the package.

Another interesting package has been developed by the Indian Institute of Young Inspirers (IIYI). Its 'adolescent counsellors' training programme' for students includes training in public speaking, drama, poster drawing and quiz competitions. The workshops are held at regular intervals over three-day periods. IIYI, which has branches in several towns and cities in the northern states of Uttar Pradesh and Bihar, is perhaps the only NGO working methodically towards developing a network of peer group counsellors.

Spreading the word

Despite their enthusiasm and innovative spirit, voluntary organisations can reach only a minute part of the adolescent population. If sex education is to have a meaningful impact on the reproductive health of adolescents and enable interventions to alter current trends relating to childbearing, abortion, sexually transmitted diseases and other afflictions plaguing adolescents, it has to have a much wider reach.

Efforts towards making sex education a part of the curriculum in schools have been underway for a long time. The National Council of Education, Research and Training (NCERT), a central government organisation which frames syllabi in an advisory capacity, has finally come up with a framework for 'adolescent education'. The framework, says J.L Pandey of the department of Population Education, addresses the critical concerns of today's adolescents through three major parts: information on the process of growing up, HIV/AIDS and drug abuse.

But how long will it take for the policy to percolate down to teenagers on the verge of unprotected sex? "At least another five years," says P.R Dasgupta, secretary, Department of Education of the central government. "We will first have to train the teachers and sensitise parents through parent-teacher societies." He admits that these bodies are weak, or often non-existent. "But it is the only way to do it," he maintains.

One mode of sex education, the 'question box activity', has already been introduced in some states. Students put their questions on sex in a box kept in the classroom. These are taken out at regular intervals and answered either by doctors invited for the purpose or by a teacher. Pandey hopes that most states will introduce this method by the end of 1999.

As for the adolescent component of the 1996 Reproductive and Child Health Care (RCH) policy, the plan is to approach adolescents through village-level health workers. "Basic physiology, dangers of early pregnancy, prevention and management of unwanted pregnancy and reproductive tract infections are the topics that will be discussed," says Dr B.R Satpathy.

But even the adolescent component of the RCH policy is only in an embryo stage. Most states are still trying to flesh out the guidelines laid down by the central government on services for adolescents. As of late 1999 in West Bengal, for instance, the health and family welfare department has just completed preliminary studies. "We are still trying to figure out the outlines of the adolescent component," says Dr Satpathy. "It will take at least another two years for the proposed adolescent services to take off." Meanwhile, the training of village-level health workers on adolescent health services is still underway. And so, for the moment, it is left to the NGOs to break the ice.

Breaking cultural taboos

Anyone attempting to break cultural taboos has an unenviable task. Sex is still very much a live wire for Indians, educated or illiterate. Anything associated with sex is not quite respectable and anyone willing to talk about it is regarded with deep suspicion.

Says Mahua Sen of the Reproductive Health Education

Project, a unit of Parivar Seva Sanstha, Calcutta, "Principals say we can talk about AIDS but not of condoms; menstruation and hygiene are OK but not pregnancy; health risks of early pregnancies is fine but not contraceptives."

The majority of parents are still unwilling to enlighten their children. "There is no need", "How can mothers talk about such things?" are the common refrains.[21] Many NGOs, in fact, had to give up attempts to take AIDS awareness campaigns to schools as principals closed their doors on them, claiming that their students came from 'good homes' and need not worry about AIDS.

Even surveys have been abandoned. The Indian Council of Medical Research (ICMR), a government body, initiated a country-wide, 18-month project in 1996 to assess the attitude of adolescents on matters of sexuality. A team of researchers doing the project in Hooghly district of West Bengal were unable to conduct the survey. "The school principals did not allow us to distribute the questionnaire to students," says Dr Arunangshu Chakraborty, a researcher with ICMR.

"We had to stop our programme on sexual information in Goa after only a few weeks," says Arindam Sengupta of HMV FM radio station. "We were accused of titillating the audience."

In 1998 two school principals in Bihar were sacked for screening a short film on menstrual hygiene, even though the audience consisted of teachers.

"This prudishness is a symptom of incipient control of women's bodies by the patriarchal system," says Jasodhara Bagchi, director, School of Women's Studies, Jadavpur University, Calcutta. "Making women aware means sharing power – especially over reproductive health decisions. If the authorities get scared to go beyond these norms, sex education will never reach its targets."

Power patterns

Women, including Indian activists, who argued in Cairo and Beijing for adolescents' right to information had visions of enlightened, empowered young women who could take decisions about their bodies, their choice of partner, their sexuality and their fertility. Both the ICPD Programme of Action and the Beijing Platform for Action speak of adolescents' rights to "privacy, confidentiality, respect and informed consent ".[22]

At home, Indian women have fought for the right to information on sexuality as a condition of empowerment. "We in the women's movement demand information on sex for deconstructing the power structure which appropriates women's sexuality and keeps it under control," says Bagchi. If these were the goals, there is little to rejoice about. With the honourable exception of a few NGOs, what passes for sex education in India is more of 'a guide to safe motherhood'. Instead of deconstructing gender stereotypes, sex education is being used by many to reinforce them.

None of the government guidelines on sex education, whether the NCERT framework for adolescent education or the ICMR Module for Primary Health Centres, mentions choice; the ICMR module talks of the development of adolescents into 'responsible adults'. Consequently, the sex education modules contain nothing on how to negotiate use of contraceptives with a partner, what to do in case of unprotected sex or how to resist sexual abuse. This, despite a 1990 Ministry of Welfare study that estimated that almost 25 percent of all rape victims are under 16.[23]

"The concept of responsible choice is undoubtedly central to sex education. But we could not keep it in our framework," admits J.L Pandey. "And this was a deliberate decision. We know that at the [official] level, there will be strong objections to the idea. The present framework, which talks mainly about the male and female body,...is only a step forward, an attempt to make sex education acceptable."

Taking shortcuts

The easiest shortcut to legitimising sex education in India is to invoke the concept of motherhood – a glorified status in a country with a strong preference for sons. The material handed out by state governments for 'population education' or 'health education' talks basically about the girls as mothers and not much else besides.

The population and health manual distributed by the Madhya Pradesh State Council of Education, Research and Training promotes equality of sons and daughters, especially in educational opportunities. But why should women be educated? Because "educated women can decide the number of children they have and can raise the children properly".[24] The 'future mother' viewpoint is strongly held by some government officials. The result is that important information comes garbed in a strict moral code. At a 1998 workshop on sex education held in West Bengal by CINI, at least 20 teachers from several neighbouring villages were asked to comment on the need for sex education. The reasons given were: "so that girls know the right time to have a baby", "so that they can look after the baby well", "so that they do not start relationships with boys before marriage".

The last, the fear of promiscuity, is the most potent of all fears. And ironically, people who a decade ago thought sex education was a foreign virus that led to promiscuity among the young, now think of it as an antidote.

Indeed, preserving traditional social mores is, to many, the primary goal of sex education. According to a researcher with ICMR, "The main aim of the adolescent component of the reproductive health policy should be to control promiscuity among adolescents." Basant Das, who heads the NGO *Sneha* (Affection) in Orissa which conducts programmes on AIDS awareness in schools of Bhubaneswar and Cuttack, says that the main message of their programme is "no sex before marriage".

But will sex education couched in moral dictums be acceptable to most adolescents? "I find the idea of love without sex ridiculous," says Swapnendu Bose, a medical student. "If I love and care for someone, why should I wait for the licence of marriage to be able to make love? Our society allows us to watch sexually explicit movies and yet expects us to stay chaste till our wedding day."

Of course, for every young man like Swapnendu, there are many others who believe in abstinence, either as a matter of principle or of policy.

Nilkantha Misra, a project officer at the Orissa State Council of Education, Research and Training, reveals that in the 20 schools where the question box activity has been introduced, questions on premarital sex are common. The answer teenagers receive is succinct: no sex before marriage.

In holding rigid ideas about adolescent sexuality, exponents of 'just-say-no' sex education deny adolescents choice and responsibility, and their attitudes often reduce sex education to a farce. "Our school had started a weekly class, where we could ask questions about anything that was bothering us," says a 15-year-old student of a highly reputed convent school in Calcutta. "After the first few months, it has now become the Bible-reading class."

"When the government itself has acknowledged that adolescents are increasingly becoming involved in premarital relationships, why should it skirt round this important issue?" asks feminist scholar Jasodhara Bagchi, director of the School of Women's Studies, Jadavpur University, Calcutta. "Unless the modules of sex education put premarital sexual activities on the agenda, they will not be able to empower women such that they can guard their own health, regardless of whether they choose to become mothers or not."

Equipping a young woman to assert control over her body and sexuality, including controlling her fertility and resisting sexual abuse within or outside the family, calls for nothing short of a transformation in the attitude of the government and the society as a whole.

"In a context like India, where adolescent marriage is often synonymous [with] and immediately followed by adolescent childbearing, it is obvious that any effort to change the way young girls are perceived is potentially revolutionary," writes Margaret Greene. "Understanding the requirements for working with adolescents will take us a long way toward grasping the meaning of the shift from family planning to reproductive health. "[25]

But if government and its officialdom are wary, hesitant or resistant to this 'perceptual revolution', adolescents themselves embrace it. Two teenage siblings who took part in a training camp organised by CINI explain.

"Earlier, I was scared to talk to boys. Now when my parents try to stop me, I try to convince them that I am not doing anything bad. My mother used to shut me up before, but now she listens to me," says 18-year-old Krishna.

"My friends and I have stopped teasing girls. We don't need to, we can talk to them when we want. If we tease now, maybe they will stop talking to us," adds 16-year-old Ramen.

Krishna and Ramen, a sister and brother from the West Bengal village Khadibedia, have changed. And that change came about in only three days. About 30 teenagers were brought together to talk about body changes during puberty, STDs, risks of early motherhood and unwanted pregnancies as well as common problems such as malnutrition, diarrhoea and environmental hygiene. Those three days were enough to destroy the inhibitions that they had inherited from a hundred prior generations. Now, young women and men aged 14-22 years sit together regularly in the village to discuss different issues.

Mita Naskar, a member of the village council and mother of a teenage daughter, said such free mixing of female and male youths was beyond the villagers' imagination. But it has not led to problems. Instead, incidents where young men tease girls, hurling comments or singing lines from raunchy Hindi film songs, have diminished. Where the law, police and ever-alert guardians failed, the adolescents themselves succeeded. And parents recognise that breeding fear and suspicion in the minds of young men and women towards each other only distorts their natural curiosity. Some 80 percent of families in a neighbouring village, Dakshinbagi, are now willing to send their teenage daughters to the CINI camp on sex education.[26]

Tested to their Limit
Sexual harassment in schools and educational institutions in Kenya

Juliana Omale

At Maseno University in Vihiga district, about 400 km from Nairobi in the south-west of Kenya, a third-year male student boasts about his exploits in humiliating female students. He specialises in embracing and groping women with or without their consent. Disregarding the opinion of a female student interviewed with him, who has been trying to make the point that someone touching your body without your consent amounts to harassment, he says, "*Ah, Mimi ninaleseni ya kudara wanawake na kila dame anajua*" ("I am licensed to embrace women and every lady knows that").

"The attitudes of male students are disturbing," says Arthur Okwemba, a recent graduate of Egerton University, Njoro, about 200 km from Nairobi. "They want to assume that when a woman agrees to be taken out on a date she is essentially giving the nod to the start of a relationship often leading to harassment and molestation," says Okwemba. At male students' hostels, while gathering information on sexual harassment at the Universities of Egerton, Kenyatta (in Nairobi) and Maseno, he encountered lewd graffiti and picture pin-ups of naked women on the walls. "The prevailing attitude is that a woman is at best a parasite on the financial resources of a man and that she should at least show her appreciation by giving sexual favours," he says.

A diet of discrimination

Women striving for higher education are tested to their limit by the hostile social and economic environments that define student life.

At university, young women make up less than 30 percent of the student body, reflecting a gender gap widened by drop-out through primary and secondary years. Deputy Vice Chancellor of Academic Affairs at Nairobi University, Professor Florida Karani notes that the socio-academic environment at the male-dominated universities "impacts negatively on women students". She says female students are often depressed, lack confidence, assertiveness and self-management skills and fall prey to early marriages and unplanned pregnancies.

Sexual harassment has been identified as a clear constraint on the educational advancement of women, according to the Nairobi-based Forum for African Women Educationalists (FAWE) comprising female education ministers, vice-chancellors and other policy-makers.

In recent years, countries as far afield as South Africa, Chile and the Philippines have joined the growing number giving legislative attention to the problem, according to the International Labour Organization.[1] Sexual harassment has been discussed primarily as a workplace issue. Definitions focus on three criteria: that conduct by a colleague is unwelcome, unreasonable and offensive; that a woman has grounds to believe her objection to such conduct would disadvantage her in connection with her employment; that the conduct creates a hostile working environment.

The negative attitudes of many male students and some university staff create an intimidating, hostile and humiliating working environment for many women students. Women students and academics are frequently without sufficient strength of numbers or institutional power to challenge male abuse of power.

Unwelcome sexual behaviour – insults, remarks and jokes, unwanted physical contact, requests and even threats – create a daily diet of discrimination against women students.

Fatuma Chege, who lectures in the Department of Education at Kenyatta University says harassment occurs all the time. She cites the examples of women students being groped and fondled as they queue for meals at the cafeteria, and of catcalling. She is concerned when harassment intrudes into tutorials and female students are afraid to contribute to discussions for fear of being drowned out by the catcalls from their male colleagues.

Chege categorises sexual harassment as any verbal or physical action that leaves the recipient uncomfortable and demeaned both physically and psychologically. "When it has a sexual orientation, it becomes sexual harassment because it is directed at the victim because of his or her gender," she says.

"The concept of sexual harassment is not African," she adds. "We have no vocabulary for sexual harassment in our local languages." But she believes that since the feelings of debasement are universal to all victims, there is no excuse for the subject to be swept under the rug. A founder of the Gender Interest Group (GIG) at Kenyatta University, she argues that "if the victim remains silent, it is used as an excuse for bad behaviour". GIG discusses current gender issues of concern to the university community. It is creating awareness, especially among girls, that they need not suffer humiliation and that it is all right to put their foot down and say "No!"

"After years of conditioning to be subservient and to step aside for the male, it isn't surprising to find that our girls feel powerless to turn the tide," she says. The result is that women students have virtually retreated into their hostels and their social life on campus is curtailed. They cook and eat from their rooms, use the library sparingly, attend class only when it is an absolute necessity and avoid social functions on campus. Even common rooms in their hostels have become no-go areas because it is no longer safe for them to use these facilities.

Chege is concerned that this isolation is diluting the quality of women's education. "This means they have no access to information, and they shun leadership roles because they are afraid to draw attention to themselves."

"Girls are compromised by their naivety and trust of authority figures from babyhood right through primary and secondary school," she adds. "In our country the authority figure is often male and cannot be talked at. I am always challenged for contravening culture, but I say we make culture by what we decide."

Reactions by universities to allegations of sexual harassment have been minimal, she claims. She takes issue with the much-flouted regulation that requires women's hostels to be locked up and inaccessible to visitors by 10.00 pm. "It is no surprise that the regulation applies to women students, but worse is that janitors can be bribed by men to look the other way."

"There are no statements or guidelines to regulate behaviour in our public universities and implementing rules and directives is difficult," she says. Sexual harassment guidelines do not exist. It becomes acceptable as a way of life that follows a woman right into the workplace.

Dr Sheila Wamahiu, a former lecturer at Kenyatta University and coordinator of the Ad Hoc Group of Women Educational Researchers, says, however, that the code of ethics for teachers is clear about the relationship between teacher and student: "A lecturer should not be giving marks to a girl because he is sleeping with her."

In December 1999 six male lecturers from Egerton University were suspended for sexual harassment. Described as notorious pursuers by female students, they were also accused by some male students of demanding money in exchange for better grades.

Peer 'pressure'

Twenty-two year old Josefynne Miingi, a third-year student at Egerton University, feels the worst offenders are students, and that most lecturers tend to be sensitive and sympathetic to the plight of female students. However, "victims don't report to the university authorities," she says. The general attitude is that discussion is a waste of time and likely to generate unnecessary publicity, especially for the woman. Although a Women and Gender Analysis Programme which has student members is open for those seeking counselling and direction, members like Miingi feel that its impact is not being felt.

Girls are constantly being pressurised for sex, and according to Miingi a lot of rape occurs under such situations. "You aren't really safe anywhere because you could be attacked in your own room," says Miingi. She says that in order to be left alone, one must learn to be loud and outspoken on women's rights. The alternative is to get a boyfriend – especially one who is well built – to fight off unwanted attention from members of the opposite sex.

Short of fighting back, a lot of women cope with the harassment by walking in large groups, especially at night. And women on campus learn soon enough where not to go. The main library is a no-go area at night because of poor lighting in the vicinity. "We stopped using the main library in our first year because getting there meant crossing a large unlit area at night," she says.

At Maseno University, female economics students complain that they are unable to leave the smaller Siriba campus at night for the main campus where the library is located because they have genuine fears for their safety. It has meant forfeiting valuable time and sacrificing the quality of their academic work.

For fourth-year student Mariam, the students' cafeteria is out of bounds. She could not stand the way some male students groped at her as they queued for meals. She says she would rather pay more to eat in peace elsewhere.

Also out of bounds to her are the rooms of male colleagues. She says it is taken for granted that one is having an affair with the occupant of the room if one is seen going there too frequently. "But even just being on friendly terms with a male student is enough to earn you trouble. They say you are loose. You can't win."

A third-year student requested anonymity for her testimony. "I was in my room when a guy who is well known to me breezed in and lunged at me. I pushed him away but he kept groping. Suddenly he stopped and sat up abruptly. Then he started to apologise and that is when I realised that he had ejaculated. I have forgiven him but this incident caused the break-up of our academic discussion group. It has changed everything for me."

At Jomo Kenyatta University College of Agriculture and Technology first-year women students say they are more likely to be harassed than seniors. Women in their first year are usually harassed by the occupants of Hall Six where most senior male students reside.

Asked why he made catcalls whenever a female student in a short skirt walked past, a male student replied in corrupted Kiswahili, *"Wanajaribu kutushoo kago na wanajua kuna wanaume ambao wanatafuta hiyo kitu"*, which translates as "They are showing off their private parts and they know very well there are men [like us] who are looking for that thing."

Another male student put it this way: *"Tuna whistle ndiyo wengine wanaofildria kuvaa vim kama hivyo wapate funzo na wajiepushe,"* which translates as "We whistle so that others who may be thinking of wearing their short skirts may learn a lesson and stop."

Poverty and prostitution

Students are in a rat race for education scholarships and loans that are too few and therefore highly competitive. Increasingly institutions are making people pay for services that were once heavily subsidised by the state. The availability of student loans schemes through the Higher Education Loans Board (HELB) since 1996 is no guarantee that a student will get adequate funds to finance his or her university career. The situation is likely to worsen following increases in tuition and boarding fees.

The harsh economic climate exposes some women to another, and distinct, threat to their sexual and reproductive health – prostitution. 'Sugar daddies' are usually family men of means – including prominent community leaders or public officials – who buy sex for money or maintain 'mistresses' in institutions of learning. They may also be single affluent young men or university colleagues and acquaintances.

Jane Awuor (a pseudonym) is an ambitious science student pursuing a diploma at a national polytechnic in Kenya's coastal town of Mombasa, 500 km south-east of Nairobi.

She uses a false name because she is also a prostitute selling her body to college mates, lecturers and well-heeled men in Mombasa town.

Her mother knows nothing of this other side to her first-born child's life and Awuor is anxious that she never learns the truth. Divorced and struggling to raise four other children on her paltry earnings as a factory secretary, she cannot give Awuor more than the tuition fee. "I understand her predicament so I am forced to 'survive' ." Her tuition fees are nearly 5,000 Kenyan shillings (US$78) per term, and hostel accommodation and food cost more. Students are also required to make financial arrangements for their internship when they will be posted to industrial plants and institutions to gain practical experience relevant to their disciplines.

A chance meeting at the college gates led to the offer of an internship for Jane with a well-known company in Mombasa paying KSh 200 (US$3) per day and payment of her rent – in exchange for sex.

Jane's relationship with her current client is strictly practical. There are no frills about it and certainly no romance. She looks on the arrangement as 'help' out of an otherwise distressing situation. She describes her predicament as "when someone uses you...[and] you have no alternative but to give in to the act".

A 'girl-unfriendly' learning environment

Young women who reach university have already survived the pitfalls at secondary and even primary school level, where many student attitudes first begin to form.

Sixty-three percent of girls of primary school age enrol in school each year. According to the Ministry of Education, just over a third of the girls and over half the boys who enrol in primary class one complete eight years in school. With Kenya's worsening economic problems, it is likely that the figures are much worse than the official statistics. Between 1985 and 1995, primary enrolment rates fell for both boys and girls.[2] The Ministry notes that girls' performance is also jeopardised by specific factors such as teenage pregnancy, forced or early marriages, son preference in certain communities, socio-cultural practices including female initiation rites, domestic work and poverty at household level.

Kenyan researchers Dr Wangoi Njau and Dr Sheila Wamahiu note that sexism, whether conscious or not, is responsible for the continuation of practices such as female circumcision, early marriage and early childbearing, which raise the drop-out rate of girls from school. It also influences family decisions to educate (or not educate) girls and produces a girl-unfriendly learning environment at home and within the community.

The heavier household workload of girls is responsible for tardiness, absenteeism, poor concentration and hence lower examination performance leading to either 'self'- or enforced withdrawal of girls from school. Girls' labour is not only a cultural demand, but in many cases it may be absolutely imperative for family survival.

Negative attitudes towards girls further permeate the classroom, manifesting themselves in gender discrimination in textbook content, the teaching/learning processes and the peer culture.

"Sexual harassment of girls, both within and outside the classroom, can be seen as a reflection of the low status accorded them in essentially sexist cultures," say Njau and Wamahiu.

Dangerous hours

The various forms of violence against girls by their male peers serve to strengthen parental fear, and that of the girls themselves, of attending school.

Anastasia Kalekye from Kangundo, nearly 60 km from Nairobi, in Machakos district, recalls how her mother threatened to withdraw her from primary school after she was harassed coming home from school.

It is common practice for primary school students in their final year at school to be detained after school for extra tuition. Teachers are under pressure to prepare their pupils for the final examinations, which are very competitive, only a small proportion of candidates making it to the better equipped and staffed national public schools. "This meant that some of us got home as late as 9.00 pm because of the distance, yet we were expected to be in school by 6.30 am the next morning," says Kalekye. "One day I was nearly raped by a man who hid up a tree near our home." She says only her screams saved her. Her mother decided that enough was enough and confronted the schoolteachers the next day.

"She told them my honour was more precious than the piece of paper [the certificate of primary education] they were preparing us for." The result was that the school relaxed the tuition hours somewhat because many other parents were unhappy at their children being detained so late and alarmed by reports of girls being sexually harassed or abused on the way home from school.

But the whole experience left Kalekye's mother unconvinced that the benefits of attending school were worth the dangers for her daughter. Anastasia dropped out of school after class eight.

In a village in Vihiga district, Veronica knows all too well how real these dangers can be. (Her name and her mother's have been altered to protect their identities.)

Veronica was forced to drop out of primary school one year short of the final examination after she became pregnant in class seven. She was 14 years old. Much as she loves her son, she cannot erase the pain from her mind that he is a product of gang rape by a group of four schoolmates.

"Before it happened, these boys used to harass us on our way to and from school," she says. "They threatened to beat us if we didn't give in to their sexual demands." The boys had a reputation for ruthless bullying. They were a class ahead of Veronica, but much older than their classmates as they had repeated some years. Repetition of classes in children's middle years at school accounts for older candidates at the end of the primary school course. It is not uncommon for a class to span an age range of three or four years.

According to Veronica, she and a friend opted to stay in after school to finish their homework and avoid being caned by their teachers the next day. It was almost inevitable that they would encounter the gang of boys on their path home. Her friend agreed to go along with them. Veronica, faced with the prospect of having to walk the remaining three kilometres home alone and in the dark, had little choice but to join them. "I thought I would be able to convince my girlfriend to find a way of escaping the clutches of the bully boys and avoid any harm."

They ended up in the home of one of the boys. In the Luhya tribe, a boy can no longer live in his mother's house and is required to build himself an *esimba* – a hut, where he is free to entertain his friends after he comes of age. It was therefore unlikely that the boys who attacked Veronica and her friend would have been interrupted by adults in the compound.

Traditionally, a boy comes of age after being circumcised at the age of 14 or older. Many parents now opt to have their sons circumcised at a younger age of seven or less since the logistics and economic burden of hosting traditional initiation rites are unrealistic for most families. However, the child misses out on the traditional sex education and instruction in clan or tribal etiquette that would have been imparted to him if the old ways were followed.

After the attack, Veronica and her mother Savita reported it to the headmaster. Her attackers got wind that the villagers had launched a search for them and they disappeared. They have not been seen since and are rumoured to be in Nairobi. The matter ended there.

Veronica would like to continue her education, but as a young mother her ambitions must be postponed. Her mother had placed her hopes for the family's betterment in her eldest daughter's education. "My husband left us, after complaining that I was not giving him sons," she says. With five other daughters she has little social standing in her community, which places a premium on the birth of sons. "When I sent my daughter to school, I expected her to show me a good KCPE (Kenya Certificate of Primary Education) at the end of eight years," says Savita with bitterness. "I got a grandson instead."

Violence in schools

School itself is not always a safe haven. Media attention has highlighted notorious cases of violence within schools over the last decade.

In July 1991, a little-known Catholic secondary school – St Kizito, in Tigania, Meru district, and 400 km north of Nairobi – erupted in an orgy of rape and anarchy. Nineteen schoolgirls died at the hands of their male schoolmates. Seventy-one others were reportedly raped.

The St Kizito incident caused public and international outrage, especially following the headmaster's casual comment that the boys had never meant to hurt the girls but "only wanted to rape".

Some of the boys involved in the violence were brought to court and charged. The school was closed and an official at the Education Department of the Kenya Catholic Secretariat said that following the St Kizito incident, the Church was shifting towards more single-sex secondary schools.

The media clamour over St Kizito had barely died down when, in January 1993, 13 girls at Hawinga Girls Secondary School in Siaya district, Western Kenya, were attacked and raped in their dormitories by a group of armed men.

And on the night of 7 July 1996 a number of girls were attacked and raped at Mareira Mixed Secondary School, a Catholic-sponsored school in Muranga, Central Province. The perpetrators were said to have been male students and villagers.

Fred Omwoyo, a curriculum developer at the Kenya Institute of Education, recalls the case of a secondary school, also in Meru district. The school was burnt down by the boys when the headmaster introduced a policy to keep the boys away from the girls at night. "It was inevitable that mutual friendships existed between the two sexes and it was considered normal for the boys to escort the girls to their dormitories after prep."

According to Omwoyo, the headmaster felt that this situation would breed sexual temptation and immorality, so he made the girls leave for their dormitories 10 minutes before the boys. "The boys were mad," says Omwoyo, "It turned out that they were angry about a lot of other things at the school, so they burnt it down."

According to researcher Dr Sheila Wamahiu, who has been involved in a pilot study on sexual harassment in primary schools, there are several documented cases of rape and violence perpetrated by schoolboys against schoolgirls. She maintains that because none of the victims died, the incidents did not attract media attention or public condemnation.

Teachers betraying trust

In 1996, Keveye Girls Secondary School, a little-known school in Vihiga district, attracted media attention after it was alleged that a number of students had become pregnant. In the aftermath of public outrage at the school administration, the provincial education officer planned to transfer the headmistress to a school in the neighbouring district. Concerned parents argued that the headmistress had in fact improved discipline and raised academic standards. With the school's board of governors and a local Member of Parliament they intervened to get the transfer rescinded.

Instead, three male teachers at the school were implicated in the pregnancies of the girls, resulting in the transfer of two of them. The third teacher remains at the school.

Even primary school girls are under pressure to sell sex to their teachers in exchange for better grades. At a primary school in Ebusakami village in Vihiga district, girls complained about two teachers who beat them if they turned down their advances and especially if they reported the harassment to the school authorities. The two teachers have since been transferred from the school.

Moses Kibet, an assistant chief in the Sambirir division of

Elgeyo Marakwet district, about 800 km north-west of Nairobi is disturbed by incidents of sexual relationships between teachers and their students. He and other parents in the area feel that cases are either not being reported often enough or receive little attention from school administrators.

Kibet abhors what he calls "acts of mercy" by poverty-stricken parents to absolve errant male teachers caught in the act with their daughters. It is a common practice for the family that has been wronged to accept 'compensation' in cash or kind from the offending individual or his family.

"They pay compensatory money and gifts to parents, knowing that they could land in a lot of trouble if the matter was brought before a court of law. So the matter ends there," he says.

For example, at a primary school in the small farming town of Kitale, situated about 400 km north-west of Nairobi in the Rift Valley Province, a class eight pupil was made pregnant by her teacher. Sensing trouble, he obtained a large loan, most of which he used to pacify his student's father who was also a teacher. The two men's colleagues were surprised at this turn of events. The least they expected of the girl's father was that he would lodge a formal complaint and follow it through the school administration system and into the courtroom if need be.

It is said the offending teacher used the remainder of his loan to grease the palms of the divisional education officer, who was well aware of the case as it had been duly reported to him earlier. The matter ended there.

At another primary school in Kitale a female teacher says that male colleagues implicated in sexual harassment and pregnancies at the school are still teaching there because they received overwhelming support from the rest of their colleagues. "They tend to side with their own, even in the most obvious of cases," she says. "During a disciplinary committee session at the school, a teacher who was asked to explain his conduct claimed that the girl in question had tempted him to molest her! No action was taken."

At yet another primary school in Kitale a pupil who reported to the headmaster that she was being harassed by her teachers was shocked when the headmaster joined her harassers' bandwagon. She reported the matter to some female teachers who opted to return her to her parents for her own safety.

According to Dr Paul Ogula, from the Department of Education at the Catholic University of Eastern Africa in Nairobi, Kenya's education system is in crisis. He believes that as long as some school heads continue to run their schools like personal fiefdoms, the violence and chaos that characterise some Kenyan schools will not end.

'Skwashing' the problem

While sexual harassment is receiving the first glimmer of official recognition in the workplace, there remains a policy vacuum when dealing with the issue in schools and educational institutions.

In the workplace

The truth for too many women is that they feel they must put up with sexual harassment if they want to get a job, keep a job or be considered for promotion. Despite the theoretical acceptance of gender equity as a development aspiration, there has been no coordinated effort at national level to incorporate commitments made to international treaties into national law, policy and planning. Kenya is signatory to the Women's Convention (the Convention on the Elimination of All Forms of Discrimination Against Women) and ratified it as early as 1984, but action taken to implement it is sporadic. In 1996, Parliament adopted a parliamentary motion on the implementation of the Beijing Plan of Action but still no budgetary provision has been made for it.

Researchers have found that sexually harassed women do not report their ordeal to the authorities because they fear being accused of inviting the harassment and are unsure of what steps to take. Even their trade unions are male-dominated and therefore likely to favour the harasser.

Women also fear that even their husbands or partners may blame them for the problem. When Jane (not her real name) complained to her husband about her employer's sexual advances towards her, he was furious – with her rather than her boss. As she was returning home late from work one day her husband grabbed her and attempted to chop off her hands. He accused her of having an affair with her employer.

Already faced with cultural barriers, lack of qualifications and the inflexibility of the workplace, women are further intimidated by sexual harassment.

"Sexual harassment is about manipulative power," says Abigail Kidero of Canadian CIDA, former executive officer of the Kenya Medical Women's Association and coordinator of the Support Kenyan Women Against Sexual Harassment (SKWASH) forum founded in 1996. A baseline survey of more than 250 men and women carried out by the Kenya Institute of Management found that one third had experienced sexual harassment at work.

Women feel that sexual harassment should be added to the list of barriers hindering the advancement of professional women. At a SKWASH presentation to the Young Career Women Association, many participants said they had experienced sexual harassment, ranging in character from the more overt and physical to the more 'subtle'. One participant said her boss's computer screen saver had a picture of a female with large breasts. This image continually intimidated her but she never quite saw it as sexual harassment. The male participants said they had thought sexual harassment was quite harmless but after the presentation they said they would be more careful in the way they related to their female colleagues and try to keep sex out of the workplace.

Cases of sexual harassment documented by SKWASH include a woman civil servant excluded from meetings and told she must transfer offices after rejecting sexual advances from her boss. She resigned. A bank worker harassed by a prestigious client who demanded she be sacked when she rejected his advances was able to keep her job after providing evidence to her boss. A saleswoman sacked after refusing the sexual advances of a client opted for an out-of-court settlement.

SKWASH has made presentations to managers, negotiated with trade unions and made contact with working women's associations. Several organisations are now in the process of developing sexual harassment policy documents. "We feel the subject should be made explicit," says Kidero.

In educational institutions

To tackle sexual harassment of female students in learning institutions, Kidero says the focus must be on working with the Ministry of Education and on policy interventions that will improve the management of schools and colleges under its jurisdiction.

FAWE executive committee member and vice chancellor at the University of Cape Town, South Africa, Dr Mamphela Ramphele, urges that greater attention be paid to the creation and promotion of an enabling environment that promotes gender equity in African learning institutions. She draws attention to "the widespread view that women have no rights over their bodies.... That is why sexual harassment and physical abuse of women thrives."

FAWE has expressed concern that sexual harassment continues to reinforce African women's and girls' exclusion from the education systems of their countries. "FAWE's primary goal is to get girls into school, keep them there and encourage excellence during their school years," says Dr Edda Gachukia, Executive Director. FAWE is also planning to address boys so that they can provide peer support to girls in and out of school.

Stymied at the start

Progress in tackling such attitudes is stymied by the controversy that surrounds mention of sex in schools. Despite evidence of early sexual relationships and high levels of schoolgirl pregnancy, sex education including AIDS education and measures to support pregnant schoolgirls remain a bone of contention between church and state.

The church feels sex education will encourage more and earlier sex. Proponents of sex education argue that many young people are already sexually active and without information to make responsible decisions, they – particularly girls – will suffer from untreated STDs, unwanted pregnancies or unsafe abortion.

A 1991 study of more than 3,000 unmarried Kenyan students aged 12-19 found levels of sexual activity far outstripped use of contraceptives or knowledge about how pregnancy occurs. Fifty-one percent of students had had sexual relations, most commonly beginning at age 13, and by age 19, nearly 80 percent of male students had had sexual relations. Paradoxically, 65 percent of those questioned did not approve of premarital sex and less than 30 percent knew that pregnancy could occur at first intercourse, without female orgasm, or if the couple practised withdrawal.[3]

Research shows large variations in sexual activity between different communities and socio-economic groups. Earlier studies showed that approaching 70 percent of unmarried women in teacher training colleges in Kenya have had sexual intercourse, most commonly starting at the age of 18.[4] In a rural area of Machakos district, 26 percent of girls and 64 percent of boys had sexual intercourse for the first time before the age of 16.[5] It is unclear whether premarital sexual activity is increasing in different communities or whether, because of later marriage and earlier menarche, it is the social context of adolescent sexuality that is changing rather than the levels of sexual activity and childbearing.[6]

While young people are caught in the middle of these changes, controversy persists over the appropriate content of school curricula. When developing materials on population and family life, the Kenya Institute of Education involved parents, pupils, students, teachers, communities and religious bodies. "No one was left out," says Omwoyo of the Kenya Institute of Education. "We made our intentions clear, and there was no explicit talk of sex. Feedback was encouraging."

Sections of the churches, especially the Catholic Church, argue that the United Nations Fund for Population Activities (UNFPA), the Family Planning Association of Kenya and other local and international population rights groups are pressurising the Ministry of Education to unload their agendas into the education system. "This is a situation of poison welling up from within," says Agousta Muthigani, acting education secretary at the Kenya Catholic Secretariat.

As a result of the AIDS epidemic, the Presiding Bishop of the Methodist Church in Kenya, the Reverend Zablon Nthamburi, has stressed the importance of sex education programmes in schools but was quoted in the *Daily Nation* as saying that such programmes should be stripped of the controversial component on contraception.

Although Kenya's laws and policies do not explicitly restrict the provision of services to adolescents, the government does not provide reproductive health programmes or services specifically geared towards their needs. Kenya's health policy framework does, however, identify the need for "promotion of fora to examine the sensitive issue of youth contraceptives".

Attempts to revise and widen the scope of Kenya's population policy by integrating the Programme of Action of the International Conference on Population and

Development, 1994, were delayed, according to Minister for Planning and National Development George Saitoti, because of controversy surrounding the family life education school curriculum.

New information about levels of violence – much of it sexual violence – against Kenyan women, highlights the urgency of new approaches to the debate about adolescent sexuality.[7] Sexual coercion does not just affect adults. As Mariam, Veronica and many others will testify, sexual harassment and violence towards girl students is well established at universities and even earlier – in primary schools.

Sacred Knots and Unholy Deals
The road towards pro-women legal reform in Egypt

Dina Ezzat

> To the nest of love
> fly pigeons fly.
> Tell the awaiting dreams
> that I am rapidly coming on my way.
> Tell them that with me
> comes my dear loving fiancé.
> Tell them that we come
> to live and love.
>
> *Egyptian wedding song*

The wedding of 26-year-old Dalia Mahmoud and 34-year-old Ahmed Noureddin, two young upper-middle-class professionals, is nearly over. The Muslim registrar takes the right hand of the bride's father, places it in the right hand of the groom and throws a white handkerchief over the joined hands. He tells the older man: "Repeat after me: I give you my daughter – virgin and adult – in marriage, in accordance with the dowry that we have agreed upon."

Next the young man is asked to declare: "And I accept to wed her." His words are met with a storm of ululation from the female guests.

Afterwards the couple is showered with congratulations, as well as exhortations and pieces of advice such as "A clever woman keeps a marriage away from troubles and always leans before a passing storm" and "Your wife is entrusted to your hands; it is your duty to look after her."

After the formal ceremony Dalia and Ahmed sign the wedding contract which, in addition to giving details of their identities, the agreed dowry and the alimony to be paid in the case of separation or divorce, has a blank space where the man and woman can add, if they choose, any other pledges they have agreed upon, providing these are consistent with Islamic Shari'a law, as well as civil law.

"I know we could have included things like my own right to divorce or to insist that if he takes another wife I could get my divorce automatically; but we agreed [not to]," says Dalia. "It's not that we're against the idea, but it's not socially acceptable. It would have made me look like a bad woman before my in-laws and made my husband look like a weak man before his family and friends."

Ahmed adds, however: "Had the new marriage contract that requests the man and woman to detail their stances on these issues been passed...it would have been all right – but we could not take the initiative." He is referring to a proposed amendment to the marriage contract which would give engaged couples the opportunity to stipulate in private, before the wedding ceremony, legal and financial details relating to their future partnership.

The respectability of marriage

Most Egyptians believe that society will only accept women, and even men, in the framework of marriage. Some describe it as a 'sacred knot', a way of life ordained by God; others view it pragmatically, as a partnership from which both parties should benefit. Some see it as a 'trap' into which every man and woman must inevitably fall.

"There is no choice.... One has to do it," says Layla Abdel-Fattah, a 55-year-old editor who has been married for 30 years. "You think about it and you decide whether you like it or not but you end up going through it.... How else will you satisfy your physical needs without compromising your religious beliefs? How else will you have someone to lean on when life gets tough? How else will you have children to look to for solace when you lose your parents?"

"Those who do not get married and have children would regret it when they get older," says Hossam Ibrahim, a marketing consultant. "Who would look after them when they are old? Who would attend...their death bed and arrange for their funeral?"

"I cannot imagine what my life would have been like if I hadn't married and had children. I would have felt like a complete outcast. I would have been so ashamed of myself," says Fawziya Mohamed, 37, who is semi-literate and lives in a poor neighbourhood in Lower Egypt. She admits her marriage is not perfect: "Sometimes we argue and he loses his temper and hits me. But such is life. And, such is the life of most...married women. But we have to get married."

Very few think otherwise. "It's all right...if you meet someone...who could really be a nice addition to your life. But if not, why trouble yourself?" says Noha El-Gharib, a 35-year-old unmarried civil servant. None of her suitors has convinced her he could offer something she does not already have. "I know people...think I'm going to be a spinster.... I know some of my married friends don't like to socialise with me because they think I could be a bad example for their daughters," she says. While society can just about tolerate an unmarried man it finds it extremely difficult to accept an unmarried woman.

The rules governing marriage are set by the two principal religions in Egypt: Islam, practised by the overwhelming majority, and Christianity – mainly Coptic Christianity – by about 8-10 percent of the total population of 60 million.

According to the Orthodox Coptic Church of Egypt, marriage is for life. Incurable physical or mental illness, adultery or criminal behaviour may be deemed sufficient reason for a *séparation des corps* but never for divorce. Those who insist on divorce have to change to another Christian denomination or even convert to Islam.

Al-A'isma: a rarely exercised right

Muslims follow the codes of the Personal Status Law (PSL), promulgated in 1925 and scarcely amended since, which is based on the Shari'a (Islamic code of conduct). Under the PSL, marriage – as well as child custody and any other family matters that relate to marital status, responsibilities and limitations – is administered by a civil contract, which requires that the woman should be at least 16 years of age, the man at least 18, and that both parties should be mentally competent. At the end of the contract is the blank space where both parties can stipulate any rights agreed between them, in particular the right of the woman to divorce her husband. But there is no requirement to fill this in; nor is the registrar bound by law to ask whether the woman wants this right written into the contract. Since most women are unaware of their legal rights or are unwilling to offend future in-laws by requesting them, the space usually remains blank.

The PSL of 1925 codified the existing Shari'a right of *Al-A'isma* – an agreement, which must be stated in the marriage contract, whereby a husband extends to his wife the right to unilateral divorce without having to go through the courts. The right is based on the 'safeguarding' of the integrity of marital life and the 'honour' of both husband and wife in respect of sexual conduct; divorce is an entitlement if the 'honour' of either partner is abused, notably through sexual misconduct.

According to Azza Soliman, director of the Centre for the Issues of Egyptian Women (CIEW), most people mistakenly think that *Al-A'isma* denies the man the right to divorce his wife when he wants to. "This makes people very sensitive about the matter, and this is why we chose to put out a flier, among other fliers on the different legal dimensions of getting married. It is basically an enlightenment campaign," he explains.

Information published by the Central Agency for Mobilisation and Statistics (CAMPAS) in 1998 revealed that only 35,000 women out of over 18 million of marriageable age had claimed the right of *Al-A'isma*, and these were mostly highly educated women living in affluent suburbs of Cairo and Alexandria.

The vast majority of women of all social classes, even those experiencing great difficulty in obtaining a divorce through the courts, are against *Al-A'isma*.

Maha Mohessin, a 26-year-old lecturer of Arabic literature in a provincial university, has been trying for three years to obtain a divorce. Her husband is physically and verbally abusive. "The problem is that I have to convince the judge that he beats me and insults me in public or that he leaves my body with bruises that are very noticeable," says Mohessin. Providing independent corroboration is not easy. She would need to knock on her neighbours' door and ask them to testify that they have heard her husband swearing at her repeatedly.

Still, Mohessin does not regret that she did not stipulate her right to *Al-A'isma* in the marriage contract. She maintains that the judge should simply accept her wish for divorce "because Islam preaches that no woman should be forced to live with a man she hates or simply does not want".

Imbaba is a very poor suburb of Greater Cairo where radical Islam gained such a hold in the late 1980s and early 1990s that it was dubbed "the Islamic republic of Imbaba". A *ma'zoun* (marriage registrar) working there for over 15 years says he has not married a single couple where the woman has stipulated her right to divorce. "No man who deserves to be called a man can accept this: a woman to decide for him or to divorce him," he says.

All the power

Al-A'isma does not affect a husband's right to divorce. Under the Personal Status Law he needs only to recite – without witnesses – the formula, "Go, you are divorced". He then has to get the marriage registrar to issue an official paper documenting the divorce. If he says these words once, he can 'reclaim' his wife within three months; if he waits for longer and wants her back he has formally to re-marry her, with her consent. But if he pronounces the words three times in succession, or divorces her on three occasions, he loses the right to reclaim or remarry her – unless she marries another man and is subsequently divorced.

Once under the conjugal roof, women are traditionally seen as the auxiliary part of the marital equation, under the 'protection' of their husbands but subservient to them. A woman must obtain written approval from her husband before the civil authorities will issue her with a passport, and he can deny her the right to travel overseas even if she wants to go to Mecca as a pilgrim, a devotion that all Muslims are encouraged to perform at least once in their lifetime.

Although research conducted by CAMPAS shows that about 30 percent of households are female-headed, this view of female dependency remains largely unaltered. As 'leader' of the family, the man has the right to take unilateral decisions on matters affecting his wife and children. He may, if he chooses, delegate authority to his wife or eldest son – not an infrequent occurrence as many men are away from the family home for long periods of time. Still, the 'representative' is expected to contact and consult with him before a final decision is made on any serious issue.

"The family, [as] the fundamental unit of society, is a most conservative institution [and the notion of] harmony and stability is often used to put pressure on women in favour of a traditional home-oriented role in society," says Aziza Hussein, prominent sociologist and chairperson of the

National Council for Population and Development. "This applies to agrarian and urban societies alike.... The man still has all the power and the wife is completely at his mercy."

"Every boat has to have a captain,...otherwise it would not sail well and might even sink," says Mohamed Sa'id, a taxi driver from Upper Egypt. "This captain has to be the man."

Steering women's reproductive lives

One area where most men assume they can play the role of 'captain' is in women's sexual and reproductive lives.

An extreme example of male control of women's sexuality is the practice of female genital mutilation (FGM), sometimes euphemistically termed female circumcision. According to several concerned non-government human and women's rights organisations, including the Egyptian Organisation for Human Rights, over 90 percent of Egyptian women, both Muslim and Christian, have been subjected to either clitoridectomy (partial or total removal of the clitoris) or excision (removal of the clitoris and partial or total removal of the labia minora). Infibulation (removal of the clitoris, partial or total removal of the labia minora and incisions made in the labia majora, with stitching or narrowing of the vaginal opening) predominates in Southern Egypt. If his fiancée has not already undergone the operation a man can insist that she does so before marriage, according to Aziza Kamil, chairperson of the Association for the Combat of Unhealthy Practices Against the Woman and the Girl Child.

Often performed in unhygienic conditions, FGM may have numerous negative health effects: agonising pain when done without anaesthesia, bleeding, anaemia, shock, tetanus, fever and infections. Long-term complications include painful menstruation, cysts, urinary leakage, prolonged obstructed labour with an increased risk that mother and infant will die, unnecessary caesarian sections and sexual and psychological difficulties.[1]

Reproductive health researchers also note that it is common for a man to believe he has the right to sex with his wife whenever he feels like it – so long as she is not menstruating – irrespective of her mood or inclination.

A survey conducted in 1997 by the El-Nadim Centre for the Management and Rehabilitation of Victims of Violence and the New Woman Research and Study Centre found that 93 percent of 500 women interviewed perceived marital sex without their consent as an act of violence. Forty-six percent of the 100 men questioned said it was their right to have sexual intercourse with their wives "even when they were arguing or...not consenting", and 70 percent of this male sample, of which over a third had university degrees, said they were sometimes "justified in beating their wives" for a variety of reasons including reluctance to have sex.

It is not surprising that one woman, an executive secretary in her late 20s and married for nine years, says: "I can't think of one time where I really enjoyed our conjugal encounter. I tried to talk to him about it but he got very upset and told me I was insulting his manhood. And my mother says to me, 'What do you want? The man is very healthy – he gave you two lovely boys."

Society says a woman's primary role is childbearing. If a couple fails to have a child within the first two years of marriage it is standard procedure for the woman to have a medical examination. "They [society as well as the couple] assume there is something wrong with the woman's ovulation," explains Sawsan Abdel-Fattah, a reproductive health activist. "Many men do not like to go for these tests, even when their wives medically prove to be healthy."

The responsibility for spacing children, too, falls to the woman. However, says gynaecologist Nahila El-Bolk, "In nine cases out of 10, we do not even suggest the idea of a condom as a potential contraceptive. We know that it is still not accepted by Egyptian men. So we try to save the time and help the woman choose the right contraceptive."

Men may also censure their wives' choice of family planning method. "Some women say they do not like to use the pill because it changes the shape of their bodies in a way that their husbands do not like," says El-Bolk. "And...some do not want to use the IUD because their husbands say it interferes with their sexual pleasure," although a correctly inserted IUD will have no such effect.

Repeated pregnancies place women's reproductive and general health at great risk. Social scientist Hind Khattab, who carried out field research in the early 1990s in two villages of rural Giza, adjacent to Cairo, found a high incidence of unattended reproductive health problems including very high rates of uterine prolapse and reproductive tract infections. Women's reluctance to seek treatment was often associated with fear of their husbands' opposition and a general sense of powerlessness in the marriage.[2]

Ahlam, the subject of one of Khattab's case studies, was first married at the age of 16 but divorced within a year, following disputes with her mother-in-law. She married again and, by the age of 40, had conceived seven times, had three miscarriages and one stillbirth, and had three surviving children. Her husband took a second wife, who bore him three more children, resulting in Ahlam overworking to prove her own worth. "He's good to me only when he feels like it," said Ahlam of her husband.[3] During the period of the research, Ahlam miscarried again. When the cause of her repeated miscarriages was found to be a dilated cervix, requiring treatment, her husband still insisted that she leave hospital and "return to her children".

It is in this oppressive context that two initiatives have been taken in recent years to try to bring about a more equal basis to the marital relationship and less restricted access to divorce on the part of women.

A binding agreement

The more controversial and radical of these is the attempt to amend the marriage contract. Initiated early in 1994 by a group of women's rights activists and supported by a few members of the governmental Supreme Council for Motherhood and Childhood to which some non-government organisations (NGOs) are affiliated, the campaign has met with widespread opposition from the religious hierarchy and the majority of politicians. As a result, six years on, it is not yet on the statute book.

The proposed new marriage contract is an amalgamation of a draft produced by several women's rights NGOs and a blueprint from the Egyptian Ministry of Justice, which is responsible for keeping records of marriages and divorces. It aims to secure for would-be married couples the right to make informed decisions about a wide range of legal and financial details relating to their future partnership.

"As stipulated by the Shari'a", reads the proposed contract, "the following items can be the subject of a binding agreement before marriage. The prospective wife and husband may agree upon any, some or all of these items."

The first three of the seven items concern ownership of the conjugal home and household furniture in the case of divorce, and compensation to a wife divorced against her will.

The fourth concerns the wife's right to obtain employment and education, and to travel abroad "with legitimate justification". The fifth point states: "The husband does not commit polygamy."

The final two proposed points, which refer to *Al A'isma*, spell out the wife's agreed right to divorce – adding, in parentheses, that this does not deprive the husband of his right to 'request' the same – and state that if she exercises this divorce option she forfeits rights to financial compensation. While this scenario is far from financially ideal, activists believe it is a realistic compromise, because they fear that many men will refuse to divorce their wives simply to avoid being made financially responsible. This proposed amendment, however, may provide a way out for those women who want and can afford to take it.

The couple may, if they wish, include additional agreements, for example in relation to custody. The contract further mandates premarital medical check-ups from both the man and woman to ensure that they are free of "infectious or birth-preventing diseases". This includes tests for HIV.

Hoda El-Sadda, one of the main activists lobbying for the amended contract, explains that it aims to cover traditional areas of dispute in problematic marriages or divorce cases. "We took into consideration, as much as possible, the different social and economic contexts," she says.

Mona Zulfickar, the main architect of the project, adds: "We included different options because...it could be easier for a husband to [agree]...not to commit polygamy, but to refuse the wife's right to divorce herself.... Remember, the contract is all based on choice and agreement. "We are not imposing any of these conditions. What we are aiming at is changing people's ideas, changing tradition, encouraging people to be aware of their rights under Shari'a."

Harsh criticism

With few exceptions, the state and independent *ulamas* (those authorised to issue religious rulings and opinions) ferociously attacked the proposed amendments to the marriage contract as an attempt by 'Westernisation forces' to undermine Islam by sowing discord in the family, the nucleus of Muslim society.

According to Zulfickar the notion that the intention of the proposed contract is to 'Westernise' marriage is absurd. "Women [were using] the rights that we suggest should be added to this contract in the early years of Islam," she insists. "We also have found contracts [from] a few centuries ago where women stipulated clearly that their husbands should not practise polygamy or should not interfere with their right to travel."

The proposed contract was roundly condemned by Gad E-Haq Ali Gad El-Haq, the late Grand Sheikh of Al-Azhar, considered one of the highest religious authorities in the Muslim world. Also critical was the charismatic and popular cleric, Mohamed Mitwali El-Shaarawi, who advocates limited education for women, the veiling of women, and female genital mutilation "for fear that women might be sexually aroused if they mounted the back of an animal".

"Most of what [is] in this contract is against the spirit of Islam," says Youssef El-Badri, a fiery preacher who sues the state, or encourages his followers to do so, every time it takes a step in the direction of women's liberation.

In the last three years El-Badri has celebrated some significant victories against women's rights, including a court ruling that reversed a ministerial decree banning the veiling of girls under the age of 12 in schools, and another that temporarily reversed the health minister's 1996 ban on doctors performing female circumcisions in public hospitals and clinics. In 1997 Egypt's highest administrative court upheld the earlier ministerial ban on doctors performing FGM as well as a 1959 law criminalising all female circumcision in the country.[4]

Unfortunately, ministerial decree alone cannot stop the practice; in July 1998 a 12-year-old girl bled to death following the procedure in a private hospital in Cairo.[5] New findings, however, from the Population Council in Cairo, show that young girls in Egypt today are more than 10 percent less likely to undergo FGM than their mothers were, due in part to the impact of the International Conference on Population and Development (ICPD) and subsequent education campaigns.[6]

According to El-Badri: "The rule in Islam is that men and women are equal but that women are more emotional and therefore they should follow the guidance of men so long as it does not contradict with the clear orders of God Almighty." He adds: "If men and women were to be on a fully equal footing in marriage then fighting would never stop."

The item in the proposed marriage contract that drew the harshest criticism was that stipulating the woman's right to divorce. "It is true that Islam grants women this right," says El-Badri, "but it should be for individual women to decide whether or not they want to use it. The ruler [in this case the government] has no business interfering in the personal lives of men and women." If a law is passed amending the contract, he intends to sue the government. "God willing, I will win," he says.

One of the few religious leaders to show cautious support for the contract was Mohamed Sayed Tantawi, then the Grand Mufti (the ultimate religious arbitrator) and now the Grand Immam of Al-Azhar University, the highest Muslim authority in the land. Tantawi's initial view was that the proposed amendments contained "nothing against Islam" and that they simply restated a right that Islam already grants to women. This ruling drew so much criticism from the traditional *ulamas* that he added the statement: "Nonetheless, the way the items are stipulated in the contract presupposes problems in a way that most people will consider as an ill omen. And since these matters are already dealt with in the PSL then there is no point in having them in the contract."

Tantawi denies that he reversed his support. "My stance remains the same," he says. "It is the people who initiated the proposed contract who chose to put it on hold."

Campaigner El-Sadda agrees that the initiative has been temporarily abandoned but for tactical reasons. "Yes, we must admit that for now the contract is shelved. The time is not right to try and dig it up again." Other advocates of the amended contract say they did not really put the project on hold but that their allies in the Ministry of Justice and the Supreme Council for Motherhood and Childhood advised a more tactful approach because of adverse public opinion.

Market analyst Khaled Mazhar is one of many who oppose the initiative. "This contract is such a shocking idea," he says. "It's like giving a man and a woman two pistols and asking them to stand opposite one another and try to shoot. The idea about marriage is that two people who presumably care for each other or want to build something together enter a common life in good faith. Presupposing the problems they may encounter is not the way to solve them," he argues.

Men from less privileged backgrounds were particularly critical, describing the proposed changes as "the way to break up homes", "an attempt to make women disobey their husbands", and "a mischievous war against men's rights".

Criticism also came from within women's rights circles, for quite different reasons.

"This is such an elitist contract," says one activist who asks for her name to be withheld. "It presupposes that women...can read the contract when in fact over 60 percent of Egyptian women are illiterate; it assumes that if women can read what is in the contract they will use it in defiance of a whole social set-up that tells them they have to follow the rules, or else; and worst of all, it presupposes that all women are Muslims, so it ignores the existence of Coptic women who also have problematic marriages."

The changing battleground

The last few decades have seen widely divergent social currents.

"The discourse of the state in the 1950s and 1960s was about women's liberation [and] the right of a woman to learn and work," says Aida Seif El-Dawla, a founder member of the New Woman Research and Study Centre. Recalling how the media echoed the debate she adds: "The movies championed the kind of woman who would defy outmoded traditions and seek economic independence and exercise her right to decision-making;

and society would sympathise with this type. Today, the opposite is true.... The state discourse about women is completely different."

Lawyer Wafa' El-Masri agrees. "Had this proposed [marriage] contract come out in the 1960s it...could have been passed with more ease," she says. "But today things are different."

The timing of the proposed contract, it is argued, is another factor that undermined its chances of success. The public debate about the amendments was followed, only a few months later, by a bigger furore over ICPD within Egypt and internationally. As the conference embarked boldly on issues relating to women's control over their bodies, such as safe and legal abortion provision, both Christian and Muslim leaders insisted that these rights should be addressed from a theological perspective.

An increasingly active Egyptian civil society praises ICPD for bringing the issues to the limelight. Moreover, "in the process of preparation [for ICPD]...we had an excellent opportunity to address the issues publicly and conduct much research on the different issues," says Seif El-Dawla. Since then, however, the increasing opposition of religious leaders has influenced government attitudes towards women's issues.

"This is because women's rights are the main front on which the state is prepared to compromise and appease the reactionary Islamist groups," says Seif El-Dawla.

All the more reason, says Farida El-Naqqash, secretary general of the women's section of the left-wing Tagammua party, that women's groups should not give up. "The women's rights movement should...forge ahead with its agenda," she declares. In her analysis, the state has its political agenda by which it wants to overcome or neutralise the Islamist factions intent on toppling the current regime and establishing a theocratic state.

Asmahan Shukri, secretary general of the women's committee in the Islamist-oriented Labour Party, and El-Naqqash both admit that in their battle for political reform most opposition political parties put women's issues at the very end of their agendas.

El-Naqqash insists that the liberation of women does not have to wait for the liberation of society. However, not everyone has the same uncompromising spirit.

"It is one thing to say that we are going to amend the law through Parliament," says Farkhunda Hasan, secretary general of the women's committee of the ruling National Democratic Party, "but it is quite another to tell a society that believes in men's superiority that men and women will be on a completely equal footing within the marriage establishment, which is like a taboo really."

At the time that the PSL was enacted in 1925 it was stipulated in the archives of the Ministry of Justice that the nature of the law "could develop with the spirit of age". Yet, the only effective amendment came in 1979 through the efforts of the former First Lady, Jihan El-Sadat. The so-called 'Jihan Law' stipulated that a woman should be informed by the *ma'zoun* if her husband took a second wife, and entitled her to a divorce within one year of notification. In the case of divorce, and if she had children, she was granted ownership of the marital home. The amendments also raised the age up to which children could remain in their mother's custody, to 12 for boys and 15 for girls.

El-Sadat says her efforts were spurred by the tragic stories women told her as she travelled throughout the country. It was then a tough job gaining the official stamp of approval on the amendments during the regime of her late husband, President Anwar El-Sadat, at a time when the Islamist forces were gaining ground. "But I did all I could and lobbied for as much support as possible," she remembers.

Four years after the assassination of President Sadat by an Islamist army officer, a Higher Constitutional Court declared all but the child custody amendments unconstitutional. The only aspect of the 'Jihan Law' that was retained was the woman's right to be informed of her husband's polygamy. The court ruling was acclaimed by traditional Islamic circles as a victory over 'Westernisation'.

Painkiller or cure?

The attempt to gain support for a proposed Personal Status Procedures Bill – the other initiative that occupied campaigners throughout the 1990s – was far less ambitious than the former first lady's attempt to change the Personal Status Law two decades before.

Women's rights activists say that it was the debate over the marriage contract, together with the challenges presented by ICPD, hosted by Egypt, and the 1995 Fourth World Conference on Women, attended by the First Lady, that spurred the government to revive the Personal Status Procedures Bill. The bill was seen by them as a compromise initiative by a government unwilling to agree to feminists' more progressive demands for changes in the institution of marriage, but equally unwilling to cave in to radical Muslim forces.

The new legislation finally passed by the male-dominated parliament in January 2000, is designed to facilitate legal procedures for more than a million women trying to seek divorce, custody of children and alimony through the courts. Government statistics show that 1.5 million divorce petitions are filed annually in Egypt, and seven million people are currently seeking legal separation.[7]

Forty-five-year-old Afaf Marzouq is one of them. A mother of four school-age children, she has been trying for three years to get her husband, who took all her life savings and abandoned her after marrying another woman, to provide for his children.

"He doesn't give us [anything]. I am practically living on charity and on the little money I get from occasional house-helping that I do behind the back of my children to avoid hurting them," says Marzouq. "I don't want much. I just want them to finish their education so that they have better luck in life than me."

For many women, the mechanism guaranteeing immediate payment of alimony is the strongest point about the new law. Bank Nasser – the state bank – will be required to pay the ex-wife alimony as soon as a judge allows it and to claim back the money from the ex-husband. "This would be great," comments Sayeda Mohamed, a divorcee in her early 30s with three children, who has not received one piaster (fractional unit of currency) from her husband since her divorce three years ago. "[He] keeps changing his address and the court of law has not been able to locate him," she explains. She has been living with her parents and doing domestic work to support her children. "[My] father is an old man with a very limited pension that barely gets him and my mother through the month and my brothers live and work abroad and have many financial responsibilities [so]...they cannot really help me."

"This alimony issue is a real concern for many, many women," commented sociologist Hoda Badran, chairwoman of the Alliance of Arab Women, prior to the passing of the bill. In her view if the new law did nothing other than deal with this problem, it would achieve something very significant.

Further, the new law insists on a judge taking no more than six months to issue a verdict on issues relating to divorce and alimony. This means that the thousands of women who spend years waiting for a verdict will quickly have their cases heard.

Moreover, no husband is entitled any longer to divorce his wife without informing her via the court, or to forcibly annul this divorce within 90 days without informing his wife. A divorcee who takes another husband a year after the break-up no longer has to worry about the outrageous situation of her 'ex-husband' informing her via the court that she is still his wife after all.

"This means...there should be no more horrible stories...of women who find themselves 'married to two' due to a legal system that allows years for a judge to issue a final and irreversible verdict," said Amina El-Guindi, the secretary general of the National Centre for Motherhood and Childhood, prior to the passing of the bill.

The reform has been welcomed by some women's rights groups as a significant, if partial, victory. Others point out that, unlike the proposed and shelved amendments to the marriage contract, the new legislation fails to spell out women's rights.

"It is more of a pain killer than a cure," says Tahani El-Gebali, a feminist and legal rights activist, referring to an additional option entitling a woman to file for an immediate divorce on the grounds of incompatibility provided that she relinquishes any claim to alimony. She argues that some, if not many, men will pressurise their wives into accepting this option rather than seeking a regular divorce with proper financial entitlements.

Other critics observe that the option will only benefit wealthy women, who can afford to forgo financial support from ex-husbands.

Moreover, if the court-appointed panel finds that spouses are incompatible, the woman must then publicly declare that she "hates" her husband and can no longer fulfil her conjugal duties "as laid down by God" – a declaration not required of a man seeking to divorce his wife.

According to El-Gebali, Islam has in fact given women

clear rights with respect to marriage and divorce but these have been undermined by male chauvinistic interpretations. To do real justice to women, she argues, society needs to recognise women's rights under Islam to choose their husbands, to divorce them if they feel the marriage or the husband is causing them harm, and to receive their financial dues as wives or as divorcees. However, although she does not believe the new law goes far enough, she sees it as a step forward.

The new legislation means a woman using the courts will no longer be required to have a lawyer represent her. "This is all very nice," warned Mohamed Abdel-A'al, head of the women's division of the Egyptian Organisation for Human Rights, "but how would an illiterate woman manage to get along with the complicated legal system without a lawyer, and how much would the litigation process be shortened?"

Much of Abdel-A'al's work is concerned with providing free counselling for poor women in preparation for their court cases. Another task is to conduct research on women's issues. From his experience on both fronts, Abdel-A'al believes that a far more radical overhaul of the Personal Status Law is required.

Zeinab Radwan, professor of Islamic philosophy at Helwan University, is also critical. "[These] are mere procedural changes that could make the misery of thousands of women who are trying to get divorce and alimony more tolerable but would not erase this misery," she insists.

Into the 21st century

Even the modest reforms of the Personal Status Procedures Bill were achieved at a cost. In addition to the harsh conditions attached to 'no-fault' divorce suits, a clause allowing women to obtain a passport or travel abroad without their husbands' permission was rejected.

Says women's rights activist Hoda El-Sadda: "We see this as a first step that will eventually pave the way [towards introducing a new marriage contract]. But of course the ultimate objective is a new Personal Status Law that takes into consideration the problems and facts of our time and [can] still be formulated within the bounds of liberal readings of Islam."

"We have to work at the grassroots level," says Seif El-Dawla. "We have to offer an alternative point of view to the anti-women codes. We have to explain our views. We need to realise that the battles about female genital mutilation or the marriage contract are primarily political."

According to a recent article by one of Egypt's leading feminists, Nawal El-Sadawi, the time is ripe for altering the views and modes that govern relationships within the institution of marriage.[8] "The relations of and within marriage will always be changing along with the economic and cultural changes that society is experiencing," she writes. In her view this process of change is what will allow society to alter its modes and rules for women's reproductive rights.

Not long ago, argues Sadawi, the mere notion of abortion was an absolute taboo, but today some Muslim clergy would countenance early abortion for women made pregnant through rape.

Not all Egyptian women will benefit, however. Coptic women still have to abide by different personal status laws that prohibit divorce except in very rare cases; the right to abortion is not discussed at all. To talk of more personal status rights for Coptic women is to talk of serious inter-church reform – another taboo altogether.

In Egypt, debate on extending women the same rights as men can be acrimonious, even apocalyptic. One parliamentarian warned ominously that if the Personal

Status Procedures Bill was passed it would lead to more murders of women because men would never accept having their wives leave them.

The longer the process of amending the PSL the more likely it is that a woman who marries in the early years of the 21st century – whether a company director or a poor market trader – will be subjected to the laws and social pressures under which her great grandmother married in 1925.

No Paradise Yet
Women and child custody laws in Bangladesh

Lamis Hossain
with additional interviews by Raffat Binte Rashid

In Bangladesh, to be referred to as '*Josna-r Ma*' or '*Alamin-er Ma*' ('so-and-so's mother') is a sign of respect for the status that only motherhood can confer on women. Children are taught: "*Ma-er pa-er tolai beheste*" ("Paradise lies at your mother's feet").

Yet paradise remains postponed for Bangladeshi mothers, denied choice or adequate care in their reproductive lives. The average age at which women married in the early 1990s was still as low as 14, and the pressure to bear a first child soon after marriage remains high.[1] Although successive governments' family planning campaigns have resulted in a dramatic decline in the birth rate, from 6.3 births per woman in the period 1971-5 to 3.4 in 1991-3, one survey in the early 1990s found that one in three births was either not wanted at the time it occurred or not wanted at all.[2] There is also a significant variation in contraceptive use between different parts of the country, with areas where community and religious leaders exert greater control showing considerably higher birth rates than elsewhere.[3]

Bangladesh remains one of the few countries in the world where women on average die younger than men[4] and still has one of the highest maternal mortality rates in the world.[5] The vast majority of babies are delivered at home without professional care or medical backup, and in nearly three out of four cases women receive no antenatal care before giving birth.[6]

Ironically, the same society that subsumes a woman's identity within motherhood routinely denies her the right to keep her children if her marriage breaks down.

A losing battle

Few experiences for a mother are as distressing as the prospect of losing a child. "What do I do when my husband snatches away the child that I have?" asks a woman from the village of Hudarajapur in the district of Jessore, about 300 km from Dhaka. "If the child is taken away from my lap, how do I live? I am the mother who bore the child."

Nasima (not her real name) is a computer operator in her mid-thirties working at a government institution in Dhaka. Five years ago, she discovered her husband was having an affair with their maidservant. Taking her son with her, she left the house in shock; however, she chose not to initiate a divorce because of the likely effects on her infant son and her own social position. "There was no support forthcoming from my family. I was simply told to adjust to the circumstances," she says.

Angered that Nasima had left him and found employment in order to support herself and her son, her husband gave her a choice: either give up her work and return to the marital home as his wife or keep her job, in which case he would divorce her. But Nasima thought that quitting her job would leave her even more vulnerable and also make it appear that her husband was right.

"It wasn't my fault that the marriage broke down," says Nasima. "Why should it be a question of whether he accepts me, and not of whether I accept him?" Her choice, however, led to her husband refusing to return her son after an agreed visit and divorcing her. She spent the next four years struggling to gain custody of her son.

When Nasima decided to take legal recourse, she knew little about the court system. If her case had been heard straightaway, the courts would have been reluctant to separate a one-year-old from his mother. But due to her own lawyers' incompetence, and the other side's obstructive tactics, four years of delay passed before a judgement. The odds were stacked against Nasima gaining custody of a five-year-old: she lost.

Nasima's experience is not unique. Maya was born and educated outside Bangladesh. When she was 16 her father arranged for her to marry a fellow Bengali Muslim. After living more than ten years with her abusive husband and bearing four children, Maya was tricked into moving to Bangladesh where her husband divorced her. "Now he is in his beloved country, protected by his Muslim laws," she says angrily. "He took away my children, including the one who was nursing, threw me out of the house, forced *talaq* [Muslim divorce] on me, deceived me and sold my property without my knowledge. Yet when he appealed for custody, the court gave him the children."

Sara Hossain, a lawyer and human rights advocate, dissects these ruthless, heart-breaking legal fights where the principal victims are the minor children: "A central issue in the breakdown of a relationship is often...the division and sharing of parental rights and responsibilities. Our experience is that women are denied their rights to custody more often, and more routinely, than men."

Mothers without rights

In Bangladesh personal laws, based on religious and customary law, govern family relations, specifically matters relating to marriage, divorce, dowry (where applicable), maintenance, inheritance, guardianship and custody of children. There are different personal laws for Muslims – the majority population – and for Hindus, Christians, tribals and other minorities. Some Muslim personal laws are derived from clear injunctions in the Qur'an, but most derive from jurisprudence under various schools of thought and often differing in their interpretation. Thus, certain Muslim laws in Bangladesh are unlike anything in Tunisia or Malaysia. Some were codified under British colonialism. The result is a kind of "Anglo-Mohammedan law where misconceived and fossilised Muslim laws based on centuries-old misinterpretations of history became the rule of law".[7]

The Bangladesh Constitution recognises fundamental rights to equality before the law and bars discrimination on the grounds of sex.[8] However, personal laws are thought of as falling outside the civil law. While there are minimum standards of equality in the public sphere of civil justice, the private sphere of home and family is relegated to an arena of variable norms outside of these minimum rights, according to lawyer Sara Hossain.[9]

In Bangladesh a man has only to make an oral pronouncement (*talaq*), followed by written notification to the Chairman of the Union Council, to obtain a divorce.[10] He has to supply a copy of the notice to his wife, but needs give no reasons for the divorce nor gain his wife's consent. A woman, on the other hand, has to seek a judicial decree to obtain a divorce and her reasons for doing so must fall within one of the categories, such as impotence, failure to perform marital obligations, or cruelty, listed under the 1939 Dissolution of Muslim Marriages Act. Women have the same right to unilateral divorce as men, but only when this has been delegated to them by their husbands in the written marriage contract, which happens rarely.

Child custody laws are based on stereotyped notions of gender roles that operate to the detriment of women. According to Muslim personal law, a woman can never be the legal guardian of her children.[11] She is entitled to the physical custody of young children on the grounds that "she is naturally not only more tender but also better qualified to cherish a child during infancy".[12]

After a divorce in the case of a male child, the mother's custody rights last only until her son no longer needs assistance to eat, drink and perform other natural functions – generally said to be at the age of seven, [13] after which the father is considered more able to provide the son with an education and to teach him the manners of men.[14] A girl is allowed to remain with her mother until, at the onset of puberty, she develops a 'carnal appetite' and is therefore handed over to her father to supervise her conduct.

Sultana Kamal is a practising lawyer in the north-eastern district of Sylhet and Bangladesh coordinator of Women Living Under Muslim Laws, an international network of women's groups within Muslim communities which publishes a regular dossier on women's experiences. Commenting on the authorities that maintain the system of personal laws, she observes: "Motherhood and [being in] control have never been associated by them. Motherhood and service have been. It's very significant that boys are allowed to stay with the mother before they are seven, which is the age when the child needs the most care in life and fathers are less willing or able to give it. So the mother is given custody, but she is not granted control."

Kamal's point is further illustrated by the fact that under Muslim law a mother can lose her right to custody under certain circumstances, which are not applicable to men: if she remarries, engages in 'immoral' conduct, or moves to a place beyond easy travelling distance of the father.

Alongside religious jurisprudence are the provisions of the Guardian and Wards Act, enacted in 1890, under British rule. The Act provides that the court can appoint a guardian for the care of the child and the administration of a minor's property, and can decide who is entitled to custody, where it is satisfied that the welfare of the minor requires such an order.[15] In ruling on custody, the court is called upon to look at the personal law of the minor for guidance on what constitutes the welfare of the child.[16]

Despite the confusion in the law, the courts sometimes make 'sane' decisions,[17] ruling, for example, that the mother's poverty is not a bar to custody.[18] Even more occasionally – in "less than a handful of cases", according to Sara Hossain – a woman who has remarried has been granted custody where doing so was deemed consistent with the child's welfare.[19]

The situation is unsatisfactory and much depends on how a judge – nearly always a male judge – interprets laws biased against women. "The consideration of the welfare [of the child] criterion is made subject to the 'law to which the minor is subject', and this is usually interpreted as meaning the personal/religious law of the child," Sara Hossain points out. "Thus, although the Guardians and Wards Act applies equally to everyone in Bangladesh, its effects are not equal, and a woman's custody rights...will depend on her religion."

The automatic application of personal laws can produce unjust, even nonsensical results. In a recent case, the High Court awarded custody of the two younger children to the mother, but automatically awarded custody of the eldest child to the father since the child was over seven.[20] It allowed no discussion of the children's welfare or the fact that the father had allegedly kidnapped them or whether it would be better for all three siblings to remain together. In another case, the court completely ignored a young child's preference so as to rule in a manner consistent with personal law. Seven-year-old Diyan, who has been the subject of a custody case since he was a toddler of 18 months, told the court: "I want to live with my mother." Unswayed, the judge ruled that Diyan live with his father, the 'natural' guardian.

Salma Sobhan is a lawyer and executive director of *Ain O Salish Kendro*, a legal aid and human rights organisation based in Dhaka. "In most cases we are seeing the worst of all possible choices," she explains, referring to the way existing laws are applied. An example is what happens when fathers abduct children where the woman has legal custody. "The court does not act under the personal law by saying that the woman should straightaway have custody of her minors, in accordance with the Shari'a [body of Islamic doctrines], and that the father can dispute this matter in court. Instead, [it] confirms the father's *de facto* custody until such time as the case is determined, and that could be two to three years. During that period the mother's right to visit the child is limited."

Nasima – the computer operator who fought for and lost custody of her son – disputes that there should be any artificial age limits attached to custody. "There should be a concrete statement that if the mother is capable and willing to take care of her child, then the child should go to her. A seven-year-old is unable to take care of himself," she points out, using her own son as an example. "He is still a child who sits on people's laps. Until the child understands bad from good he should stay with his mother. After that age, he or she should be able to decide."

Asked what the father's rights should be, Nasima says: "Fathers should be able to see their sons – as long as they can be trusted not to take the child away from the mother as a result. My son needs both of us. He sometimes asks me, 'Why don't you and *Abbuji* [father] get houses next to each other?'"

Custody disputes beg the wider question of guardianship, within marriage as well as after its break-up. Rights lawyer Sobhan believes that reforming the law in relation to guardianship is the highest priority "Both parents should be allowed to be the guardians," she says.

Her sentiment is shared by Nasima. "I've competed with men in my job and no one made it easier for me just because I'm a woman. So why can't I be the equal guardian of my child as well?"

Although Nasima is a working mother living in the city, some of her views are shared by village women like those of Dakatia, in Jessore, about 150 km west of Dhaka. The Dakatia women are members of a *mahila samity* (women's group) formed under the auspices of Banchete Sheka, a long-established and well-respected development NGO (non-government organisation) that provides women with services such as credit, training in income generation, and legal rights awareness.

"There should be equal rights," one woman says about guardianship. "The father raises the child by providing for them and feeding them. But the mother expends as much effort and energy. She keeps the child in her belly. In the winter, how many times does the mother get up for the child and how many times does the father? If you kept an account, you would find the mother does more work."

Rokeya, the Banchete Sheka legal aid advisor present at the meeting, adds that it is illogical for the father to be named automatically as the children's guardian. "I knew this woman with three kids who used to support herself. Her children did not want to be admitted to school in their father's name. They had never seen their father, who had since married someone else. 'Our father has done nothing for us,' they said, 'Why should we put his name? Our mother represents everything for us, so we want to put her name.' When their mother tried to register them in her own name, the school flatly told her: 'We cannot allow that. We don't have that kind of society here.'"

Personal law gives men the upper hand outside the court room, in villages where mediation is the common way of resolving disputes and legal rules are little known. Sufia Begum, a widowed mother and leader of the *samity*, is unaware of the welfare-of-the-child criterion sometimes enforced by courts under the Guardian and Wards Act. She sees the relative bargaining strength of the parties as determined by personal law. "In one of our mediations we agreed that the child would stay with his mother up to the age of seven only, but does any mother want to give away her child? How grown-up is a seven year old, anyway?" Sufia asks.

"*Apa* [elder sister], this law would be better," Sufia says. "The child stays with the mother while the father provides for the expenses. When the child is able to stand on his own two feet and says he wants to be with his father, then one should let him go."

Constant insecurity

Legal aid adviser Rokeya regularly receives applications for assistance from rural women. Although most are concerned with demands for dowry or with second marriages, they rarely involve only one issue, as the application from Ratna Begum of Fultala, Jessore, reveals: "My marriage was registered in 1992. But for the past five to six months I have not received any maintenance. My husband then married a second wife without my consent. He has taken away my child. I have been driven away from my house. I am now seeking your help."

The letter shows how, in Sultana Kamal's words, "the combined forces of family laws...keep women in a constant state of fear and insecurity". Begum's husband can take a second wife if he wishes. Technically, the first wife's consent is required, but he can simply divorce her if she withholds it. He only has to pay her maintenance for a limited period. He can also take her child, secure in the knowledge that by the time the courts do anything about it, the child may be deemed too old to live with her.

With personal laws so biased towards men, a husband can easily use them to 'punish' his wife, according to Sandra Kabir of Population Concern. "A father often retains custody of the child to...blackmail her into accepting his terms for the marriage and relationship." [21]

Despite the numbers of women who are divorced or

abandoned by their husbands – the 1993-1994 Demographic and Health Survey states that among ever-married women three percent are divorced or separated [22] – the consequences for women have attracted less discussion than other personal laws such as inheritance. For women, marriage is almost mandatory, but they have little choice as to whether or not to stay married. Divorce is seen as a method by which a husband punishes his wife or disciplines her, according to Sultana Kamal. In marriage, as in its dissolution, Sandra Kabir points out, "it is important to recognise the pressures exerted by traditional culture, religion and society – on both women and men".[23]

The dissolution of their marriage may result in women losing their children, their source of income and their social status. Their chances of remarrying are slim in a society that allows men to take two wives but looks down on divorced women. Young women often have much older spouses and consequently face widowhood, divorce and abandonment at a younger age than men. In one rural survey, 95 percent of the divorced women were found to be under 29 years of age.[24] Women struggle to survive: 40 percent of female-headed households are categorised as "extremely poor", compared with eight percent of male-headed households.[25]

Obedience before health

The fear of divorce in the absence of any blame on their part traps women in unsatisfactory – even dangerous – marriages. They tend to suppress their own needs, to the detriment of their physical and mental health, and to report their husbands' illnesses rather than their own.[26] Dr Turo Rosario, a young woman doctor working in a one-room clinic on the outskirts of Jessore deals with this daily. "They are so oppressed," she says, "that they can't even open their mouths and say what they want.... Where both the husband and wife come to consult me, the wife will say, 'See my husband first.'"

Personal laws "most certainly" influence a woman's reproductive rights and health, according to Habibunnessa, a lawyer involved in legal aid work. "A woman has no say in matters relating to her reproductive function," she states. "She cannot bear or space her children according to her convenience. This, I believe, is so with women from all strata of society. Take for instance my case. I have a child, whom I conceived according to my husband's desire, and want no more. My husband certainly wants more and questions my right to deny him this.... I am a working woman capable of supporting myself, yet I have to defend my reproductive choices every other day."

Habibunnessa gives another example: "One of my clients, frustrated after having four girls, seeks my help because he wants an heir. When I questioned him as to how his wife felt about bearing another child he replied: 'What would she say? It's my child she bears. She simply has to do it.' Men believe that since it is they who are paying for their child's welfare, maintenance, and they who are their natural guardians, it is entirely their decision. In my opinion our personal laws are always discriminatory towards women...[and place us] always under the protection of fathers, husbands, and sons."

Although approximately one third of reproductive-age couples now use some form of modern contraception, many women who want to use contraceptives still face opposition from their husbands, in-laws and community leaders.[27]

Bangladesh is a country with an extreme preference for sons. Josna, in her mid-thirties, is visiting the Model Family Planning Clinic in Sylhet clandestinely. Her husband told her he would be satisfied with a family of two sons and two daughters, but by trying to grant his wish Josna has already had five children, all girls. "If he asks me why I have stopped conceiving, I will just say, 'It must be Allah's will.'" She does not know how he will react if he finds out she has been to the clinic. "He may or may not scold me. It's hard to tell what a man thinks," she says.

It is not rare for women such as Josna to be severely punished for using contraceptives without their husbands' approval. Shahana, a housemaid in Dhaka, was abandoned by her husband because she was "too bold". "After my first child was born, I was determined not to have any more because my husband had no income and no desire to earn either," Shahana explains. "We lived on what his parents or my parents gave us, and occasionally what he brought home after gambling. I was not allowed to work either. 'No wife of mine will step outside my house' was his order. He discouraged me from using pills because he had heard from other villagers that these...would remain inside my body and form into a cyst. If I fell sick, he would not want to bear the expenses."

But Shahana was determined, and went to a health care centre to get contraceptives. "I told my husband and mother-in-law I was taking the child for vaccination," she recounts. "When he discovered the truth I was really scolded by his mother and beaten by him, because I defied them. [And] they said the IUD would go up to my liver and I would die," she says.

A recent study shows that such misconceptions about contraceptives are found in all regions.[28] About 25-32 percent of respondents believed that vasectomy was a form of castration. Researchers have also found that significant numbers of husbands and relatives often oppose contraceptive use, believing that it reduces women's ability to do physical work.[29]

Rahima, a 40-year-old cook who has lived in Dhaka since the age of 20, says: "Allah will strike those who manipulate his desire. Children are his gifts to us and...He surely sees to their wellbeing as well. Man need not think about who is going to feed the child." Rahima cites the experience of her own family: "My mother never allowed my sisters nor my sisters-in-law to use anything. My grandmother didn't allow my mother or aunts to do so. Look, I had seven children, four died and three remained. You see, Allah takes care of all things on earth."

Rahima is proud of her "very obedient" sisters-in-law. "My mother is very strict and...her daughter-in-laws never talked to any strangers, like family planning workers. [They] never went to the hospital except with my mother for the children. If they were ever sick, home-made relief was given to them," she explains.

Dr Tahmina Sarker, in charge of the medical section of Concerned Women for Family Planning, feels that a woman's choices are above all influenced by her husband's beliefs. "The husband's and the mother-in-law's word, because sons depend on mothers regarding such decisions, is law for these women. They believe that barring childbirth is a taboo according to the Qur'an and their blind faith is doubled by the *moulanas*' [priests'] sermons," she says.

"When a family planning worker visits clients their prime job is to involve all members of the family," Dr Sarker explains. "[Yet] even in urban areas women wait for their husband's yes or no, they say it is not a matter of individual choice, especially when someone wants to use copper-T or Norplant. Because of prolonged bleeding husbands disapprove, but if proper counselling is given they tend to continue."

Induced abortion is restricted in Bangladesh except to save the life of the woman.[30] Nevertheless, the government does provide for menstrual regulation (MR) services for women who fear they may have an unwanted pregnancy. The practice of MR is thought to save well over 100,000 women from the dangers of unsafe abortion every year.[31]

The Bangladesh Women's Health Coalition (BWHC) was founded in 1980, and initially consisted of one clinic in Dhaka, providing MR. It has now has seven multi-service clinics in urban and rural areas, attending to women's gynaecological, obstetrical and health problems and children's health needs, as well as providing contraception,

MR and general counselling.

While NGOs such as BWHC may transform the lives of some women, many women remain isolated, dependent and without access to reproductive health services. As a result, every year an estimated 750,000 resort to unsafe abortion, mostly in clandestine circumstances.[32]

Much ado about...rights

According to some, complaining about the effect of religious laws on women is all much ado about nothing. The Islamic Foundation is an educational and missionary organisation involved in social work and the dissemination of Islam. Syed Mustafa Kamal, Deputy Director of its branch in Sylhet, a district known for its conservatism, does not perceive personal laws but people's ignorance of religion as the problem. "We asked a group of women graduates what their *kabinnama* [marriage contracts] contained and no one knew," Kamal says. "Even educated people don't have any knowledge of Islam and their rights under it."

Women's rights would be ensured if the provisions of personal laws were followed strictly, believes Kamal. "Women do not even receive what they are due under the inheritance laws, for instance. If a father fails to give land to his daughter, then he is acting outside his religion." On the subject of guardianship and custody, he denies that the law works against mothers. "Fathers normally don't want to keep the child," he adds.

This view is questioned by Ayesha Khanum, General Secretary of Mahila Parishad, a nationwide women's organisation with 45,000 members at the grassroots level. "When proceedings for divorce are brought and maintenance is demanded, the fathers want their child back."

The women of Hudarajapur also disagree with Mustafa Kamal's view. "You say that fathers do not want to take their children?" one woman retorts, "So many snatch their children away. The men believe, 'It's my child, why shouldn't I keep it?'" But would a father on a low income really want the added burden of an extra child in practice? "[He] just gets another woman to mind the child," the woman explains. Another says that if men realise they are to blame for the break-up of the marriage they fear problems later on. "They think, 'When the son grows up and realises [this], then he may side with the mother and cause me trouble. But if I educate him and feed him, he will be with me,'" she says. "Many fathers do want the child for this reason."

Syed Hassan, is a bank employee and father in his mid-thirties who feels wronged by his ex-wife. He is considering bringing legal action to regain custody of his son, who was just three months old at the time of the divorce. "I didn't file a custody case [then] because I didn't want to scar my son – it's not his fault," he explains, "but this doesn't change the fact that I am his natural guardian and that my ex-wife is just the custodian. She cannot make any decision on his behalf without my consent. But she violated the law, she took my son away from the country, denied my visiting rights, refused to acknowledge my desire to pay maintenance. If I sue her now I am positive I would win the case." His confidence reflects his belief that the law is on men's side.

The campaign for legal uniformity: progress and backlash

Breaking the vicious cycle of women's subjugation, however, requires more than intervention at the individual level. The Mahila Parishad has launched a campaign to introduce a Uniform Personal Code in order to redress the inequalities between men and women of different communities perpetuated by different personal laws and other antiquated legislation.[33] The draft Code, presented to the government in 1992, proposes new legislation on the registration and dissolution of marriages, and on maintenance, inheritance, adoption and guardianship.

"From our point of view, the spiritual and ritual aspects of life should be followed according to one's community but there should be civil uniformity where the legal aspect is concerned," says Ayesha Khanum of Mahila Parishad. "There is uniformity in criminal law. We need uniformity where women are concerned as well. The spirit, attitude and structure of the laws have now become an obstacle to the women's movement. It is not such a rigid code that we cannot change it," she adds.

Moulana Amini, General Secretary of Islami Okhiya Jote, a fundamentalist political party, disagrees: "Time may change but not Allah's laws," he says. In his view, Allah created men to rule women and "Muslim law [ensures] proper rights to women over their children and their own selves. Allah's laws cannot be discriminatory – women are getting what they deserve." Likewise, Syed Mustafa Kamal of the Islamic Foundation sees no need for a uniform code. "Allah is the creator of the whole world. His is the uniform code," he asserts.

Islamic groups are not the only ones with doubts about reforming personal laws. Members of minority religions are also wary of attempts by the Muslim majority to change their religious practices. Subrato Choudhury, a Hindu and an advocate at the high court in Dhaka, believes that Hindu personal laws require modification and in theory supports proposals for a uniform code. "We need groundwork first," he qualifies.

Choudhury says there is still rampant discrimination against minorities in all aspects of life and any attempt to change traditions risks looking like a further attack on their cultures. "Ten years ago, the Bangladesh Puja Ujjapon Parishad [Bangladesh Hindu Celebration of Worship Forum] took the initiative to discuss reforms in divorce and property laws to benefit women. But [objections] came in from different districts, from Hindu lawyers, judges, university professors."

Even those who support the idea of reforming personal laws are cautious. Aftab Choudhury, a journalist in Sylhet, says: "There should be changes in the personal laws. But with greater education, society itself will want it. If it is done suddenly, the religious leaders will agitate against it."

The comment is a telling one in a country that has seen a sharp increase in recent years in the number of *fatwas* (religious decrees) issued against individual women deemed to have transgressed social norms or women who have strongly asserted their human rights, including their sexual and reproductive rights.

NGOs seeking to empower women have also been persecuted. The Bangladesh Women's Health Coalition (BWHC), which raises awareness of personal laws governing marriage, divorce, inheritance and the guardianship and custody of children – as well as providing reproductive health services – found its offices in Sylhet burnt down by a frenzied mob in 1994.[34] On the same day, Islamic fundamentalists called for a nationwide strike against author Tasleema Nasrin following a *fatwa* sentencing her to death for criticising the persecution of both Hindus and women.

There have been many less publicised cases of *fatwa* victims brutalised, killed or driven to commit suicide because of "the organised efforts of radical clerics to spread the culture of *fatwa* all across the country", according to one NGO worker.[35]

Religious conservatism remains the greatest stumbling block to change. According to Ayesha Khanum, Mahila Parishad's campaign for a uniform code is backed by 90 percent of women's organisations in Bangladesh, as well as enlightened professionals. "But the political climate is not conducive. There is a large gap between leaders of women's groups and the political leaders. When religion is used in politics, it is bad news for women's emancipation."

Although Bangladesh Law Minister Abdul Matin Khasru maintains that his government is committed to affirmative action for women, he defends official reluctance to enact the 1992 draft Uniform Personal Code, stating: "...it is not possible for a democratic government to take a step that might hurt the religious faith of the people".[36]

Prospects for change

The gap, however, is not unbridgeable. Women's groups and the government are in agreement at least on the pressing need to improve the status of girls and women. The Ministry of Social Welfare has formulated a Decade Action Plan for the Girl Child in Bangladesh in order to pursue the objectives of the South Asia Association for Regional Cooperation (SAARC) Decade Action Plan 1991-2000. Although personal laws are not specifically mentioned, the plan states that the intention is to "reconstruct...the socio-economic and legal system to become more supportive of women's development on an equal footing with that of men".

The government has also prepared a Draft Participatory Perspective Plan (1995-2010) aimed towards eliminating all forms of discrimination against women. Unlike previous drafts, this one includes "equality in the family and society" as one of its targets. The Fifth Five Year Plan, which is currently being prepared, and the National Policy on Women's Advancement, approved in February 1997, also mention the need to achieve equality between men and women in *all* spheres.[37] Further, as the government's 1997 report to the Committee on the Elimination of All Forms of Discrimination Against Women (CEDAW) frankly acknowledges, the protection accorded through the civil laws is "outweighed by the inequalities reflected in many areas of personal laws governing the life of women".[38]

In the same report the government also recognised that Shari'a law is "not immutable" [39] and withdrew its reservations to two articles of the Women's Convention (the Convention on the Elimination of All Forms of

Discrimination Against Women), including Article 16(1)(f) which gives women the same right to custody and guardianship of their children as men have. This is in addition to its original acceptance of 16(1) (d) which gives men and women the "same rights and responsibilities as parents, irrespective of their marital status", but adds that children's interests are paramount. The government still holds a reservation against 16(1) (c), which ensures the "same rights and responsibilities during marriage and at its dissolution". As a result, Bangladesh is now theoretically committed to providing men and women with equal rights and responsibilities as parents and guardians, while at the same time failing to grant equality of the sexes within marriage and at its dissolution.

The country report also claims that other reservations to the Women's Convention are currently being reviewed. The most important of these is its reservation to Article 2 which requires states "to pursue by all appropriate steps and without delay a policy of eliminating discrimination against women". Without this provision the ratification of the Convention is arguably a symbolic exercise only.

In April 1999 Bangladesh Prime Minister Sheikh Hasina announced a national policy to promote "equality between men and women in all spheres of life".[40] "Nobody will give you your rights, you have to achieve [them] through struggle and fight," she told a gathering of women officials, urging them to insist on equal treatment. But while official recognition of equality is welcome, Hasina's message seems to imply that empowerment is more a matter of individual – not governmental – responsibility.

There are signs of change at the grassroots, too, even in conservative districts. BWHC was able to resume its work in Sylhet after holding discussions with district authorities and local officials, negotiating with religious leaders and their followers, and organising public meetings – attended by the husbands, fathers and brothers of the women of the community – at which prominent people spoke in the organisation's favour.

Rights lawyer Sultana Kamal observes that when changes were last made to the codified personal laws, in 1961, Bangladesh was "a religious society...[and] there was no resistance from the people". Although Bangladesh is still a religious society, this does not preclude a growing awareness of women's rights. According to Kamal, religious leaders nowadays purport to speak "in the name of the people" when they oppose reforms, but do not bother to find out what 'the people' really think. Other activists emphasise the flexibility of Islam to accommodate change.

Changes cannot come too soon for Nasima. Unlike most Bangladeshi women, she did not grow up acutely aware of her inferior status in society. "I was always a confident young girl," she says. "My father died when I was a baby and my mother singlehandedly raised my sisters and me. I was told that I could do anything." Nasima went to college, completed a Master's degree and even married a man of her own choice despite the disapproval of some family members. "I thought I was a person; I never really made a distinction between being a man or a woman," she says, until her marriage fell apart and the bricks of the legal system came crashing down on her head.

It has been more than five years since her husband took their son. After years in court, she has only been able to obtain visiting rights twice a week. For Nasima, the greatest betrayal has been that of the legal system. In her bitter experience, paradise lies nowhere near a mother's feet.

A Field of her Own
Women and land rights in Zimbabwe

Pat Made

Farmers Virginia Manyange, a 30-year-old mother of three, and her sisters-in-law are officially landless. They live in one of Zimbabwe's Resettlement Areas (RAs), Jompani, 250 km west of the capital, Harare, where government permits to land are usually not issued jointly to spouses but to men only. The women and other family members of the Manyange homestead labour on 12 acres of arable land where they grow cash crops. Working conditions are tough. "You spend several hours walking to the fields and by the time you get there you are totally exhausted," says Virginia.

In addition, each woman cultivates a *gandiwa*, a one-acre plot traditionally granted by husbands for their wives' exclusive use. Here they grow crops for their families, some of which they sell locally to meet school fees, purchase school uniforms and buy nappies for their babies. The extra income also funds personal items such as sanitary pads, covers bus fares to visit relatives or attend funerals and supplements general family expenditure. Like other women at Jompani, however, the women of the Manyange family have little power to determine the pattern of family spending – despite making a substantial contribution.

The women's access to resettlement land is precarious. Should a husband die, a land permit does not automatically transfer to his widow unless both spouses were joint signatories. For a wife abandoned or forced to leave an abusive marriage, divorce usually spells economic ruin. It is she who must leave the resettlement land where she has laboured. She can try to apply for a land permit elsewhere; however, she may be sent packing. "When we want to register...we are tossed back to our ex-husband's village," one Jompani divorcee reports bitterly. More often a divorced woman will try and return to her parents' home – but her family may not welcome her back.

Neighbour Monica Makubalo concurs. "It's worse if you get divorced and are chased away from your husband's plot, because back home your own family does not even want to see you. They, too, are scrambling for land."

Unable to register for resettlement elsewhere, a divorced woman may be left in limbo. One woman at Jompani, who asks to remain anonymous, reports that she and other divorced women are treated "like beggars" because they have no access to land and are forced to seek assistance to care for their children.

"What is very shocking is married women's...pervasive fear of being chased away from their marital homes," says Maia Chenaux-Repond, a former civil servant who has devoted the past 18 years to investigating gender issues and land rights. "Wives are acutely aware of how vulnerable they are. As a result they tend to be unassertive within marriage.... If they are divorced, men retain the home and property and [the women] are destitute."

Dependency on men for access to land means that women may stay in marriages even when these put their health, including their reproductive health, at risk. In 1996, the Harare-based Musasa Project, the first Zimbabwean non-government organisation to investigate and confront violence against women, conducted a survey in rural Midlands Province.[1] Of the 966 women (of all ethnic backgrounds) interviewed, one in three had been sexually abused, sexually harassed or forced to have sex against her will, and one in 12 had been assaulted (beaten, kicked or hit) while pregnant. Yet most had tolerated the abuse for fear of being driven out of the marital home.

"If I am chucked out by my husband and with only my Grade 3 education, where would I go and what would I do?" asked one woman in Matebeleland Province during a Musasa gender training and information seminar.

"What! No such thing!"

The Zimbabwean government prides itself on its progress in implementing women's rights, including legislation to change inheritance and child custody practices. But even a new inheritance law does not cover land rights.

Progress on all fronts, however, has been overshadowed by a March 1999 Supreme Court decision stripping women of their legal adult status. If the ruling is not overturned, it makes a mockery of step-by-step attempts over two decades to improve the lot of Zimbabwean women.

Ironically, in January 1998, the government delegation to the Committee for the Convention on the Elimination of All Forms of Discrimination Against Women (CEDAW), cited the 1982 Legal Age of Majority Act (LAMA) as one of Zimbabwe's chief achievements. In granting majority status to women – like men – at the age of 18, LAMA had been hailed by many as a major piece of legislation that moved women from the realm of minors to full adult citizenship with the rights and entitlements of this status.

Yet soon after the delegation's return, some parliamentarians once again clamoured for the law to be repealed, as they had done periodically since its enactment. The reason? LAMA was "destroying" traditional culture and families. "What is good in England and America does not... mean the same should apply to Zimbabwe," MP Livingstone Manhombo objected. "The executive should [say] it loud and clear that, beyond [women] voting, this House is against the Legal Age of Majority Act."

In July 1998, the minister without portfolio in charge of resettlement, Joseph Msika, was similarly dismissive of the Women's Land Lobby Group, a coalition of activist organisations, when he rejected outright their demands for land permits to be registered in the name of both spouses, and for the 5 million hectares earmarked for redistribution to be given to single, unmarried women or women heads of households. His reason: such policies would lead to the break-up of homes.

This fear is echoed by some Jompani men. "What! There is no such thing as...women owning land in their own right. If it's for widows, that is understood," says Phineas Gwafa, a respected village elder and warden for 17 villages.

"I totally disagree with a [land] quota system for women; it will lead to increased divorce cases. A single woman has no capacity to run her own land. What happens to it when she decides to marry and move to her husband's village?" argues 31-year-old Sabelo Makubalo.

Opponents of LAMA were, therefore, jubilant when the March 1999 Supreme Court decision over inheritance relegated women to the category of "junior males" in their families. In a controversial ruling that made international headlines, all five male judges declared that 58-year-old Venia Magaya was not entitled to inherit her deceased father's land – although she had been appointed his heir – because of her sex, and awarded it to a half-brother. In his decision, Justice Gibson Muchechetere stated that under customary law African women are subordinate to the male household head, both in their families of birth and marriage. The Court also reinterpreted LAMA, declaring that it was never intended to supersede customary laws governing marriage, divorce, inheritance and custody and to grant women "additional rights which interfered with and distorted some aspects of customary law".[2]

The ruling, which wiped out 20 years of women's legal rights by "elevating customary law over constitutional rights", according to women's and human rights organisations in Zimbabwe, [3] provoked disbelief and anger, and galvanised opponents into action. A petition has been presented to Parliament calling for legislation making all Zimbabwean women – black and white – equal to men. "We are determined to see that women have access to justice," said Lydia Zigomo, director of the Zimbabwe Women's Lawyers' Association. Calling the decision a "setback", she declared, "It will not change our goal. We will continue working for justice." [4]

Magaya had appealed to the Supreme Court because of a lower court ruling that upheld the right of her half-brother to evict her from her deceased father's home and land.

Gender on the land agenda

Various categories of land exist in Zimbabwe: commercial farmland, which is the most fertile land, traditionally settled and owned by whites (now also by members of the black middle-class); the communal lands, formerly known as 'tribal trustlands' or 'the reserves', inferior in quality, overcrowded and allocated by the former colonial regime to the black majority population; and resettlement areas (RAs) where, since the country's independence in 1981, land has been redistributed to the black population.

In October 1997, President Robert Mugabe captured international attention when he instituted the second phase of land redistribution in which over 1,400 farms, still largely white-owned, were targeted. "We are going to take the land and we are not going to pay a cent for the soil," he announced. Unsurprisingly, landowners mounted vociferous protests.

Again, gender concerns were left out of the controversial land equation, women lobbyists say, forcing them to band together with other civic organisations to put 'gender on the land agenda'. "Land is such a political issue," says Shereen Essof, Programme Coordinator at the Zimbabwe Women's Resource Centre Network (ZWRCN). "The government seems totally closed to land rights for women. There has been a gradual attitude change in some quarters, but no huge success for women on this issue," she says.

"Women are already managing the land," points out Rudo Kwaramba of the Musasa Project. "But having land rights would give women more control over the income from the land they now manage, and would be one more step towards empowerment."

Subsistence farming is a largely female domain owing to the historical migration of men to the towns, a trend that has continued since independence. More than 70 percent of Zimbabwe's agricultural labour force are women whose economic and social survival depends on access to land. As producers of agricultural and other goods, women contribute to the nation's Gross Domestic Product (GDP) and generate income for the family. But the extent of their involvement in small-scale agriculture, the informal sector and within the household has been inadequately documented, resulting in an underestimation of their economic contribution. [5]

Women did not benefit directly from the first phase of land redistribution in the 1980s; and a 1994 Land Tenure Commission, although confirming that women have unequal access to land, presented no recommendations to address their marginalisation. In a report, 'The Gender Dimension of Access and Land Use Rights in Zimbabwe', prepared by ZWRCN as evidence to the Commission, the precarious nature of women on the land is highlighted: "Married women in the communal lands only have secondary land use rights through their husbands, single women find that preference is given to their brothers, while divorced women are forced to leave the land with no guarantee that they will have access to land in their own home areas. And widows may be evicted from the land they have worked on for years by male relatives of their husbands."

In the RAs, female-headed households (widowed and divorced women with dependants) can, in theory, acquire permits to land, but married women still only have secondary land use rights through their husbands.

To gather data to present to the Land Tenure Commission, Women and Law in Southern Africa (WLSA) carried out research on women's and men's land rights in three 'Model A' resettlement schemes (where individual plots are worked with family labour). Among its findings,[6] published in 1994, were that 87 percent of permit holders were male, that almost all women permit holders were widowed or divorced women with children, and that wives had lost some of the independence they had under traditional land tenure.

Although less than one percent of the black majority population lives in the RAs, these have become a focus for the women's land rights campaign because they represent the government's showpiece pledge to restructure land access. WLSA argues that because there is "little that is traditional about resettlement" - where people willingly uproot themselves and begin a new life away from ancestral lands and traditions - "resettlement schemes are a good place for government to remove discrimination as regards land rights for women". [7]

Although pressure for reform has come mainly from women, there is evidence that a substantial minority of men would support it, too.

A 1993 survey involving 398 settlers, 145 of whom were men, studied attitudes towards women's ownership to land. [8] It found that 38 percent of men supported the idea of spousal ownership of land.

Not even a field of her own

Under the traditional land tenure system, it was customary for a man to give his wife a piece of land for her own use – to farm or even to sell. Proceeds from this land – typically a single acre – went to her estate, but in practice most of her earnings went to family consumption. "One of the reasons women wanted that portion of land was that when she died, her relatives would know that she was honoured and respected in the family in which she married," says Chenaux-Repond, an expert on women's issues and land rights.

Unfortunately, the practice is getting rarer, in both the RA and communal areas; only 60 percent of women in the RAs benefit from their husband's goodwill, according to Chenaux-Repond. Husbands justify this by claiming that since they are named as sole permit holders, they are forbidden to give their wives a field. Others defend the decision because land is already scarce and argue that women are not good managers. "Some husbands have given their wives fields, but they turn around and claim the proceeds. It boils down to the fact that he owns the land, wants control and therefore claims the proceeds," says Chenaux-Repond.

Emma Muyeye, wife of a Jompani councilman, believes that some men are still honouring the old tradition, giving their wives plots as generous as four acres. "But those who face the biggest problem are the ones with more than one wife. It is very difficult to allocate enough land for three or four wives – there just isn't enough," she says.

Phineas Gwafa, the 56-year-old village warden for Jompani, stresses the importance of wives' right to their traditional plot. "Some women even committed suicide when men took away the land," says Gwafa, who has two wives.

Intimate connections: production and reproduction

In a publication entitled 'Reproductive Health Rights in Zimbabwe' authors Rene Lowenson, Orna Edwards and Priscilla Ndlovu-Hove note that, historically, "relationships between men and women, production relations, property rights and inheritance procedures and social roles were often shaped by reproductive roles". [9]

At the heart of women's low status in Zimbabwe is the traditional system of *lobola*, or bridewealth, according to which, through payments in cash and in kind to the bride's family, a husband acquires rights, including sexual rights, over his wife. *Lobola* also gives the village elders and traditional leaders control over women's right to property. Married women may be granted secondary rights to land allocated to their husbands. But even this is a cultural and social obligation, and not enforceable by law.

Aquiline Mashoko, a widow on the Jompani RA, blames *lobola* for men's unwillingness to give women the profits from their labour. "The main problem...is that a man feels he paid *lobola* for you and he feels you are his property."

Independent of education or class, Zimbabwean women's security derives from their "belonging" within a family structure as wives and mothers, according to Musasa Project director Kwaramba. Women's dependency typically leads to a situation where they "hand over their reproductive health [and] rights to men or they try to use sex to control men", she believes. "Women still tend to have children even when they've been told that it is medically dangerous, to maintain security within a marriage."

Husbands who believe they are entitled to make unilateral reproductive decisions perceive themselves both as the chief earner and uncontested authority figure. "If I decide to have five children this is because I know I can look after them," one man told researcher N Wekwete. "The husband is the head of the family, and the wife can never tell me the number of children she wants to have."[10]

Thomas Deve, a political analyst formerly with the Southern African Political and Economic Society (SAPES), notes that women in the rural areas tend to have a large number of children, with a preference for boys. "A woman's failure to provide children leads to big problems," he says. Rumbidzai Nhundu of the Women's Action Group (WAG), part of the Women's Land Lobby Group, emphasises the psychological pressure that women are under. "Women still believe that bearing children will keep them within a marriage and on the land," she says.

Although the number of children born to Zimbabwean women in the rural areas has dropped from an average of six to four[11] due to the government's strong emphasis on family planning during the 1980s, women's reproductive choice remains limited. "Women may, at times, be able to space their children, but the man still can determine how many she will have. If she refuses, this leads to men taking other wives," says Elsie, a farmer who requested her surname not be mentioned. She has only one child and would like to have control over both the spacing and the number of further children.

Women also dread the emotional and economic fallout should they be unable to conceive; recent data show high infertility rates in Zimbabwe.[12] If reproductive tract infections go untreated they can cause pelvic inflammatory disease, which often results in infertility, ectopic pregnancy and chronic and debilitating pelvic pain.[13] Nhundu says health surveys among rural women by her organisation show that infertility is listed by women as a major reproductive health issue, as childlessness can result in divorce or husbands taking second wives, threatening their access to land. "[Women] also believe that having children will help to stabilise a man's character, again providing them security within the marriage," she says.

Not all Zimbabwean men insist on their unilateral right to sexual control. "These days every woman has a right to choose the number of children she wants, if anything we men are preferring fewer children," says Jompani village elder Gwafa. "It's very old-fashioned to insist on many children especially when the cost of living is so high."

Newly married Maidei Chatyoka, also of the Jompani RA, takes a less rosy view of the Zimbabwean 'new man'. She agrees that some now accept that their wives can use contraceptives to prevent unwanted births; however, women cannot insist that their partners use condoms to prevent sexually transmitted diseases (STDs), including HIV, the virus that causes AIDS. "You can never raise [that] issue because a man will tell you that condoms are used with prostitutes and not with their wives," Chatyoka says.

Internationally, women's reproductive health and rights have been recognised as a fundamental aspect of social justice. Zimbabwean women, too, have clear opinions about what their basic sexual and familial rights should be. Mabvuku Women's Group, a women's club sponsored by the non-government organisation the Makinah Carey Trust, brings together participants from different areas of Zimbabwe to a centre in Mabvuku, a high-density suburb of Harare. Asked to list the rights they thought they were entitled to, the women immediately identified "the right to know how to be protected against STDs, the right to keep children after a divorce, the right to say 'no' in sexual relations". But exercising these rights is quite a different matter.

Sex and violence

If women try to assert their reproductive rights with husbands, violence is all too often the consequence. "Communications around sex in the home is still a taboo," says Musasa Project's Rudo Kwaramba. "Sex is something women provide; it is not something to talk about," she adds, noting that the likelihood of violence means most women "won't even dream" of negotiating sexual issues with their partners. Project researchers have consistently found that not only outright violence, but the threat of violence, can be used by men to maintain control over women's sexuality and childbearing. Musasa clients – fearing attacks should they try to initiate a discussion on family planning – even report burying or hiding contraceptive pills.

Pregnancy does not always offer a respite from violence – despite the widely held perception in Zimbabwe that because fecundity is so culturally valued, violence against pregnant women would not be tolerated. A recent household survey conducted by the Musasa Project among 966 respondents – the first large-scale study to document women's experiences of violence in sub-Saharan Africa – found almost half (45 percent) of the women who had ever been pregnant reported at least one act of psychological or physical abuse. Of these, 22 percent reported being physically assaulted while pregnant, with 9 percent reporting blows to the abdomen and 4 percent reporting attacks with a weapon.[14]

Battering during pregnancy may cause, in addition to injury or death to the mother, premature labour, miscarriage or delivery of a premature or low-birthweight infant with reduced chances of survival. The Ministry of Health and Child Welfare has identified domestic violence as an important factor contributing to maternal mortality.[15]

Culturally, strict controls are placed on women's sexual behaviour to prevent the offspring of children outside of marriage, but no such controls are placed on men. It is widely accepted that men will have sexual relations outside marriage. This puts women more at risk of contracting HIV. According to Ministry of Health estimates, AIDS now claims 700 lives a week in Zimbabwe.[16]

Although rural women with little economic means or education have the fewest options, even educated, urban women often lack the sense of confidence and self-worth to ensure that they protect themselves. According to Lowenson, "Studies are beginning to suggest that the...behaviour [of the male partner] determines a woman's HIV status," regardless of her economic and educational status. [17]

"In my own right"

Kwaramba reports that women of all backgrounds may subject themselves to domestic violence rather than leave a marriage, so as to hang on to the identity and respected status that marriage confers. "'He can beat me as long as he keeps me' appears to be women's thinking," Kwaramba says, adding that the two things women fear are being "beaten to death" and being "sent away". "Women only talk about violence when they fear they are going to lose everything," she says. "We find that when they come to [the Musasa Project] they don't talk about the violence right away. This only comes out in the course of the conversation. What is clear now is that women can allude to their fears without naming them."

She says the country is at a stage where people now talk about violence, but not at the stage of legislation against it being put in place. "Zimbabweans, at all levels, now know what is 'politically correct', so men will openly say that it is not good for a man to beat his wife, but it is difficult to get to the heart of a person and for them to accept it at a personal level," Kwaramba says.

Lack of land rights, or insecure access to land, affects women of every marital status ('never-married' - both younger and older women), divorced, separated, widowed and married. Edna, from Chivu in the Midlands Province, is single. "My younger brother has a portion of land that is being kept for him at our home," she says. "But there is nothing for me, because it was assumed that I would get married. I want land of my own, too. It is culture that says we must get married to have access to land and a home."

Sara, a farmer's wife who also wishes to remain unidentified, feels that to be divorced (or "sent away") by her husband, or to find herself widowed, would leave her equally vulnerable. "Women are afraid to be on their own without a husband," she says. "Culturally, women must be under a man and it is still like that now. There is a stigma to women being alone."

"Yes, I need land in my own right, land that is for me and that does not belong to my husband," she continues. "Then when there is an argument, I don't have to worry when he says 'this is my land, you have to go'."

From grassroots to government

In 1998, 19 organisations formed the Women's Land Lobby Group to create a more cohesive lobbying force involving women and men. One of the group's strategies is to begin to mobilise women in the rural areas around the land issue so that their voices become more audible.

"The Lobby Group needs to bring in more women from the grassroots level so that they can own the process," says Rumbidzai Nhundu of WAG. "Pressure for women's land rights must come from women on the ground too.... We need women at all levels telling policy-makers the same thing as we are here in Harare. We must go out and see how we can mobilise rural women."

Despite the fact that none of the several dozen women and men interviewed at the Jompani RA knew about the Land Lobby Group, ordinary farming women have long recognised the need for women's land rights. According to widow Aquiline Mashoko, this consciousness is demonstrated whenever the District Administrator (DA) calls a meeting; the majority who attend are women seeking access to the land and official recognition in the RA programmes.

"Usually when there is a meeting at the DA's office, some three quarters of the people are women. [Nevertheless] it is their sons that get land, while they are left out, simply because they are women," Mashoko reports.

Winning over policy-makers is no easy task. Karen Dzumbira of Women in Law and Development in Africa (WILDAF), a pan-African organisation with a Zimbabwean branch, believes there is a genuine lack of understanding among Zimbabwean policy-makers of gender equality and women's human rights issues, although they may speak the 'politically correct' language. This new wave of conservatism, she says, may be because policy-makers are thinking more as men than as leaders: "They are not aware or do not understand what they are doing."

Rumbidzai Nhundu, too, refers to policy-makers' "lack of understanding", but adds that men, who are the majority of those in positions of power, "are not ready to give up the benefits of being men and the privilege that this bestows". "Political will to change is lacking," she says. "But men of quality are not afraid of equality."

Women are citizens, too

Feminist researcher Dr Patricia McFadden who works for SAPES believes that a central issue yet to be taken on in the women's land rights campaign is the question of citizenship. "Land is a scarce resource...an entitlement that derives from the right of citizenship," McFadden says. "Women need to start from the question 'who is a citizen?' Citizenship entitles one to exercise one's rights, have access to resources."

The notion of citizenship is not central to Zimbabwean women's sense of identity. "Men are centred as citizens and they demand their rights based on this," McFadden says. "It is clear that Zimbabwean policy-makers are coming from a different ideological perspective when it comes to women's entitlements and access to certain rights. It is believed that women are catered for by men." And, she adds, "when the state gives any right to women, they view it as a favour, as a privilege and not a right."

Says Thomas Deve: "We still operate according to...traditional customary law where women's identities are shaped by a sense of 'belonging' to the family." Rumbidzai Nhundu of WAG agrees. "The message that comes across," she says, "is that women are not citizens unless they are within a marriage".

The Women's Land Lobby Group has not yet addressed the issue of rural women's reproductive rights. "We have not reached that depth of analysis yet [of the connection between] land rights and reproductive rights," says Unity Chari, an activist and member of the coalition. The Women's Action Group is one organisation in the land lobby coalition that has specifically concentrated on women's health. But it, too, has not yet focused on the relationship between reproductive health and access to land except for examining the physical and mental health problems associated with farming in the resettlement areas.

For Priscilla Misiharabwi, director of the Women and AIDS Support Network, such analysis of the linkages between land rights and reproductive rights is more than timely. "The issue of land plays a big role in the socio-economic empowerment of women. Control and protection of reproductive health is still a problem and remains the main issue now."

Women's development on hold

"The land redistribution policies have been enforced by stereotypical attitudes," says Nhundu of WAG. "Heads of household should no longer be defined as just men, but as men and women."

Activists argue that women's land rights are integral to

national development. "We must begin to talk about the economic and development aspects of land rights for women," says Karen Dzumbira of WILDAF. "Development will be slowed down if 50 percent of the population is not involved."

"Women being able to own land is a poverty alleviation strategy," says Shereen Essof of ZWRCN. "If you give a woman her right to own land, she will invest more in the land and this will in turn have an impact on family sustainability. By giving the woman her land rights, this is a step towards economic empowerment.... [Her own] health and the health of her children will begin to improve."

"The financial rewards she reaps from the land will be used to develop herself and her children," Essof continues, adding that women will begin to invest more in the education of their children and in better health care. "The land lobby is not just to ensure rights to land, but rights to other resources."

International leaders are now hearing the message that women's land rights are integral to national development. In November 1999, 1,500 policy-makers gathered to discuss progress on the continent in implementing the recommendations of the 1995 World Conference on Women at the Sixth African Regional Conference on Women in Addis Ababa, Ethiopia. "Gender differences in ownership and control of land might be one of the most important factors [explaining] the gap in economic wellbeing, social status and empowerment between men and women," Angela E.V King, Special Advisor to the UN Secretary-General on Gender Issues and the Advancement of Women, told the meeting.

But calls for women's complete integration into Zimbabwean society intersect an economy in free-fall – in part due to demands for debt repayment under the World Bank/International Monetary Fund Structural Adjustment

Programme – with rising unemployment, rapid inflation, high interest rates and declining living and health standards. Domestically, students and workers have protested against anti-democratic measures such as banning strikes, press censorship and alleged corruption of the Mugabe executive.

President Mugabe is believed by many to have thrown the country into a constitutional crisis in February 1999 when he backed the army in opposition to the Supreme Court over the illegal detention and torture of two black journalists by military police for reporting an alleged coup among officers to end the government's unpopular and costly involvement in the civil war in the Congo (formerly Zaire). Mugabe's attack on his perceived enemies, particularly the judiciary, is also causing alarm among the donor community, which has been asked to help bankroll the government's compensation scheme to the 841 white-owned farms it intends to take over for distribution among the black majority.

One step forward, two steps back

In September 1998 the Women's Land Lobby Group made a presentation to an International Donors Conference on the Land Reform and Resettlement Programme. It also organised a women's workshop on land which ran concurrently with the official conference. Neither event changed the government's position on women's access to land.

Undeterred, the Land Lobby Group, in cooperation with the Zimbabwe Farmers Union, next mobilised a series of community workshops. "We are still in a process of sharing information across the board on women and land," says Shereen Essof. "But as a result of our presentation at the donors meeting, people are now taking us seriously and we have become a reference point on the...issue. We have been contacted by donors and others for more information. One woman was selected to be part of a government mission to Brazil to study the land reform process in that country."

Since Zimbabwe is a signatory to the UN Convention on the Elimination of All Forms of Discrimination Against Women (Women's Convention), activists say they will draw the government's attention to Article 14 of the Convention which recognises rural women as a distinct group who should be empowered to participate in, and benefit from, rural development. Their rights in respect of land and agrarian reform as well as land resettlement schemes are particularly mentioned, the Women's Land Lobby Group notes.

However, in the wake of the March 1999 Supreme Court decision denying Venia Magaya the right to inherit her father's land – a ruling that opponents say violates the country's constitution and international rights treaties – acquainting legislators with the fine print of the Women's Convention may be a non-starter.

Ordinary women, who could be the beneficiaries of the Land Lobby Group's efforts, say that in addition to legal changes in land distribution, including joint spousal ownership, they need strategies to help them negotiate and discuss their rights.

"Some men think that when you start talking about rights, you are not straight [faithful], or that you've picked up ideas from the women's club you belong to," says Georgiana, a young woman from Harare who regularly travels to her husband's rural home to help grow crops on his land there. "We need to know how to express the issue of rights in the home to men."

Another of men's fears is that with legal rights women might control cropping and income and spirit away profits to their parents – a notion Sabelo Makubalo, of the Jompani RA, rejects. "It's best that land get registered in both our names because my wife is aware of our family needs and there is no way she will siphon income from our fields to her own relatives. I trust her," he affirms.

"If you have a field of your own...you are then not like a child," was the comment of one rural woman interviewed by Women and Law in Southern Africa.[18] What Zimbabwean women – and their advocates – want is more than an individual husband's goodwill: they want equal access to land enshrined by law.

Women no Cry
Female-headed households in the Caribbean

Suzanne Francis Brown

Tradition paints the picture of a strong, independent Caribbean matriarch, ruler of her family within the domestic sphere. She is sturdy like the mountain backbone of Jamaica, assertive and feisty like the lyrical calypso music that springs from Trinidad and as loving as the many islands that dip and rise in a great chain around the Caribbean Sea. "We have the strength, the will, the mind and the ability to cope," says Diane, 37, from Trinidad and Tobago, a single mother with two teenage sons.

Take a closer look at the 'strength-of-black-women' thesis – a "near-glamourised picture of the resourcefulness, initiative and endurance of poor black women", according to Jamaican social scientist Pat Anderson – and another woman may be seen. In this woman's life, male partners – even if they are non-resident ones – may have a decisive say in her major life decisions: contraceptive use, childbearing and strategies for economic survival.

Caribbean patterns

Women-headed households are not unique to the Anglophone Caribbean. Industrial and urban development in contemporary developing countries – often accompanied by male labour migration – are associated with a worldwide increase in women-headed families, according to researchers.[1] However, women-headed households are more numerous in the Caribbean than in any other region in the developing world. Understanding why this is so, and exploring how Caribbean women experience family headship may provide insight into the lives of women worldwide.

The number of women-headed households varies across the Caribbean, with estimates ranging from 22 percent of all households in Belize, on the Central American mainland, to over 50 percent in Antigua and Barbuda, according to a 1995 Caribbean Community (CARICOM) study.[2] But the real extent of female-headed households – which are also overwhelmingly single-parent households – is thought to be even higher. Many women are 'de facto' household heads, whether through temporary absence of the man or because the woman is, in fact, the chief provider, although the man maintains titular headship.

Throughout the Caribbean, legal marriage and the nuclear family are viewed as an ideal, but they are more the exception than the rule. Younger women and men normally maintain 'visiting unions' [where men do not reside with their partners], gradually moving to common-law or legal marital unions in their middle years. A 1980 Pathfinder International study found that just one-quarter of Jamaican couples were married and that more than 70 percent of children were born to unmarried women. A 1995 St Lucia Family Survey shows that, in half the homes visited, children under 15 years of age were not living with their biological fathers.

Some 5 million people live in the 16 countries that make up the Commonwealth Caribbean. The majority are descended from West Africans transported to the region as plantation labour. After slavery was abolished in the 19th century, plantation owners imported indentured labourers from India. Chinese, Syrian, Lebanese and Jewish populations have also found their way to the region, making for a complex ethnic mix.

Within the African-Caribbean population, the historically high rate of households headed by single women has been explained as a consequence of slavery. Women were likely to keep close contact with their children over an extended period, whereas adult men might have been sold away from their families. In more recent times, female-headed households have tended to emerge when children, born of visiting relationships, remain with their mothers after the unions have ended.

Asian households, found mostly in Trinidad and Tobago and Guyana, are more likely to become headed by women because of male migration in search of employment. There is often a long gap before the wife is sent for, and sometimes she is not sent for at all.

The reasons that women come to head their households – whether by choice, circumstance or default – speak volumes about their relationships with Caribbean men, their hopes for their children and the social, cultural and economic systems within which they live.

Halima is an Indo-Guyanese woman who shares headship of her small household with her mother. She has one 10-year-old son. "The child's father gone his own way," she says. "Supporting my son is my responsibility. I wouldn't say the father helps." Asked if she would welcome another relationship, Halima replies: "I don't think I want somebody else.... He tell you that you can't go here and can't go there, and can't wear this and can't wear that."

Cora is a 50-year-old Afro-Guyanese woman who had her first child at age 15. Her last was born 24 years later. "Myself and the child's father separated about 18 years now," she says. "I've headed my household since then. I didn't choose it, but as the years go by, I got used to things and I leave it like that. When you have children, especially girl children, and you take somebody else, there's always problems – if not with yourself, with the children. A lot of things going on in Guyana with stepfathers. I didn't want that."

Cora refers to the problem of abuse, especially of girls, by men attached to their households – whether half-brothers, fathers, stepfathers or 'uncles'.

To manage economically, she did domestic and then supervisory work. "At one time I had three jobs. Sometimes I had to take the oldest children with me to assist.... I would [also] make things to sell – sugar cake and so on." As is often the case in the Caribbean, networks of relatives and friends helped out. Guyana has a legal framework of child support laws with suggested child maintenance rates for fathers, but Cora never sought to use them. The maintenance rates were too low to bother with, she says. Besides, "I've never seen my father or mother go to court, so I didn't want to go either."

Cora now works as a facilitator with Red Thread, a non-government organisation (NGO) that runs a women's centre. Her pain is evident when she reveals that – despite knowing first-hand the hardship of a woman raising a family alone, despite having contraceptive knowledge, despite their mother's consciousness-raising efforts – two of her daughters became pregnant while teenagers. One lives at home; the other has moved out.

Matriarchs in patriarchy

The mother-centredness of Caribbean families is often accompanied by male marginality and high numbers of children born outside marriage. Families may consist of a mother, several children who may or may not share a father, and other relatives of the same or different generations. These commonly include the children of the household's young adults, especially of daughters.

Many social scientists argue that the mother-centred family is a functional response to adverse conditions like poverty and unemployment, providing "a level of flexibility and adaptability in the face of economic change", according to Professor Elsa Leo-Rynie of the University of the West

Indies. Other coping strategies of female household heads include setting up small businesses, building strong support networks of family and friends and relying on male partners to provide some financial assistance.

Historically, Caribbean women have had a strong sense of self and place. During slavery, women, alongside their men, engaged in active rebellion, as well as using more subtle methods to subvert the system. One technique used by female slaves was to prolong breastfeeding, a time when they received extra allowances and benefits from plantation bosses. During the early 20th century women played a significant role in the region's nascent labour and welfare movements.

Despite women's activism, both private and public, the region's underlying systems – particularly the formal economy, religious institutions and many cultural norms – remained patriarchal.

The rise of the women's movement in the 1970s, with its focus on gender roles, demands for equality and reproductive rights and criticisms of 'macho' attitudes, has sparked a backlash of male defensiveness. "In our culture," says Audrey George, of the St Lucia Planned Parenthood Federation, "the man has always been the dominant figure. Now, when a lot of jobs are being held by women and we are doing well, many men see that as a threat. [They're saying that] a woman shouldn't be able to head [a family] and a woman shouldn't get the same salary as a man. Some young men are beginning to say that it's time the men take over their role again."

In St Lucia, a 1998 calypso competition featured an entry entitled "Where is you [your] husband?" The song, which targeted prominent women, challenged women's demands for rights. To Audrey George, its message was: "Don't come and tell me anything about rights [if] you don't have a husband. Because if you don't have a husband, that means something is wrong with you. If a woman doesn't have a man, she's not considered a woman. If she doesn't have a child, she's not considered a woman. And if a man doesn't have a child, he's not considered a man, either."

Joy, a Barbadian woman who is childless by choice, has felt pressure from friends and family. "Most women I come in contact with feel they should have children, even if it's only one." In fact, she experiences more pressure from women than from men. But she also recalls an otherwise enlightened male friend telling her: "Is time I see that belly big, you know."

In many poor rural and inner-city communities, a woman who chooses to postpone motherhood is called a 'mule'. Young motherhood is accepted almost as a rite of passage. "For many women, motherhood might present itself as a socially acceptable way...of maintaining an alliance with a man," writes researcher Hugutte Dagenais.[3] "Such a strategy is especially inviting to teenagers, for whom motherhood also constitutes the passage to adulthood."

But too early pregnancies can endanger young women's health and life. Complications include a higher rate of caesarian sections, premature labour, miscarriage and stillbirths among adolescents, especially those younger than 15, than among older women.[4] Pregnant teenagers are up to four times as likely as women older than 20 to die from pregnancy-related causes.[5] Pregnancy-related illnesses such as hypertension and anaemia are more common among adolescents than among adult women.[6] Early sexual activity also increases the possibility of developing cervical cancer – since it is linked to infection with the sexually transmitted human papilloma virus (HPV). The region has one of the world's highest mortality rates for this cancer.

Cultural trends are changing, however. A 1990-94 survey on sexual decision-making among Jamaicans, in which 2,580 people aged 15-50 were interviewed, found a general trend indicating that having many children is becoming less important in the lives of many Jamaican women.[7]

The study also found evidence of "a growing disdain

among Caribbean women for dependency on men", one aspect of which may relate to the traditional and quite open predilection of Caribbean men for many partners and, often, many families. Notes Guyanese researcher Nesha Haniff: "This double standard regarding the place of 'other women' in men's lives has bred cynicism and the belief that men lack discipline when it comes to women, and that the women in their lives are expected to indulge them."

Research shows that women may also have more than one partner, though discreetly. The sexual decision-making study found that among those surveyed the average number of partners in one year was seven for men and two for women. Joy, from Barbados, comments that among her women friends, most between the ages of 30 and 40, many might have two boyfriends, "but the two together wouldn't add up to one".

While it is broadly accepted that men will have multiple partners, women who have more than one partner, or even a succession of partners, are often castigated. One young man in Jamaica, visiting his 'baby-mother' (the mother of his baby) after an absence of many months, found her pregnant by another man. His reaction: "I take money to give to her for the baby and find her with a big belly, not one year after my baby is born. She's a whore. I won't take money round there to look after another man's baby."

Vexed relations

The comment raises the vexed matter of how Caribbean men and women view economic reponsibilities to each other and their families.

Many women in the Caribbean would say that men are irresponsible. Many Caribbean men would characterise women as nagging and greedy.

Janet Brown, of the Caribbean Child Development Centre, cites a study in which men and women in four

Jamaican communities concurred that man's primary role is as breadwinner.[8] A complicating factor is that men are often expected to contribute to several households, including those of their mothers who raised them, their sisters to whom they owe some responsibility, as well as their 'baby-mothers' and, where relevant, their wife and formal family. There is, says Brown, a tremendous demand upon the men. And where men do not have the will or the resources, they may simply stay away.

One study invited adolescent mothers in a back-to-school programme to comment on the men in their lives. "I know some baby-fathers...say their baby-mother come first, and they think their baby-mother special," said one. "Most of the ones I talk to feel that way." Another remarked, to general laughter, "But sometimes they have more than one baby-mother, so which baby-mother they calling special?" [9]

A 1994 United Nations survey notes that a significant factor behind the rising number of female-headed households is the perception that children are a private cost to be borne primarily by women. One indicator of male attention, or inattention, to their children may be the number who register their names on the child's birth certificate. In Jamaica, the Registrar General's Department reports that, of the 53,000 births occurring each year, less than a quarter are recorded in the names of both parents.

Indeed, many men distinguish between 'getting a child', which is treated like a notch on a gun, and 'having a child', which is more deliberate and usually comes with a degree of economic and social involvement.

But whether or not the men contribute, financially or otherwise, they remain important participants in many female-headed households.

"The fact that women are heads of household and single doesn't mean they are not in relationships and that they don't put up with abuse from men who don't necessarily live in the house," says researcher Haniff, who criticises Caribbean society which socialises women into romanticising both relationships with men and motherhood.

In Jamaica, Beryl Chevannes, the Executive Director of the National Family Planning Board, agrees: "No matter how much she may be single, be responsible for her own household, if she has a boyfriend, sex is going to come up as an issue and 10 chances to one, he is going to want her to have a baby for him and she is going to say 'yes'. Even a strong woman may be worn down. We've had women who've tied their tubes and a man comes along and wants them to have a baby and they come wanting to reverse the operation."

The cultural norm and belief that Caribbean men are not capable of devoting themselves to one woman also places their partners at risk of infection with sexually transmitted diseases (STDs), including HIV – the virus that causes AIDS, notes Sheila Stuart, executive director of Caribbean Rights, a regional NGO network. While AIDS in the Caribbean is more prevalent among men, most new cases are occurring among women who contract the disease unknowingly or from unfaithful partners who refuse to use condoms.

"Women will continue to be vulnerable to HIV/AIDS infection unless there is some behaviour modification among men," says Stuart, warning that those women who themselves have multiple partners or have a series of partners in swift succession, will be at even greater risk.

Pat Mohammed, of the University of West Indies Department of Gender Studies, maintains that "many [men] show signs of wishing to meet up to women's aspirations [for] joint partnerships. But distrust still seems to be a dominant feature of gender relations in the Caribbean."

A small number of Jamaican men have set up a group called Fathers Inc. to try to combat male parental irresponsibility and give Jamaican fathers a better image. It contends that many, if not most, men are good fathers who do their best to meet their obligations. But, as founding member and sociologist Barry Chevannes admits, "Tell that to a woman who has had to deal with the worst sort of situation and you run into a wall of scepticism, even anger."

Wielding power, taking decisions

Interviews throughout the Caribbean suggest that some women experience male violence as the norm – even a sign of love. "Beating is common and most women think it's normal," says Red Thread activist Cora, in Guyana. "In workshops, few will say that a man doesn't have a right to beat a woman.... Most say that if their man don't beat them, they don't love them. The man is showing his power over them. But they not seeing it."

In most Caribbean territories, the problem of domestic abuse goes far beyond the occasional beating. Although many cases are never reported to the police and few women seek prosecution, researchers from the Caribbean Association for Feminist Research and Action (CAFRA) found that 30 percent of women surveyed in an islandwide sample in Barbados in 1997 reported being battered as adults, with one in 17 noting severe, continuous abuse. Nearly one in three reported sexual abuse during childhood or adolescence. [10]

In Jamaica, recent statistics suggest that one in seven women between five and 60 years of age experience gender violence, with the rate for the 15-55 age group rising to one in four.[11] As many as 40 percent of Jamaican girls aged 11-15 interviewed for a study on teenage pregnancy reported that first intercourse was forced.[12]

Women throughout the region suffer blows rained down by spouses or visiting males – often where economic contributions have conferred an element of power. During a group discussion, Randy, a young Barbadian male, explains that violence is a frequent recourse especially among poor Barbadian men who rationalise, "If you take my money, you got to take my lashes as well".

As Beryl Chevannes of Jamaica's Family Planning Board states: "Poor women may have reproductive rights but they can't exercise them, due to dependency."

Joy, from Barbados, disagrees: "We as women, we love the man, we put up with nonsense...until we reach the position where we say, 'I done with this shit'". In the end, Joy says, women act.

Female household heads who achieve economic independence may be freer to take charge of their emotional and sexual lives; however, such change is neither easy nor automatic. There are, increasingly, a number of high-profile, professional women whose economic independence has meant more autonomous decision-making. Many head their household by choice, refusing live-in male partners or expelling abusive ones. Some women, when deciding to have a child, seek to raise it themselves, allowing the man no parenting role.

For other economically independent women, though well educated and assertive in their jobs, "when it comes to their sexuality they are very vulnerable [and] there appears to be other psychological factors operating", says Stuart of the NGO Caribbean Rights. "A lot of them remain in very abusive relationships even though they are financially and socially independent."

It took Angela, a 41-year-old office worker in Trinidad, many years to leave her husband after years of trying to resolve an abusive marriage. "Because of my religious and family upbringing, I thought that my husband was within his right to beat and verbally abuse me," she recalls, noting that each time she left, family, friends and her priest encouraged her to return and "make the marriage work". She is now the sole supporter of her two children. "Being economically independent played an important part in the choices I made," she says.

Romance and finance

Comments Dr Tirbani Jagdeo, executive director of the Caribbean Family Planning Affiliation: "If a woman has a job and has that level of independence, she is more likely to make decisions consistent with her interests than if she is dependent on the flow of income from a man. For women without other sources of income, their decisions are influenced by the guy."

Jagdeo comments: "On many, many occasions when a woman with a child from a previous partner establishes a new relationship, the man will say: 'I'm feeding this other man's child. Why shouldn't I have a child, too?' And, frankly, from his perspective, he makes sense.... But if that relationship doesn't last, she ends up with two children and she's going to be headed towards a third." When the resulting large households have limited resources the long-term economic and health impacts may be considerable.

Up to three quarters of women heading their households lack formal employment. Yet, as author Merle Hodge points out, there has never been a time in Caribbean society when women did not go out to work: "Women here have been 'going out to work' from morning – first as enslaved or indentured labourers, and after that as small farmers, cane cutters, domestic workers, market vendors, seamstresses, washers and ironers, inter-island traders, child minders, sellers of food at the roadside." [13]

Today, although some women have high-profile professional and managerial jobs, the majority of female-headed householders are concentrated in low-paid and low-status occupations, such as domestic work, factory work, waitressing, cleaning and working as shop assistants. Women also predominate among teachers, nurses and office clerks, traditionally lower-paid professionals. World Bank studies indicate that women earn just 70 percent of male earnings, with even greater gaps when female-headed households are compared to households headed by men.

Few female heads of household even have the security of a regular job. According to a 1993 study by Barry Chevannes, only a minority are in regular employment (25 percent in Barbados, 33 percent in Jamaica and Guyana, and 45 percent in St Lucia) compared with a majority of male household heads (66 percent in Jamaica, 75 percent in Barbados, 85 percent in St Lucia and Guyana).[14]

Joyce, a housekeeper, has a teenage daughter and three grown sons. She manages on a small salary, grows food at her 'ground' some miles from home, and benefits from extended family, friends and community networks. She describes the large number of working women who head households in her small village, located amid the coffee fields of Jamaica's Blue Mountains. "About 80 percent of the women up here have to go out and work for themselves and their children, judging by the number you can see in the square in the morning, going to the coffee. Some never lived with any man. The man just comes and gives them a child."

Changing the future

Few teenage mothers would be classifed as household heads. Most are in unstable visiting unions and most still live with parents. But teenage motherhood disrupts educational and career paths and may foreshadow future female-headed households.

For St Lucian physician Deborah Louisy-Charles, the major consequence of early pregnancy is its effect on the educational opportunities of the young women involved. Though there are noteworthy exceptions, in most Caribbean nations, pregnancy effectively ends a young woman's school career, which also affects her future earning potential and steers her towards the cycle of economic dependence.

The good news is that teenage pregnancy rates have dropped somewhat – from average regional rates of about

150 pregnancies per 1,000 teenagers in 1950 to about 90-95 per 1,000 today.[15] Changing times explain some of the decrease. Teenage girls whose expected course of action 50 years ago would have been to leave school early and start their families are now expected to remain in secondary school until at least age 15, with the possibility of building a career. Many of them are postponing pregnancy and even postponing their first sexual experience.

One programme, the Women's Centre Foundation in Jamaica, has turned around the lives of thousands of young Jamaican women, whose average age is 14 years, by providing the opportunity for pregnant schoolgirls to continue their education until their babies are born and they can return to their classrooms. Girls attending the Centre also receive skills training, contraceptive information and counselling, along with their parents and 'baby-fathers'. Fewer than two percent of girls who pass through the Centre become pregnant again during their teen years; the list of graduates include doctors, nurses, bank clerks, insurance agents and administrators. But while the Centre reaches thousands of teenagers, its target audience numbers tens of thousands.

Controlling fertility

Despite cutbacks due to economic recession and structural adjustment programmes, family-planning services are widely available in the region, supplied by both governmental and non-governmental agencies. Widespread use of contraceptives has cut average family size by half over the past 40 years, from six children in 1960 to less than three today. Caribbean women use modern methods of contraception, with the pill and female sterilization (tubal ligation) the most popular. Condoms, IUDs and injectables are available in various family-planning programmes across the region. "Having said that," Dr Jagdeo of the Caribbean Family Planning Affiliation adds, "only about 60 percent of sexually active women...use a good method of contraception."

Contraception and childrearing are generally considered to be a woman's responsibility. In a study of men's attitudes, conducted in St Lucia, half of those surveyed claimed to have discussed the subject with their partners. Most expected their partner to deal with the matter. "I never use contraceptive in my life," said a 21-year-old labourer and father of two. "If she get pregnant, she get pregnant." Among the few men who did use a contraceptive method, the following comment was typical: "My girlfriend uses the pill, and I use the condom with my other girlfriend." [16]

Nesha Haniff, who conducted the study, hypothesises that the way men value children is reflected in their contraceptive use: "If a man values his children little and has minimal responsibility for them in emotional and financial terms, his contraceptive use is likely to be correspondingly minimal."

In married couples and common-law unions, Dr Jagdeo believes that "male opposition to family planning doesn't play a significant role in a woman's contraceptive decision-making. The men oppose, but the number of women who take that opposition to the point where they don't use a method is pretty small." Women in married or stable partnerships know they are going to have regular sex and can organise their contraceptive methods appropriately.

Preventing pregnancy is more difficult for women in relationships "where the guy pops in now and then", he notes, or where women have more than one partner. "Levels of contraceptive use in visiting unions tend to be lower," he says. "They end up...having a first, second and third child."

When contraception isn't used, or when it fails, and unwanted pregnancy occurs, some women turn to abortion. In Barbados and Guyana, abortion is legally available for a broad range of health reasons, guaranteeing that the procedure is usually a safe one. In both Jamaica and Trinidad and Tobago abortion is illegal, with waivers allowed if a woman's life, physical or mental health is threatened, although Jamaican minors must obtain parental consent.[17] In other countries in the region where legal abortion is restricted, women who have the economic means pay for a safe abortion in a private clinic. Poor women and desperate teenagers must rely on unsafe, backstreet abortionists, putting their health and life at risk. Complications from unsafe abortion damage women's health and can claim lives, though there are no official statistics for illnesses or deaths resulting from illegal abortions. Given the battles raging over legalisation of abortion in many places, most Caribbean law and policy-makers prefer to be silent and "let NGOs take on the battle", says Jagdeo.

Local NGOs have fought other reproductive health battles in the past, he adds. "Family planning in the Caribbean was established by NGOs, sometimes without the support of governments, often with the silent support of government. NGOs had to bear the criticism, the stress, the vilification of people who thought that family planning was something to kill off black people, to make women free and loose, to undermine the moral fabric of society. But they took on that battle and now family planning has legitimate status in every single Caribbean country."

Emancipate yourself

From a legal perspective, Caribbean countries have a framework broadly supportive of women's rights, although laws relating to sexual and reproductive rights are rarely in one neat package.

Independent Caribbean states are all signatories to the United Nations Convention on the Elimination of All Forms of Discrimination Against Women (CEDAW – the Women's Convention). The Caribbean Community Secretariat is helping governments to revise legislation in compliance with this convention. Model laws have been developed in such areas as domestic violence, equal pay, sexual harassment and property, inheritance and financial maintenance rights.

Andaiye, an NGO activist and researcher who ran the Women's Desk at the Caribbean Community (CARICOM) Secretariat, believes that long-term changes in gender roles are required for women's lives truly to improve. In particular, education can help empower young women by increasing their chances of employment and, consequently, of greater independence. Dr Jagdeo is hopeful that this will soon be the trend, since the proportion of Caribbean girls attending and completing secondary school is now higher than that of boys. "The more this pattern continues," he says, "the more teenage pregnancy in the Caribbean will recede."

"It may not affect the number of female-headed households," he adds, "because women may still choose to head their households. But they wouldn't be headed by women dependent on other sources of income."

Family Life Education, including sex education, is also a key. While it is currently taught, to varying extents, in secondary schools, Beryl Chevannes in Jamaica advocates an earlier start. "We need to begin at age six with children in schools and the home, for them to understand that your life is your responsibility and you must be prepared to look after yourself in your own life. You need education. You need to have a skill, a job, earn your own living, be able to buy your own food, pay your own way and make your decisions."

Education for independence must also incorporate gender views, she adds: "what is expected of a man, what is expected of a woman, and how the two get together and plan their lives".

Jamaica's Fathers Inc raises these issues by showing videos on sexuality and parenthood, counselling men attending family court, consciousness-raising around annual Father's Day celebrations and organising a football competition for inner-city teams as a means of reaching young men. But the numbers they reach are admittedly limited.

"Despite the limitations, we have succeeded in putting a new dimension of fatherhood on the national agenda and the national consciousness," says Barry Chevannes. "People are aware that it's not so bleak. At the least, it has made people stop to think that there are men who are ready to stand up and say 'Hey, don't stereotype us'."

Yet among the St Lucian men interviewed by Haniff, awareness was not enough to break established patterns. Although they had suffered from the absence of a father in their own lives and had promised themselves that they would be different, many "ended up having a child outside of marriage, a child from whose life they were often absent".[18]

For their part, notes physician Louisy-Charles of St Lucia, "women are more aware of their bodies, more concerned about reproductive health issues. They're seeking answers to questions, not just being passive. They know more about theoretical things. But they're holding back about asserting themselves."

Women are increasingly conscious of the need for changed gender relations, but economic and cultural constraints continue to obstruct the transition from awareness to action. A Caribbean ministerial conference on gender issues, held in October 1999, highlighted obstacles to gender equality, particularly "poverty and violence against women [which cripple] women's capacities to secure the enjoyment of their human rights," according to Len Ishmael, director of the sub-regional office of the UN Economic Commission for Latin America and the Caribbean.[19]

Meanwhile, the myth of the indomitable, independent matriarch both obscures and simplifies an altogether more complex reality.

Legalised Cruelty
Anti-women laws in Pakistan

Hilda Saeed and Ayesha Khan

Karachi, 1981. It should have been a routine meeting for members of the Shirkat Gah Women's Resource Centre, but the mood of the small group of young women was quiet, tense, deeply concerned. They had just heard the news of an inhuman sentence passed on a young couple found guilty of adultery: a hundred lashes for the woman – who was pregnant – and stoning to death for the man.

Fehmida, the young woman in question, had married a man of her own choice, Allah Bux. Her irate father, believing his honour compromised, had lodged a case of kidnapping against the young man. In court, the couple was accused of adultery because their marriage was considered invalid. The punishment was alarming, cruel and unexpected.

The news of the judgement came like a bombshell. Most of urban educated Pakistani society, including the women at Shirkat Gah, were generally progressive in their outlook; they firmly shared the beliefs of their country's founder, Mohammed Ali Jinnah, that Pakistan should be a homeland for Muslims, but the government should remain secular. They had gradually become aware of the programme of 'Islamisation' pursued by the government of military dictator General Zia ul-Haq, who had seized power in 1977. But until this court ruling, they had failed to realise the full implications of laws passed in 1979 – the

Hudood Ordinances – under which the young couple had been sentenced.

The women at Shirkat Gah felt ill-equipped to deal with the crisis, but their anger won out. A meeting was called of all women's groups in Karachi, and Pakistan's activist group, the Women's Action Forum (WAF), was born. Its mandate: to ensure equality for women, and to work for the repeal of all discriminatory laws that were not in accordance with the Universal Declaration of Human Rights, to which Pakistan was a signatory.

WAF organised simultaneous rallies in Karachi and Lahore against the Hudood Ordinances. The police in Karachi were relatively restrained; those in Lahore tear-gassed the peaceful but large procession and beat several demonstrators, including popular national poet Habib Jalib. They arrested some of the activists, and forced the rally to disperse.

Fortunately, continuing WAF pressure and agitation helped to secure an honourable acquittal for Fehmida and Allah Bux.

Two decades later the Hudood Ordinances are still in place. In January 1998, Riffat Afridi, an 18-year-old university student from a Pathan family, married a fellow student from another ethnic group against her parents' wishes. Her enraged family charged her husband with kidnapping and claimed that Riffat was already married to a cousin. Riots broke out in Karachi, as opposing clans accused each other of violating their traditional values. When Riffat's husband appeared in court for trial, he was critically wounded by machine-gunfire. Subsequently the court acquitted him of kidnapping charges, but the couple faced conviction for adultery if Riffat's other alleged marriage should be proved.[1]

Fearing for their lives, the two students went into hiding while seeking asylum. Unfortunately, their applications were rejected by a number of Western countries, prompting Asma Jehangir, then chairperson of the non-governmental Human Rights Commission of Pakistan (HRCP), to argue that such cases should qualify for political asylum because the lives of individuals are at risk due to their wish to assert a fundamental human right to choose their own spouse.

A year later, in 1999, Samia Sarwar, an abused mother-of-two seeking divorce from a drug-addicted husband, was executed in her lawyer's office by a gunman hired by her own family. Her attorney Hina Jilani, sister and law partner of Asma Jehangir, narrowly escaped death in the attack. Because her parents had vehemently opposed her wish to divorce and threatened her for bringing shame on the family's 'honour' if she did so, Sarwar had taken refuge in a shelter for abused women in Lahore. Fearing to meet alone with her father, the current president of the Peshwar Chamber of Commerce, she had agreed to see her mother, a gynaecologist, in Jilani's office in April to discuss her situation.

Despite identification and witnesses, no arrests have been made – an outrage that has led to protests and demonstrations for justice in cities across the country. Instead, Sarwar's family continues a campaign of slander, death threats and *fatwas* (religious edicts) from the Peshwar Chamber of Commerce against Jehangir, demanding she be punished according to religious and tribal law.

According to a WAF statement, the Sarwar murder "illustrates the degree of brutalisation in society where parents can plan and execute the murder of their daughter for daring to exercise her rights as sanctioned by both law and religion".[2] Several hundred women are killed in the name of honour every year, but their murderers are rarely brought to justice, according to a September 1999 Amnesty International report [3] published in the wake of the military coup against the Muslim League-led government the same month. The All Pakistan Women's Association has asked the new military regime to treat honour killings as wilful murder under criminal laws.[4]

An editorial in the Karachi newspaper *Dawn* titled 'A grim reminder' blames Sarwar's death – and those of thousands more women since 1981 – on, among other factors, "the presence of Zia-era anti-women legislation [which] has been tolerated by successive governments and has been bent to suit the whims of male chauvinists".[5]

Targeting the vulnerable

Since its birth, Pakistan has experienced a series of swift changes of government, including two long spells of military dictatorship: the first from 1958 to 1969, followed by a short period of democracy, and the second – under General Zia-ul-Haq – from 1977 to 1988. Although he did not enjoy his people's mandate, Zia took power with a self-appointed mission to turn Pakistan into an Islamic state.

Zia's right-wing policies served a critical political purpose in developing something of a constituency comprised of small urban business, Islamist political parties, and of course, the powerful military. He appointed to his Cabinet three members of the Jamaat-e-Islami, an Islamist party without broad electoral support but commonly believed to be backed financially by Saudi Arabia. Prior to 1979, Pakistan's legal system had been a mix of colonial legislation, common law and religious personal law. With the support of his backers – and in a milieu of strict conservatism, inadequate communication, poverty and illiteracy – it was relatively easy for Zia to introduce constitutional and legal amendments in the name of Islam.

Fundamental rights were suspended, the country's constitution heavily amended and the new, anti-women laws came swiftly. The changes set in motion created an atmosphere of fear, brutality, divisiveness, intimidation and tension, which still exists today.

The Hudood Ordinances, based ostensibly on the Islamic Shari'a (or legal code of conduct), are a collection of five criminal laws, covering rape, adultery, theft, robbery, and prohibition of the use of alcohol and narcotics. Their stated aim, when introduced by Zia, was to bring the Pakistan Penal Code (PPC) and the Code of Criminal Procedure into conformity with the injunctions of Islam.[6] The word Hudood stems from *hadd* or limit: crimes under Hudood are punishable because they have crossed societal limits. The Ordinances apply to both Muslims and (with some differences) non-Muslims.

The Law of Evidence[7] promulgated in 1984 excludes women's testimony altogether in *hadd* (maximum) punishments and halves the value of their evidence in lesser *tazir* punishments and in civil matters. Non-Muslims are not allowed to give evidence,[8] in direct contravention of the 1973 Pakistan Constitution, which guarantees equality to all citizens irrespective of caste, creed or sex.

The new laws had a direct impact on the lives of women and non-Muslim minorities. Shahnaz Wazir Ali, educationist and member of the People's Party deposed by Zia, says that Zia avoided upsetting the status quo by targeting "the weakest and most vulnerable sections of society". "Secluding women and putting them out of the mainstream are visible and concrete manifestations of a conservative society," she says. As Shahla Zia, lawyer and activist, explains: "Almost all over the world where orthodox groups haven't been able to access political power, their move has been to retain a grasp on the personal or the family."

Zina: a dangerously fine line

Under the Hudood Ordinances, the offence of *zina* (unlawful sexual relations before or outside marriage) has had the worst impact on women. False allegations of adultery or fornication have been brought against women to intimidate them. Blatant miscarriages of justice have become synonymous with *zina*, punishing women who are already deeply vulnerable to abuse by the criminal justice system.

In rape cases (*zina-bil-jabar*), a woman, if unable to prove she has not given her consent to sexual intercourse, may find herself convicted instead. After nearly two decades of Hudood enforcement, it is rare for the accused male 'partner' to be convicted of rape. "In the earlier version of the Pakistan Penal Code...there was strong reliance on forensic evidence," says

Jilani. "Now, on the other hand, eye-witness evidence is considered primary, and forensic evidence is only accepted as corroborative or circumstantial evidence."

Women find themselves treading a dangerously fine line. A woman's situation is weakened by inadequate access to immediate and proper medical examination. If she conceives as a result of rape, the courts can interpret the pregnancy as proof of consent to sex and she may be liable to punishment.

Matters are further complicated by the fact that under Shari'a law a girl is considered an adult once she reaches puberty. Thus, a 10-year-old girl can be categorised as an adult if she has begun to menstruate, while a 16-year-old boy is considered a minor under the Majority Act.

When Safia Bibi, a blind 18-year old, filed a charge of rape in 1983 she was pregnant. The court found no evidence that she had been raped. Instead, she herself was sentenced to three years in jail and 15 lashes for engaging in sex outside marriage. This was a relatively light sentence, according to the judge, in view of her youth and blindness. It was only because of enormous domestic and international protest that she was acquitted on appeal in 1985.

According to Jilani and Jehangir: "While the alleged rapist is innocent in the eyes of the law until proven guilty, the victim is presumed to be guilty until she proves her innocence." [9]

The trauma of alleging rape, undergoing examination, facing an intimidating judicial process and the real possibility of finding themselves accused and punished under *zina* has prevented many rape victims from filing charges.

After the Hudood Ordinances came into effect, cases of reported adultery went from a handful to thousands in a short period of time. According to the Human Rights Commission of Pakistan (HRCP), 70 women were in prison in Pakistan in 1980. By 1988 over 6,000 women were in jail, accused of crimes under Hudood. [10] According to a 1995 Human Rights Watch report, between 50 and 80 percent of female detainees in Pakistani prisons were held under the Hudood laws; moreover, over 70 percent of women in police custody experience physical abuse, including sexual abuse, at the hands of their jailers.[11]

Some of the falsely accused and imprisoned are children. Amina, a bright 13-year-old from a town in Punjab, is in jail in Karachi. In an interview Amina says: "I was only five or six years old when an 'aunt' asked my mother if she could take me to Karachi with her, to help with housework, and to put me in school as well. My mother believed her. For some time, things were all right, though I didn't go to school. But when I was about 10, I was raped, and forced into prostitution. When I refused, I was beaten. And then one day I was caught, charged under Hudood, and brought here. My parents still don't know.... I don't even know how they will receive me now, even if I do go back. Anyway, I'd rather stay here – I'll never go back, not unless my mother or father comes for me."

In one women's police station in Karachi, out of the 113 cases filed between 1994 and 1996, 94 were under *zina*. Out of the 473 women admitted to Lahore's central jail between March 1996 and June 1997, an astonishing 158 were accused of *zina*. Courts habitually fail to offer bail, parole or probation to women. Unlike men co-accused, women are unlikely to have money for bail. Nor do they often have a relative who is willing to provide this to the satisfaction of the court. According to a new report by HRCP, most accused women face long periods of incarceration. Figures collected in 1998 from 20 jails in the Punjab found that of nearly 1,000 women prisoners, almost 90 percent were awaiting trial. The Commission also found that more than one-third of women undergoing trials did not have a lawyer to defend them.[12]

Because many female inmates have no access to legal help, they "languish for months in jail in a state of legal limbo", charged an editorial in the Karachi *Dawn* newspaper.[13]

However a huge number of women are tried for *zina* and not convicted, and the few cases that make it to appeal usually end in acquittal. Human rights activists believe this is proof that the law is being exploited in order to lodge false cases against women.[14]

One such case is that of Samina, a middle-class woman

married for 18 years. She had seven children, yet every time her husband found out that she was using family planning, he would beat her. Once, when she refused to sleep with him, he threw a padlock at her. When she could bear the situation no longer, she filed for divorce. On the days of the court hearings her husband used to tie her up and once threw acid on her. She finally fled to a women's shelter.

Realising that she would never return to him, her husband lodged a false case of *zina* against Samina and another man, alleging that they had run away together. With legal assistance from women's rights activist and lawyer Jilani, Samina was eventually able to secure bail, and then to get the case cancelled. Her divorce has been granted, but she remains in a state of fear. "He's still lurking in my neighbourhood. I'm scared for my life."

Justice Tanzil-ur-Rahman, former Chairman of the Council of Islamic Ideology in the early 1980s and a member of the Islamist party Jamaat-e-Islami, acknowledges a problem of implementation: "I agree, it has been *zulm* (cruelty, oppression) for women. These judges are corrupt, inefficient. They don't believe in humanity, let alone in Islam." Like other supporters of the controversial laws, he believes the solution is to Islamise all laws and remove any clash between Islamic legal provisions and the existing statute books.

While scholars debate the religious merits of the legislation, it remains in place to the advantage of anyone who wishes to exploit it. Among the thousands of registered cases against women under Hudood, there are husbands who have used the law to intimidate their wives, police who have used it to blackmail women, and feudal landlords who have used it to browbeat their tenants.

Salma is a 16-year-old mother. A few days after her marriage at the age of 14, she was alone in her new home one morning, when her father-in-law jumped over the courtyard wall, and overpowered and raped her. He did this on three further occasions when his son was out of the house. Each time Salma threatened to tell her husband, her father-in-law beat her. Unable to bear the situation any longer, she escaped from her house, not knowing what she would do next.

In a state of extreme distress, Salma bartered her gold nosering for a rickshaw ride to a city bus stop. A police officer who was passing heard her frantic cries, stopped and inquired. He contacted War Against Rape (WAR), a citizens' group formed to deal with the growing problem, which helped her to register a case and be medically examined. In one of the few cases under Hudood where the rapist has been punished, Salma's father-in-law has been in prison for nearly two years. But he is soon to be released and Salma's husband is putting pressure on her to forgive his father. Salma sees little option but to run away again. "My relatives say I'm a fallen woman and I'm constantly taunted by neighbouring women that my son is really my father-in-law's. Even my own father thinks that my father-in-law should be released. What am I to do? I'm scared that he'll rape me again if he's released."

The social straightjacket

The image of the self-effacing, self-sacrificing woman, an adjunct to her man and confined to her biological role, was constantly promoted in the state media during the Zia regime. Coercion and disempowerment of women spread to other institutions of society. Educational institutions limited the entry of women, as in the case of medical colleges, where, until recently, higher entrance marks were required for female candidates.[15] The government even attempted to force female students to cover their heads in school; a measure that met with such disdain it was never enforced. Female promotion to managerial and executive jobs was curtailed.

According to traditional values, a man is a woman's *majazi khuda* (god on earth). She is his property and lives to please him. These beliefs are reinforced by Pakistan's woefully inadequate development, with its wide social and economic disparities.

Equally, a high premium is placed on a woman's fertility. A girl's virginity, and her youth, are prized virtues; the measure of a man's virility is the number of his children, preferably sons. A woman's infertility, chronic illness or inability to bear a son (although the sex of the child is determined by the man) may lead to violent abuse by husbands and in-laws, the possibility that the man will take a second wife or outright abandonment by husband and family.

A woman is considered the symbol of her family's honour. Any deviation from social norms or tribal laws can result in her death. *Karo kari* (not an Islamic practice) is a frightening form of such killing, which takes the life of one woman a month in the provinces of Sindh and Balochistan.[16] The expression refers to the 'blackening' of one person by another: a man who has been dishonoured – whose name has been 'blackened' - has the right to kill both his wife and her suspected paramour. "The ritual of *karo kari*," states journalist Nafisa Shah, "has survived all the legal, political, and ethical developments of our times, and is now a convenient cover for all kinds of murders. [It remains] an integral part of the feudal and tribal system."[17] According to Shah, the practice is believed to predate the advent of Islam in the region.

Child marriage still takes place to a significant extent, despite the Child Marriage Restraint Act, 1929, according to which it is illegal for a girl to be married if she is below the age of 14 years. The Muslim Family Laws Ordinances, 1961, raised the age of marriage to 16, but the law is not strictly enforced. It has also been adversely affected by the Hudood Ordinances with the addition of the clause "or if she has attained the age of puberty", qualifying the definition of adulthood.[18]

It is hard to reverse the trend and bring about progressive laws and policies in favour of women. Zohra Yousuf, Secretary General of HRCP, explains: "Because these laws have been 'Islamised' [they are]...considered Pakistani." According to activist and lawyer Jilani: "[The state] has let loose a brutal dispensation. The same law that proposes to act from high moral ground has no answer to the dilemma of a raped 13-year-old. There is no abortion available. What will be the social implications for her life? The psychological impact? No one cares."

Marital rape is not identified as a form of rape in the Hudood Ordinances – or in the Pakistan Penal Code. In the absence of laws offering specific protection to victims of domestic rape or violence, the police are not bound to take strong action. In a famous 1994 case, that of Zainab, who literally caught fire after her husband inserted a live electric rod in her vagina, her husband was charged only with 'grievous bodily harm and sexual abuse'.

WAR handles many marital rape cases in Karachi. "The police have been most uncooperative," says Danish Zuberi, a lawyer with WAR. "Often, in spite of our continued efforts the victims who come to us, or contact us with hysterical phone calls, get no protection. It's just treated as a husband-wife thing. We really need to have separate legislation for domestic violence."

Activism increases

WAF emerged as a strong pressure group challenging Zia's anti-women laws. The public protests organised in the 1980s against the Ordinances and the Law of Evidence – and the violent police reaction in Lahore – left a lasting impression. February 12, the anniversary of the demonstrations, is commemorated each year as a day of action for Pakistani women. In 1999 women in major cities held marches and torch-lit vigils under banners of joint action committees organised by WAF. The demonstrations highlighted recent cases of women punished under the Hudood Ordinances for marrying men of their own choice.

Before her death, the late Raana Liaquat Ali Khan, founder of the All Pakistan Women's Association, and wife of the country's first prime minister, joined the younger generation of activists in bravely opposing the government. "With the dictatorship of the army meddling in politics and religion, what can one expect?" she said in 1982. "Zia...says we have to put the *chador* [veil] around us, that we have to cover our heads. Why should we? Would the founders of Pakistan have permitted the chopping off of limbs, the flogging of citizens, including women? Never. Never. They are using Islam and the archaic interpretations of bigots. The next thing you know, they will have us walking on different sides of the road."[19]

Over the years activists have attempted various strategies to achieve their goal of removing discriminatory laws. Rasheeda Patel is President of the Pakistan Women Lawyers' Association (PAWLA) which, along with several women's groups including the Women's Action Forum (WAF), petitioned the Federal Shariat Court (FSC) [20]. Although the FSC was originally sympathetic to some arguments, later jurists were not; after several hearings the FSC dismissed the appeal.

"The jurists who came later,...if anything, made matters worse," explains Patel, "because along with *zina*, they wanted to add *badkari* [improper behaviour] which was a broad term, and could be applied to a variety of real or perceived behaviours." The petition to the FSC was followed by another petition, to the Supreme Court, for abolition of the Hudood Ordinances on the grounds that they violate fundamental rights, but to date the petition has not been taken up, despite repeated requests. "They keep telling me the climate's not right," says Patel.[21]

"The politics of rape"

While the establishment failed to deliver on legal reform, even after the death of General Zia in 1987 and the return to civilian democracy, violence against women only worsened. But in spite of the hostile criminal justice system, two women, from opposite ends of the social spectrum, boldly filed charges of rape when the odds of a fair hearing were stacked against them. Between September and November 1991 a series of rapes took place by law-enforcement officers. When it became clear they were part of a campaign of political victimisation, the wider Pakistani public expressed open outrage for the first time.

Veena Hayat, daughter of a veteran politician and friend of Benazir Bhutto (later the prime minister), was brutally gang-raped after the Muslim League had been elected to government for the first time in 1991. The man she pressed charges against was the head of the government Central Intelligence Agency and the son-in-law of President Ghulam Ishaq Khan. It was widely believed that the attack was designed to intimidate Bhutto and the People's Party, which had become a formidable opposition to the government. Veena Hayat and her family publicly accused the President's son-in-law and demanded his arrest.

Khursheed Begum, an impoverished mother of four, and wife of a People's Party activist, was also gang-raped, this time by police officers. Said Idrees Bakhtiar of the leading monthly magazine *Herald*, which featured the rape as its cover story: "For one long month the politics of rape seemed to take precedence over just about everything. It nearly shook the government." [22]

WAF activists took to the streets alongside women from the Jamaat-e-Islami and the People's Party, to demonstrate in front of Parliament against the government and its collusion with such crimes. Other demonstrations took place across the country, as the public responded to the appeals for justice. "As a direct result of the [Hayat] case," wrote journalist Bakhtiar, "the President's address to...Parliament degenerated to a raucous slanging match, with opposition members screaming down the president before staging a walk-out." [23] Although the press gave the issue of rape unprecedented coverage for the first time, and public outcry made world headlines, none of the accused was ever arrested and tried for the rapes, compounding the trauma of the attacked women.

The promise of equality?

Asma Jehangir, chairperson of the Human Rights Commission of Pakistan, voices the disillusionment of women and activists: "We have moth-ridden institutes of law, and there are cobwebs in the minds of the legislature. They have no consciences left; their ears are closed. This law has been made to suppress those less fortunate than us. We have said we don't need the Federal Shariat Court. We'll never leave our fight."[24]

Women activists are now taking one of two tactical approaches in challenging the 'Islamist' legacy of Zia. WAF and lawyers such as Jilani and Jehangir rely on secular arguments to critique discriminatory legislation. They refer to Pakistan's Constitution, which guarantees equal fundamental rights to men and women, and the UN Convention on the Elimination of All Forms of Discrimination Against Women (the Women's Convention) to which Pakistan is a signatory.[25]

Rashida Patel of PAWLA favours a different strategy, while agreeing that the state should be secular: "Until that is achieved, we have to research and find out what's Islamic and what's not – this seems the only way out. The reality is that Islam is the state religion – our leaders, rightly or wrongly, brought it in." Muslim feminist scholarship has indeed increased over the years, and although Pakistani women eagerly listen to new interpretations of Islamic law,[26] the government has not invited any official debate on the Islamic merits of its own legislation.

The prevailing mood among legislators with regard to discriminatory laws has been apathy.

"Most legislators do not know the contents of the Ordinances," says Shahla Zia, a member of the government-appointed Inquiry Commission on the Status of Women. She also observes that there has never been a conviction of a middle-class woman under the Hudood laws. "Women's rights issues are not a priority. If you are sitting on a separate plane, divorced from reality, these things don't affect you."

Although politicians from the two main political parties – the Muslim League, deposed in a 'bloodless' military coup in September 1999, and the opposition People's Party led by Benazir Bhutto – admit that the consequences of the Hudood Ordinances have not been ideal, they take no steps to address the gravity of the problem.

Benazir Bhutto has twice been elected prime minister but did not push for the reform of discriminatory legislation. According to Shahnaz Wazir Ali, her former Special Advisor on Social Sectors, if Bhutto had raised the question of legislation against women, the opposition would automatically have opposed any reform. It would have become, she says, "a political issue of confrontation and disagreement: a negotiating item". Although the Bhutto government, in its own political manifesto, had called for drastic reform in legislation, it never finalised its position on the controversial laws, not wanting unnecessarily to provoke negative reactions, according to Ali. "Why add another problem and bring the *mullahs* [religious leaders] out?" she says.

The deposed Muslim League government, headed by Nawaz Sharif, held power twice. Former Parliamentary secretary Zafar Ali Shah acknowledges that the Shariat Act, passed during his party's first government, was initiated under pressure from the Jamaat-e-Islami, which at that time figured prominently in the Muslim League's coalition government. Although the influence of the Jamaat dwindled to almost nothing in Parliament, the Muslim League made no move to address the Hudood Ordinances. "We can amend the Ordinances," says Shah, "but we will only do so when we feel it is inevitable." Since public activism against discriminatory legislation has remained confined to the tiny upper middle class, Shah admits that his government was under no compulsion to respond.

"Repeal requires political expediency," says Zohra Yousuf, Secretary General of HRCP. "Unfortunately, political bigwigs have this fear of being considered un-Islamic, because fundamentalist Islamic factions are well organised and have the power to create trouble."

The recently deposed civilian government remained coolly pragmatic in its attitude towards the legal status of women, and its officials were either unaware of, or denigrated, the consequences of the Hudood Ordinances. According to Shah, "neither the legal rights nor freedom of women have been curtailed by the Hudood laws." He implies that men are more often victimised, claiming that thousands of false rape cases against men have been registered over the years. Of the thousands of women charged with commiting *zina*, he insists: "It is unthinkable that someone would falsely accuse a woman...of such a thing."

Since the vast majority of women arrested under Hudood are eventually acquitted, the Muslim League spokesman concludes that the law actually protects women. What he and his government ignored are the tragic consequences for women incarcerated for months and years which "alienate [them] from their families and children and for which they receive no redress or compensation".[27]

Owing its continued existence to a combination of political stalemate and official inertia, the Hudood Ordinances continue to destroy women's lives. Further, elected governments have resorted to even more harsh and authoritarian means to control the populace. For example, special 'speedy' courts to try terrorists have been set up and abolished several times in the last decade, despite outcry from human rights activists that they destroy the integrity of the judiciary and fundamental rights. On Pakistan's 50th anniversary (14 August 1997) an Anti-Terrorist Bill was passed that allows the police to enter any area, including homes, without search or arrest warrant, if they suspect the presence of a terrorist. Police are authorised to shoot a suspect at sight.

In such circumstances, the fundamental rights of citizens protected by the Constitution ring hollow. So, too, does Pakistan's commitment to international conventions,[28] and its adoption of the Programme of Action issued at the 1994 UN International Conference on Population and Development in Cairo, Egypt, the Platform for Action issued by the 1995 UN Fourth World Conference on Women in

Beijing, and its own National Plan of Action officially endorsed in August 1998. Although a shift in vocabulary from 'population control' to 'reproductive health' has taken place in health and population programmes, what is missing is a broad-based acceptance and understanding of women's reproductive rights and sexual rights as the cornerstone of any reproductive health programme.

Even when Benazir Bhutto's government set up an Inquiry Commission on the Status of Women in 1994 – mandating it to review and examine existing laws discriminatory to women or that affect their equal rights as citizens – subsequent leaders ignored its findings. The high-powered group, consisting of human rights lawyers, Islamic scholars, legislators and headed by a justice of the Supreme Court, termed the discriminatory legislation "obscurantist" and stated: "The promise of equality has not only been ignored, it has been blatantly violated".[29] Its 1997 Report recommended sweeping changes, including the repeal of the Hudood Ordinances, making 'honour killing' a criminal offence, amending family laws relating to marriage, divorce, dowry and child marriage which disadvantage women and calling for the removal of discriminatory clauses in the Constitution of Pakistan.

There has been no official acknowledgement or discussion by Parliament of the Inquiry Commission's report, according to Amnesty International, and the human rights of women continue to be routinely ignored or violated since the Commission submitted its findings. As military tension heightens between India and Pakistan – in the wake of underground nuclear testing carried out by both countries in 1998 – women have also raised fears of the repercussions of 'nuclearisation' upon Pakistani women, citing fears that shifting scarce resources from the social to the military sector and "subsequent sanctions may adversely affect the most vulnerable sections of society, women and children...[due] to the shrinking public space for women, their ideas and their rights".[30]

Such fears have been borne out. At a December 1999 debate on reproductive health organised by the Human Rights Forum on Women, delegates charged that the last civilian government had allocated only 1-2 percent of the country's total budget to education and health.[31] Some 30,000 women die from pregnancy-related complications each year, and 400,000 more suffer life-long disabilities relating to pregnancy and childbirth.[32]

Law-making, particularly in the name of Islam, has become a standard political tool. The former government – seeking to distract public attention from Pakistan's eventual capitulation to international pressure to restrict its nuclear weapons programme – submitted a Bill to amend the Constitution – the 15th Amendment – in order to make the Qur'an and Sunnah (the life and teachings of the Prophet Mohammed) the law of the land and appointed a new executive authority to enforce Islam as it deems fit.

Women's groups fear that if the proposed 15th Amendment is implemented, further curtailment of women's freedoms will follow. For the first time, not only women and non-Muslims, but a range of political parties united in protest.

Against a backdrop of severe constraints and internal political strife, the agonising situation for women was not a priority for the last civilian government. Despite some rhetoric in favour of change, it upheld the status quo.

As Muslim League Advisor for Information Mushahid Hussain said in a rare public appearance at a meeting organised by women activists: "Our government has done so much for women. What more do you want?"

Democracy in the Nation, but not at Home

Domestic violence and women's reproductive health in Chile

Lezak Shallat

An anguished woman petitions the Santiago Ecclesiastical Court for permission to separate from her abusive husband. His adulterous relations are "exposing her to contracting one of those fatal diseases that sap one's life".[1] He began to beat her when she complained about his infidelity. When she became pregnant the beatings escalated, the most severe occurring 13 days after she gave birth. The year is 1820.

Today, much has changed for Chilean women – and much has not. Adultery only recently ceased to be a criminal offence and divorce is still illegal in this predominantly Roman Catholic country.[2] In 1994, however, Chile passed a Domestic Violence Law to revolutionise how courts, police and health facilities respond to wife-beating and other forms of abuse within families – physical, psychological and sexual.

'Paper' reforms are making a difference in the way that domestic violence is viewed by authorities, victims and perpetrators. But making violence between partners a public issue has not brought automatic changes to more intimate domains. Failure to uproot sexism and discrimination from cultural norms and social structures contributes to the violence that occurs in one in four Chilean homes.[3]

The Chilean government's legal and policy campaign against domestic violence is perhaps its greatest human rights achievement since the country's 1990 return to civilian rule. Ironically, it is not widely viewed as such in Chile, where human rights efforts have been concerned almost exclusively with reparations for state violence committed during 17 years of military dictatorship.

Recognition of violence against women

Abuse of women by their male partners is the most widespread form of violence against women.[4] The 1993 World Development Report states that among women aged 15-44 violence against women is a greater cause of death and disability than either cancer, malaria or traffic accidents.[5]

In Chile, a survey of admittance to a northern city hospital during the month of November 1991 showed that one-third of women seeking emergency care had been battered by their partner.[6] A 1997 study of 310 women in Santiago showed that 23 percent of women had been assaulted by an intimate partner in the previous 12 months.[7]

Despite its pervasiveness, violence against women has only recently emerged as an international issue. Milestones include the "conceptual revolution", in the words of US lawyer and activist Rhonda Copelon, at the 1993 UN World Conference on Human Rights, which broke through the "illusory division" between public and private domains. Previously, human rights discussions had focused on abuses by the state in the public sphere. The 1993 Conference signalled that violence against women in homes and communities also belonged on the human rights map.[8] In 1994, the UN International Conference on Population and Development made freedom from violence and coercion a central plank in its platform for reproductive and sexual health.

In the Americas, as of 1998, 27 countries had ratified the 1994 Inter-American Convention on Prevention, Punishment and Eradication of Violence Against Women (the Belem do Para Convention). At least nine countries (Chile, Argentina, Panama, Uruguay, Ecuador, Bolivia, Costa Rica, Mexico, and Colombia) have passed national laws against domestic violence.

These accomplishments are the product of two decades of grassroots activism during which women linked gender-based abuse to issues already high on the international agenda: human rights and socio-economic development (including health).[9] Tactics such as local and global mobilisations for the annual Day Against Violence Against Women (25 November), launched by Latin American feminists in 1981, have expanded into a worldwide campaign capable of placing half-a-million signatures against gender abuse on the UN Secretary General's desk a decade later.

When "no" is not an option

Less explored than the physical and mental health consequences of spousal abuse is its impact on women's reproductive health. Yet domestic violence is a reproductive health problem because it is so often intertwined with sexuality, fidelity, pregnancy and childbearing.[10]

According to Lori Heise, author of several pioneering studies: "Evidence is fast accumulating that physical and sexual abuse are linked to some of the most intractable reproductive health issues of our time: teenage pregnancy, high-risk sexual behaviour (unprotected sex with multiple partners; prostitution), sexually transmitted diseases and chronic pelvic pain. Violence has also been implicated in pregnancy complications, low birthweight, miscarriage and maternal mortality."[11]

Violence affects women's sexual and reproductive lives in direct and indirect ways.

Women living with a violent partner are at risk of coercive sex. Abuse can lead directly to unwanted pregnancy – and sexually transmitted diseases, including infection with HIV, the virus that causes AIDS – through marital rape or inability to negotiate contraceptive use. Women may be reluctant to raise the issue; some may opt for less reliable contraceptive methods, such as periodic abstinence, or attempt to avoid sexual relations altogether. But an abusive partner may not respect such strategies. Women in a poor Santiago neighbourhood told of partners who beat them and even refused them money for food until they conceded to sex.[12] For many women, "no" is not an option.

Persistent abuse can lead indirectly to infections and pregnancy by lowering women's self-esteem, leaving them vulnerable to alcohol or drug abuse and therefore less able to protect themselves from unsafe sex.[13]

One potential outcome of unwanted pregnancy is abortion. In Chile, all abortion – even to save the life of the woman – is illegal, causing an estimated 30 percent of maternal deaths.[14] Nonetheless, some 35 percent of pregnancies are terminated.[15] Nearly one-fifth (18 percent) of the estimated 159,000 abortions performed each year result in complications that require hospitalisation.[16]

In Chile, a woman may be jailed for having undergone an abortion. Violent partners appear with depressing regularity in the court records of women prosecuted for having aborted. A 1996 review by lawyer Lidia Casas of 80 testimonies identified several cases where women cited physical abuse by their partner as the reason for seeking an abortion. It was reported that some of the men became violent because they were angry that their partner had become pregnant in the first place. Four women cited being coerced, through threats or blows, into aborting.[17]

The legal system ignores male responsibility and violence in abortion. Beatings, threats, coercion and sexual violence by their partners can "place the woman in a precarious, if not devastating situation", notes Casas. Yet, "she alone is made fully responsible by the justice system." Her research found that 60 percent of abused women prosecuted for abortion were found guilty at the trial court level.[18]

"A time of special care"?

Pregnancy is an uncertain time in the life of an abused woman. For some women, it brings a respite from abuse. Other women find themselves fending off blows and the accusation that "this child isn't mine". A Santiago study conducted in 1992 among 1,000 women revealed that two out of five battered wives faced greater abuse while pregnant – a finding that "flies in the face of the myth in Chile that maternity is a time of special care and protection", notes psychologist Soledad Larrain, who directed the research.[19]

Battering during pregnancy has been linked to increased risk of pregnancy complications, premature labour, miscarriage and delivery of low birthweight infants. Studies cited by Heise show that physically abused women are three times more likely than non-abused women to start prenatal care late in the third trimester.[20] Abusive partners may prevent pregnant woman from keeping medical appointments.[21] One study found that pregnant women who were abused were – unsurprisingly – more emotionally distressed than non-abused women and thus "more likely to feel that 'chance' rather than their own behavior played the most important role in the outcome of their pregnancy".[22]

Domestic abuse usually operates in combination with external factors. A study of 161 women in Santiago found that high levels of socio-political violence were associated with a fivefold increase in pregnancy complications. "If the stress and trauma of living in a violent neighborhood can induce complications," Heise observes, "it is reasonable to assume that living in the private hell of an abusive relationship could as well." [23]

The physical and emotional toll

Battered women often complain of multiple physical complaints with no clear medical cause, especially headaches, vaginal discharge and chronic pelvic pain. "The symptom may act as a symbolic message," notes Larrain. "For example, urinary tract problems can indicate sexual abuse or permanent pressure to have sexual relations. The illness emerges precisely where the women is being harmed." [24]

More invisible still is the toll that domestic violence takes on women's sexual pleasure and self-esteem. Sexual relations can become a battleground where the abusive male exerts his power and dominance.

"I almost always feel pain," a battered wife told Santiago therapist Solange Bertrand. "It's hard for me to become excited because I don't want to have relations. But he forces me, even though I say no." In Bertrand's study of 30 battered women, 19 said they felt no sexual desire towards their partners, citing violence as the reason.[25]

Worse than the physical pain, however, is the emotional anguish of being forced into sex. Fear and shame – "the worst form of degradation" - is how women describe their feelings. Some react by blaming themselves. Counsellors at the Women's Institute, a non-government oganisation (NGO) in the southern city of Concepción, say the most common complaint they hear from battered women is: "I don't want to have sex with him. He says I'm frigid."

In Bertrand's study, however, nearly all the women reporting no pleasure in sex with their abusive partner had experienced pleasure in the past, either with this partner, before abuse began, or another. "I don't want to have relations with him because I don't enjoy it," one woman said. "I don't feel anything for him. With the insults and blows, how could I?"

The dimensions of domestic violence

Much of what is known about the dimensions of domestic violence in Chile comes from a study conducted by Soledad Larrain. [26] Completed in 1992, this was the first large-scale survey not limited to abused women.

The results took Chile by surprise: one in four women (25.9 percent) said they had suffered physical abuse at the hands of a partner, citing incidents of lesser violence ("pushes, slaps, punches or having an object thrown at them") and more severe ("biting, kicking, assault with an object or weapon, forced sexual relations and burning").[27] Some 41.4 percent of women who reported abuse had experienced incidents of "serious violence", including kicks, blows and forced sex.[28] Seventy percent of those battered said they experienced episodes of violence more than once a year [29]; 36 percent said that abuse had begun before or during the first year of living together.[30]

While an estimated 20,000 rapes a year occur in Chile,[31] marital rape is not counted among them. Yet a 1989 study that focused on 222 women survivors of violence in a poor Santiago neighbourhood reported that 29 percent had experienced being forced by their partners to have sexual relations.[32]

Information about rape in marriage is hard to ascertain. Therapists working with the victims of violence say that talk about sexual abuse in marriage is virtually taboo. But although a woman may be unwilling – for reasons of shame or notions of wifely 'duty' - to describe her experience as rape she may still feel violated. As Sudanese activist Dr Nahid Toubia noted: "She may not have the language, or she may never have been asked."[33] Cultural and personal definitions come into play, as expressed by women who 'reframe' their experience in the light of new information, as did this Latin American woman:

"My sex life in marriage has been dominated by rape, rape, rape – and nothing to do with love. I didn't know that what I experienced was rape. I first found out about that when I went into therapy – that what I described was nothing other than rape. I thought that rape was something that happened in a dark, remote street in the middle of the night. I didn't know that it could also happen in a marriage bed."[34]

Statistics from Chile's Medical Legal Service suggest a growing awareness of marital rape as a violation of women's bodily integrity. Whereas marital rape used to be denounced only rarely, the Service now receives reports of two or three cases a week.[35]

Why abuse occurs

Myths about why abuse occurs often surface when Chileans explain – or justify – family violence. Among them: that domestic violence is a 'lower-class' problem; that alcohol is the real culprit; that men are inherently violent; that victims are guilty of provocation; that violence in a family precludes love. None of these common beliefs are true.[36] But cross-cultural research into patterns of domestic violence does suggest certain 'predictive' factors.[37]

'Real' men, 'real' women

Male chauvinism is so characteristic of Latin American culture that the Spanish word *machismo* has crossed linguistic borders to describe it. Nor is *machismo* limited to men. Women are socialised to accept male authority. The concept of patriarchal 'possession' of women and children is strong within Chilean families, and authoritarianism – representing hierarchy, order and control – is respected. Consider the Chilean law – in force up until the enactment of a new Sexual Crimes Code in July 1999 – that exonerated a rapist if he married his victim and thus restored her honour.

Just as the male 'mystique' prizes dominance, qualities associated with submissiveness are praised as feminine. *Marianismo*, a term harking back to the Virgin Mary, describes attitudes of self-sacrifice and subservience that are highly valued as maternal traits.

Community health worker Valeria Garcia says it is common to hear of criticism of the Church for promoting the "outdated ideas of our grandmothers – the more you suffer, the greater your reward in heaven". Many women believe that priests fail to speak out strongly enough against spousal abuse or to understand battered women's need for independence.

In Chile, acceptance of physical chastisement as a legitimate means of resolving problems is widespread, as shown by a 1995 survey of batterers attending a treatment programme run by Dr Marina Casanova in Concepción.[38] Casanova also heads a post-dictatorship programme providing health services to victims of political repression. She sees parallels between family and political violence: feelings of despair and abandonment extending over generations; abnormal situations lived as normal; aggression springing from those who are meant to protect, not harm. Both types of violence are often justified as legitimate means of exercising authority and guardianship. And both can reach physical extremes approaching torture.

Characteristics that constitute 'appropriate' male or female behaviour are largely culturally determined. In Latin America, 'real' men are "obliged to be providers, protectors, rational, dominant and sexual artists", in the words of Nicaragua's Men's Group Against Violence.[39] Women are supposed to be dependent, vulnerable, emotional, submissive and sexually naive. A man with a strong sense of male 'entitlement' may act as if women exist to fulfil his 'gendered' expectations – a clean house, a hot meal on the table when he returns from work, sexual relations on demand. Some studies suggest that gender-based abuse is less prevalent in societies that accept more flexible gender roles [40] while other research suggests that in times of change, as currently experienced in Chile, women question more and men grow less secure. This is a formula, in Larrain's view, that can trigger domestic violence.

Class and family background

While domestic violence is found in all social strata, certain socio-economic factors increase its likelihood. Larrain's Santiago study, conducted in 1992 among 1,000 women, found that physical aggression was 5.4 times less frequent in wealthy families than in poor ones,[41] where women have less economic independence and more children. But whereas six percent of upper-class women said they suffered physical battery, more than one third (35.4 percent) reported psychological abuse. Sexual assault by husbands was present in both lower and upper income groups.[42]

However, external factors do not explain why violence happens between certain couples and not others. Idealised views of love and marriage – the expectation that the 'other' will fulfil the one's inadequacies – underlie many abusive relationships. Couples may develop strong mutual dependencies, where growth or change – or pregnancy or childbirth – generate frustration, fear of abandonment and aggression.

Love and violence coexist in complex ways. For some men, violence is linked not to hate but to love: "I hit you because you're going to leave me...and you're going to leave me because I hit you." Insecurity often manifests itself as jealousy, a prime detonator of blows. Some wives view their partners' jealous rages as an illness, like a seizure, or condition, like drunkenness, that temporarily alters the conduct of an otherwise decent man. Women may even take pride in partners' possessiveness: "He hits me because he loves me."

Women's responses

Women react in various ways to violence. The most frequent response is an individual one: defensive (crying, protecting oneself) and/or aggressive (hitting back). Returning blows is a feature of many abusive relationships but usually provokes even greater violence.

"Why do I stay?" is a question that both baffles and torments many battered women. Violence may invoke fear and helplessness; many women retreat into passivity. When the batterer – or police, or society – blames the victim, she may internalise feelings of culpability. In Heise's view, battered women are more apt to accept victimisation as part of being female.[43] In Larrain's study, 30 percent had never told anyone of the abuse.[44]

Experiencing contradictory emotions of love and hate can be paralysing. Motherhood can make the battered woman feel even more trapped, less able to leave an abusive relationship and provide for herself and her children. The batterer often has access to the woman through the children once the relationship has ended – and abuse may continue.

Women do break out of violent relationships; sometimes on the strength of their own anger, sometimes through peer or professional counselling. A typical treatment programme in Chile is a several-month group therapy session run by a women's group or public health facility and geared at empowering the battered woman.

"I lived alone with my pain," recalls a woman living in Santiago's La Bandera neighbourhood, where the La

Llareta community health group has been operating for over a decade. "The monitors saw I needed support and helped me find it. They helped me to see that I could change. It wasn't easy, but I did. I saw that I couldn't change him – that's something only he could do – but neither could he stop me from growing. And it was my growing that made him change."

Treatment programmes for batterers are designed to help men take responsibility for their violence and manage their anger. According to Santiago psychologist Cristian Walker, therapy is often effective, especially with younger men. But it is hard to gauge what is attributable to treatment and what is due to public humiliation or legal intervention.

Fighting back

"Democracy in the Nation and at Home"

In Chile, as in Argentina and Brazil, organising against the military regime led women to question the oppression in their own lives. The mid-1980s brought the anti-Pinochet rallying cry of "Democracy in the Nation and at Home". By 1988, women were taking to the streets in protests against both the 'disappearance' of female political prisoners and the battering of women in their homes. Nonetheless, championing women's rights was viewed as "superfluous and insignificant" by the human rights community, recalls Veronica Matus of the Chilean Human Rights Commission.

Meanwhile, a handful of feminists were taking matters into their own hands, providing legal and support services and eventually forming the Chilean Network Against Domestic and Sexual Violence.

Women's participation in toppling the military regime brought political payoffs when democracy was restored in

1990. Foremost was the creation of the National Women's Service (SERNAM), whose special attention to women's needs was quickly denounced by its detractors as a first step in undermining the authority of the Chilean family. SERNAM immediately went to work on a domestic violence law and a much-needed programme to create awareness of family violence in every branch of public service – police, courts, clinics, schools, municipalities – likely to come into contact with battered women or their children. The degree of tolerance afforded domestic violence by the health sector, in particular, was apparent in this finding from 1992: three out of five battered women seeking medical care in hospitals or health services were given no information on how to file a complaint, nor was any legal record kept of the aggression.[45]

A top priority was to 'sensitise' the police force. Given the distrust built up over years of repression, "work with such a hierarchical institution on a topic that touches so deeply on concepts of power and obedience with the family...contributes to [the national process of] healing", programme director Ximena Ahumada wrote.[46]

Evidence of this can be seen in La Bandera, where a street mural depicts a policewoman as an ally against domestic violence, not an agent of repression as she would have been seen in the years of dictatorship. Or in the incessant ringing of the family violence hotline in Santiago's 48th Precinct, where a young officer takes notes on where to send the mobile unit. His empathy for callers is clear, as is the information he gives on how to file a complaint.

Yet, downstairs, a policeman books a 14-year-old who has just been discharged from the hospital following treatment for an incomplete abortion. "Probably sexually abused," remarks the receiving officer. "But the law is the law. Find out if she did it herself or if she's covering up for someone." [47]

The Intra-Family Violence Law

Chile passed the Intra-Family Violence (*Violencia Intra-Familiar*, VIF) Law in 1994. Critics in the women's movement believe it has had mixed results. Among its innovations, however, are its broad definition of family, inclusion of sexual and psychological abuse, introduction of protective measures (such as restraining orders) and mandatory therapy for batterers. However, no special funding was earmarked to carry these out.

The number of complaints filed has sky-rocketed under its relatively streamlined procedures – to 61,015 cases in 1997. By all accounts, the VIF law is a 'communication success' that carries significant symbolic weight in Chile's highly legalistic society. "Just leaving a VIF brochure on the night table can have a dissuasive effect," says lawyer Luz Rio Seco of Santiago's Women's Institute.

But the Institute's 1995 review of 2,619 court cases revealed less optimistic outcomes. Although protective measures were solicited in 59 percent of cases in a Santiago court, they were granted in only 15 percent; in just 1.7 percent of the cases were offenders sentenced.[48] As community health monitor Valeria Garcia put it: "Despite the law, women still live crying into their pillows."

Some critics believe that the most innovative aspects of the VIF law (like community service as a sentencing alternative) are its weakest points. "Chilean society lacks the innovative mentality that would allow them to be effective," says Veronica Matus. "Judges...want to re-unite families at whatever cost. Nor do they want to be involved in private affairs," she adds, grimacing with mock distaste and pretending to flick a speck of dirt from her clothes. Although large numbers of police and court officials have taken VIF training, women still encounter blame-the-victim attitudes. Making a complaint can be "a second torture", says a health monitor.

Feminists criticise the primacy of family over women in the VIF law. "What is the legal asset being protected by the law?" asks Luz Rio Seco. "Some say it is the family. For us, it must be the health of all individuals."

Reform on the agenda

In Chile, change is measured in years and decades. Legal equality for children born out of wedlock with those born to married couples was recently granted despite tenacious opposition; however, the right to divorce and the effective establishment of special family courts remain stalled. However in May 1999, a joint session of Congress finally ratified equal rights for men and women. The reform replaces the word "men" in the Constitution with the word "person", and Article 19 now reads: "Men and women are equal under the law."

One long-awaited development has been legislation to reform the Sexual Crimes Code, which was under debate since 1994 and finally passed in July 1999. Although Congress approved the reformed Code in December 1998, its fate remained uncertain for another 18 months due to the opposition's outcry that it was too lenient on offenders who sexually assault children under the age of 12. President Eduardo Frei postponed a January 1999 ceremony to sign the bill into law and returned it to Congress with recommendations for approval.

Among the changes introduced are the criminalising of marital rape and abolition of the provision that, controversially, allowed a rapist to go free if he married his victim. The new legislation also seeks to avoid re-traumatising people who have been raped by eliminating the practice of bringing rapist and victim together to testify in court.

Under the new law, testimony from relatives and minors, and medical exams conducted by hospital staff, are admissible, and semen samples will be preserved for eventual

DNA testing. The reforms also require the identity of the victim to be protected, unless permission is given to reveal it.

Progress at the grassroots

SERNAM's violence prevention strategy aims to link public services (health, justice, education) at the community level, especially in low-income areas. However, its efforts to connect with NGOs and grassroots groups have been fairly ineffective.

Chile's NGOs offer services that the government can't – or won't – provide. While this makes for a more diverse range of programmes (HIV/AIDS prevention for gays, for example, or contraceptives for teenagers), it creates tension and competition for funds as foreign development aid dries up in response to Chile's much-touted economic 'success'.

Activists from Concepción's La Fogata, for example, focus on community awareness. "We want to make people understand that they have to intervene," explains Adriana Wenger. "We promote the 'Can I borrow a red thread?' tactic among neighbours: when you hear something going on, run over."

At a day care programme in nearby Hualpencillo, mothers identify their own *machista* attitudes in childrearing and examine how to support each other. As one participant notes: "Telling a friend that she 'must' leave her husband might not help her, if she doesn't have the means."

Other responses include community conferences to discuss the links between violence and AIDS, sexual abuse prevention programmes for teenagers, and workshops to examine the theological underpinnings of male dominance. But no government office provides battered women with the one facility they need most in times of crisis – a shelter – and NGO provision is negligible. Instead, women can be found late at night in police stations and emergency rooms, frightened children clustered around them.

Coronel: one community's experiences

In the town of Coronel, in southern Chile, the demise of the coal mining culture and heightened awareness of women's rights have brought a community response to domestic violence.

The coal miner is a worker and a father, respected as a good provider with a strong sense of responsibility to his family. In return, wives and children stood steadfast alongside husbands and fathers when miners went on strike to defend their jobs in 1994 and 1996.

The men's livelihood relied on a combination of brute force, technical skill and toughness. The closure of the mines jeopardised not only jobs, but places of residence, friendships, history and pride. The prospect of losing this identity generated insecurity, confusion, loss of control.

It is one more facet of Chilean mining lore that the miner beats his wife. A sub-culture that was always indulgent towards domestic violence is now having to come to terms with transformations that exacerbate household tensions: women working outside the home, selling clothes or Avon cosmetics, and entering into competition with out-of-work husbands.

The same women's NGO that acted as strike headquarters holds anti-violence workshops and had hoped, before the last wave of strikes, to open Chile's first battered women's shelter. At the same time, the community's strong tradition of organisation has prompted a broad range of actions. In the one-act play *Taco Alto* (The High-Heeled Shoe), author Elena Troncoso revives the local legend of a murdered wife to generate audience debate about infidelity and revenge. A treatment programme at the primary health clinic works hand in hand with the local court. "This place is like the Wild West," says psychologist Luis González. "Authority is the only thing these guys respect. That's why we push for legal sanctions while working towards behavioural change."

Police are also part of Coronel's anti-violence network, enforcing restraining orders even though they feel it is 'belittling' for a man to have to leave his house. "It's true that men's and women's roles are changing," says an officer on the beat. "I think husbands need to learn from today's women and start to champion their rights."

The long and winding road

While Chilean feminists have placed domestic violence firmly on the public agenda, they have had no similar success with issues related to reproduction and sexuality. Women are often asked to indicate spousal consent for sterilisation, and bills to decriminalise abortion have met with counterproposals for stiffer penalties and plea bargaining.

Because it championed human rights under the Pinochet dictatorship, the Catholic Church enjoys an influential political role in Chile. Its discourse on the dignity of women supports political moves to eradicate violence within the family – but not to the extent of sanctioning divorce, sex education or modern contraceptives. In 1995, when the government introduced a pilot sex education programme in state schools, featuring condom demonstrations and frank talk about birth control, the Church objected that it subverted parental rights and demanded it be withdrawn. In a move that surprised many observers, the government refused to back down and extended the programme into schools nationwide. "I think it is interesting that these fissures, however timid, are surfacing," notes sociologist Teresa Valdes.

Chile's VIF law illustrates the limits of legal and top-down approaches to stopping domestic violence. At the same time, its enactment has given impetus to the grassroots and community efforts in education and prevention that could bring about the attitudinal and behavioural changes necessary to halt this form of gender abuse.

Efforts are underway to educate future generations away

from the authoritarian models prevailing in Chilean homes and schools. A recent educational spot on TV surprised many viewers when a young child who spilt his milk received a helping hand instead of a slap. A few schools include human rights education in the curriculum (although women's human rights are largely ignored.) Young people also need to receive more adequate preparation for adulthood: sexuality education (not just biology, or even just sex); skills to build egalitarian couple relationships; preparation for parenting that is free from rigid gender roles and stereotypes.

Specific steps can address the immediate needs of battered women, particularly in terms of their reproductive and sexual health. Women who are raped, for example, need guidance regarding unwanted pregnancy and STDs. Heise calls upon reproductive health providers to offer emergency contraception as well as counselling on abortion options, should unwanted pregnancy occur – a response that Chile's politically cautious policy-makers are unlikely to adopt speedily.[49]

Health professionals are widely seen as being more sympathetic to women's problems than are legal professionals. Nonetheless, they need to take the reality of violence and power relationships into account and be more attuned to the possibility of abuse.

Contact with family planning services can serve to put women in touch with domestic violence prevention and treatment programmes. Pre-natal care could provide ample opportunities to identify women and inform them of services.

One obstacle to mobilising the health sector, Heise notes, is its discomfort with sexuality. "The family planning industry didn't talk about sex until the subject was introduced by HIV/AIDS prevention. And we still need to hit the AIDS people over the heads with the reality of sexual coercion in women's lives."

The story of Monica (not her real name) illustrates much of what is new – and not – for Chilean women faced with abuse. Like many anti-violence activists, her involvement is informed by personal experience. Violence entered her relationship as she grew in stature in her profession as a nurse. Her partner José was not abusive, as far as anyone knew. However, one evening Monica showed up at a friend's house with a burst eardrum. The beating came after an argument about her leaving the house to do a work-related task. José, a self-proclaimed feminist, was upset over, among other things, Monica's pro-choice activism.

Monica hid where José couldn't find her and summoned him to court. But his remorse convinced her to drop charges. Now, instead of court-mandated therapy, they have long talks about the ways in which ingrained cultural models can overpower reasonable behaviour.

File under "Hurt"
Domestic violence in Sri Lanka

Rahal Saeed

Sri Lanka is often cited as the South Asian success story for its achievements in primary health care and women's advancement. The country is in many ways "remarkable", writes Amita Shastri.[1] Its women were the first in Asia to vote. In the half-century since independence, sex differentials in education and literacy have narrowed. Nearly nine out of 10 women can read, and a higher percentage of girls and young women stay in school than boys.[2] The age of marriage has risen,[3] two-thirds of married women use some form of contraceptive, and fertility rates (the average number of children born to a woman) have declined sharply to 2.4.[4]

"To some extent, women have a good quality of life in Sri Lanka," says Dr Radhika Coomaraswamy, the Sri Lankan lawyer who is the United Nations Special Rapporteur on Violence Against Women. "Education and health indicators for women are quite high, much higher than in Pakistan and Bangladesh." But she notes that women are barely visible as leaders in the public arena of government, civil service or industry. "Basically, there is violence against women.... Decision-making and power is another area," she adds.

Coomaraswamy is referring to the endemic violence against women in the country, and the failure of parliamentarians to enact legislation to criminalise it. Domestic violence is not a defined offence in the Criminal

Penal Code. Instead, spousal abuse is registered under the category "Hurt". Police officers are reluctant to make arrests, and courts will only issue restraining orders against a brutal husband if the wife has filed for divorce. Marital rape is not recognised, except when the couple is judicially separated. Should wives become pregnant as a result of rape they have little recourse. Sri Lanka does not permit abortion under any circumstances, except to save the mother's life.

Despite the country's high scores in the Physical Quality of Life Index, the lives of many Sri Lankan women, whether Hindu, Muslim, Buddhist or Christian, are ones of endurance and suffering. Society remains conservative, traditional and patriarchal. What happens between a couple is considered a private matter; the institution of marriage is enshrined over women's rights within it; the common perception is that men are superior and their sexual urges indomitable, that they need more to eat and need more freedom.

Marriage is an institution "based on hierarchy, sacred, binding and to be preserved at all costs", writes Ameena Hussein-Uvais. In her Muslim community, marriage is seen as the exchange of sexual availability by the wife for economic maintenance by the husband. A wife's consent to sex is a "non-issue". [5]

Some abused women are driven to desperate measures. In Chilaw, a coastal town about 65 km north of the capital, Colombo, a 65-year-old woman committed suicide. Her situation was known to everyone in her community. Her husband would come home drunk almost every day, beat her and force sex on her. He had done so throughout their married life. Once, he hit her and raped her in front of her children. Unable to cope with the 'shame' - though she was the victim – she took her own life.

The need to conform to socially mandated gender roles can have a paralysing effect on abused women. Many Buddhist and Hindu women rationalise their predicament in terms of a preordained destiny, which "seems to tie up with the traditional belief in 'fate' in Asian societies, including Sri Lanka," writes researcher A.G Seelawathi. [6]

Rani, a 38-year-old mother of three separated from her husband after 17 years of abuse, says: "I think it is my fate. I am paying for a past sin, what else?" [7]

An epidemic of violence

Most Sri Lankan women – restricted by patriarchal attitudes, as well as culture and religion – cannot make autonomous decisions about their private lives. Rather than having individual rights they are expected to be the "bearers of culture and tradition...responsible for the maintenance of a community's identity", says activist Sunila Abeyesekera of INFORM, a human rights non-government organisation (NGO) that focuses on women's rights.

Culture condones violence against women not just within the intimate realm of marriage and the family – but in the public space too. The country has been torn apart by nearly three decades of ethnic tension and guerrilla war between the majority Sinhalese Buddhists and the significantly poorer Tamil minority, who are Hindus. While warfare is concentrated in the Tamil-dominated north, its repercussions have been felt throughout the nation. "Everyone becomes part of a larger system of brutality," says Sharmini Fernando of the Home for Human Rights, a national NGO that provides legal services for communities affected by the ongoing conflict and operates a Women's Desk, which addresses violations against women. "There are a lot of cases [of abuse] but the attitude seems to be that it's nothing to fuss about. Violence is increasing in Sri Lanka partly because of the war going on for the past 26 years.... [It] seems to be...an epidemic."

The World Organisation Against Torture in Geneva, Switzerland, has expressed "its grave concern over the continued reports of torture, including rape, of both women and young girls by Sri Lankan soldiers during the ongoing conflict". [8]

The unrecorded war against women

No national studies of violence against women have been conducted, but findings from the small number of urban and rural investigations are disturbing. A study of 200 lower-income women in the capital city of Colombo, conducted by the Women In Need (WIN) shelter in the late 1980s, showed that 60 percent suffered physical abuse at the hands of their husbands, and 29 percent said their children had been beaten. [9] Gerard Snowball, an Australian health officer at the Bio tea plantation in Idalgashina, 100 km east of Colombo, estimates that between 30 and 40 percent of the women in the community experience some degree of domestic violence.

Small-scale studies confirm that violence among intimates exists countrywide. A study conducted in a village in Kalutara district, 37 km south of Colombo, with a low-income group of 40 married women, aged 20-40 years, reports: "As regards violence directed against women, the majority did not question the 'rights' of men to beat them, especially in a marital dispute." [10] Another study carried out in five villages in the Kandy District, about 100 km north-east of Colombo, also with 40 women from a low-income group, stated, "We were able to identify 29 women who have faced domestic violence in the sample we surveyed. In the majority of cases it involves assault. Of this number 12 seem to face intensive assault daily and it involves bodily injury." [11]

Police records for 1996 show nearly 50,000 cases of violence recorded under the police category, "Family Problems: Crimes Against Women". Most crimes in this category are assaults on wives, according to Shalani Premachandra, officer-in-charge at the National Desk of the Sri Lankan Police Force, Women and Children Unit. An estimated one in four incidents is reported. No system exists to record the number of deaths or suicides linked to domestic violence. According to lawyer Grace Poore, who specialises in domestic violence cases, every incident reported is recorded separately, making it impossible to identify repeat incidents for any eventual legal or service follow-up.

But lack of statistics does not mean that domestic violence is invisible. In fact, according to Coomaraswamy, there has been a dramatic increase in the number of cases reported in the papers, as a result of heightened awareness of what was once a hidden subject. Monitoring the press media over the first 10 months of 1998, Women's Rights Watch found a total of 71 cases of assault and 87 cases of murder – 57 committed by husbands. [12]

In the study by WIN, three-quarters of the women interviewed said their partners were not violent to anyone outside the home. Half had items ranging from sticks and furniture to knives and daggers used against them.

"He uses anything at hand, even an iron rod or a plate of food," said a 24-year-old Sinhalese woman with one child (all names are withheld for confidentiality). "He drags me across the floor by my hair. He tells me to crawl under the bed and remain there. He throws things on the floor. He burns my clothes and destroys them."

It is not uncommon to see women with marks on their faces or even to see men hitting women in public, says health officer Snowball. His clinic, which attends a population of 2,500 villagers, receives an average of five to six women a week with burns, cuts, abrasions and even skull fractures that suggest domestic violence.

The living conditions of the plantation workers are generally unsatisfactory: long rows of 'line houses' made up of single, or sometimes double, rooms which serve as home for the entire family. The men often drink a very strong, illegally brewed liquor called *kassipu*, and then become violent. While domestic violence is found in all economic strata, it can easily be fuelled by the frustrations, disillusionment, alcohol abuse and powerlessness that often accompany poverty.

The demon drink

The WIN study concluded that alcoholism is one of the leading causes of violence. According to Coomaraswamy, Sri Lanka has an extremely high rate of alcohol consumption which, she stresses, is also used as a justification for violent behaviour.

Interviews with battered women are threaded with accounts of men drinking. Incidents of aggression that begin early in a marriage under the influence of alcohol often escalate into steady abuse, with or without this pretext.

Olu is 37 years old, married with two sons. She works as a stenographer. The first time her husband hit her he apologised and said it would never happen again. "At the beginning, he would always apologise after hitting me. He doesn't apologise any more, though.... Now, when I tell his mother he hits me, she says that I must learn to endure it for the sake of the marriage and the children. She said that her husband used to hit her too, but she would put up with it. He still abuses me. Anything and everything can trigger it. At first, he would do it when he was drunk, but not any more. Now, he does not have to be inebriated."

"When he is drunk, he is like a different man. He says hurtful things, and tells me I didn't bring enough money [dowry] with me when I got married. He calls me fat and ugly, then he kicks or punches me and tells me to leave the house. He has also threatened to kill me. If I want to leave him, he will never let me have the children. Also, where can I go? My parents are dead.... I have no savings, since he stopped working last year. We have to manage everything on my salary. He also beats me up when he wants money for his bottles and his cigarettes." [13]

Forty-year-old Ramini is separated from her husband; she and her three children stay with her mother. She says her husband, a heavy drinker, became violent the day after their wedding. Before she had her first child, she wanted to leave him and tried going back to her parents' house. But her mother said that, socially, it would be humiliating for them if she returned. So she 'advised' the husband, and sent her daughter back to him.

A year after the birth of her second child, Ramini tried to commit suicide by drinking poison. Some members of her family found her in time to save her. After that incident, though, she said that her husband tried to force her to drink poison. A year ago, she finally came to her parents with her children, though she says her sisters and brothers do not like her being there after 'breaking up' her marriage. "They say it is shameful for them," Ramini says. [14]

A 32-year-old Sinhalese mother of three describes her domestic ordeal: "He drinks daily. He chases me away and doesn't give me food. I have spent some nights in the nearby jungle. Sometimes he tries to kill me. Once he attacked me with a kerosene oil lamp. I was in hospital for a week with burn injuries."

Rape and marriage

It was not until 1995 that the Penal Code was amended to make marital rape a crime – but only if it occurs when a husband is judicially separated from his wife. Even though it rarely appears in legal complaints, the incidence of marital rape is believed to be high. The fact that "women from South Asian societies are more likely to suffer in silence a situation of domestic disharmony than women in the West", writes Lasanda Kurukulasuriya, "doesn't mean that marital rape doesn't occur." [15]

Forced sex in marriage is not generally perceived as rape, or even as violence, because it is widely believed that marriage gives a husband licence to have sex at will. Women are taught that it's a part of married life. When they get married, the grandmother and aunts advise them: "He's a man, he has an appetite for sex. Whenever he comes to you, you should not refuse him."

Extra-marital affairs – not the wife's infidelity, but the husband's – are also cited as common flashpoints for violence between spouses. Wives rarely question the man's 'right' to philander, but may challenge the draining effect that womanising (or drinking) has on his economic contribution to family welfare.

On the basis of interviews with battered women throughout Sri Lanka, women's rights activist Abeyesekera observes: "It's interesting to see...how much domestic violence has to do with sex and the withholding of sex."

Says a 34-year-old Sinhalese woman: "His sexual appetite has no limits. Sometimes he wants to have sex four or five times in one night. If I refuse, he starts fighting with me, accusing me of having other boyfriends. Then he beats me. When he gets angry, I am afraid to even look at his face because it becomes so cruel." She complained to the police; they 'advised' him to stop, which made no difference to the situation.

Shalini, from Kurunegela, is the mother of three children. She says her husband physically abuses her when she refuses to sleep with him. When she screams, he threatens her, saying he will pull out all her teeth.

"Women don't conceptualise rape by their husbands as battery," explains Coomaraswamy. "They just think they're doing their duty."

Some service providers may also share this attitude. A counsellor at one of the country's two women's shelters believes: "If you are married...you must fulfil his needs. That is the duty of a wife." A senior colleague agrees: "Men have a higher sex drive than women. If a woman wants to refuse to have sex with her husband, why did she marry him?"

The 1995 proposal to amend the Penal Code to recognise

marital rape sparked vehement protests by some Members of Parliament. Mr H.M.H Ashraff, leader of the Sri Lanka Muslim Congress and Minister of Ports and Shipping, said that the marital rape law "...could destroy the very institution of marriage in Sri Lanka and destabilise the family system.... If the wife takes her husband to court on the grounds that he coerced her into sexual intercourse against her will, a whole lot of dirty linen gets washed in public, including distastefully intimate details of the couple's sex life." [16] Such protests led to the confining of the legal sanction to the context of judicial separation. Women's and human rights groups are still lobbying for further amendment of the law.

Sometimes, the women are battered badly enough to seek hospitalisation or medical care. They may be raped, beaten and locked out of the house, ending up spending all night in the nearby jungle, or elsewhere, or creeping back into the house after the man has fallen asleep.

The consequences of marital rape

Violent men who rape their partners – or who insist on unprotected sex – endanger women's physical and mental health. Reproductive health risks include increased rates of sexually transmitted infections (STIs), including HIV, the virus that causes AIDS, unwanted pregnancy, gynaecological problems, miscarriage, and complications from unsafe abortion. Mental health repercussions include anxiety, low self-esteem and depression; some women commit suicide. There is no legal obligation on the part of health officials to record domestic violence in medical records.

Unprotected sex may result in unintended, often unwanted, pregnancy. One potential outcome is unsafe abortion. Although abortion in Sri Lanka is illegal except to save the mother's life, an estimated 170,000 take place annually, according to Dr Ramanathan, Director of the Marie Stopes Clinic in Colombo. One study estimates that 20 percent of hospital beds in gynaecological wards are occupied by women suffering from complications as a result of unsafe abortions. [17] Dr Lalini Rajapakse, a member of the Task Force on Reproductive Health, estimates that 12 percent of all maternal deaths are attributed to abortion.

Pregnancy is no guarantee of freedom from violence. Some 42 percent of women interviewed by WIN said they were physically abused while pregnant. It is not uncommon for the first episodes of abuse to coincide with a first pregnancy, as happened to a 37-year-old stenographer from a middle-class English-speaking family who married at 25 and became pregnant almost immediately. She explains: "I was pregnant the first time he beat me; I was stunned. But now, I can't remember.... [When] it was over...I did not tell anyone. I was so scared. And anyway, his family lives all around." [18]

Violence can have negative impacts on the outcome of a pregnancy, with abused women likely to seek prenatal care at a later date. Physical assault and the associated stress have been linked to premature births and low birthweight of infants. [19]

A woman's fear of unwanted pregnancy may not deter an aggressive husband – even if he also does not want more children. This is the dilemma of a 36-year-old mother of five whose husband becomes violent "especially when there are more children and financial problems increase. Whenever I talk to him about family planning, he fights with me – he is totally against it."

"We don't want to sleep with our husbands because we don't want babies," one woman told Abeyesekera. Another said: "They don't allow us to use contraceptives, but they still want us to sleep with them. And when we refuse, we get beaten."

The pressure to endure

Advances in women's literacy and employment mean that many Sri Lankan women now work outside the home.

Although employment gives women greater freedom of movement, domestic violence increasingly revolves around "money, control of movement or ensuring that wives don't leave the house", believes human rights activist Fernando. She says women still face violent attitudes in the public space; widespread sexual harassment on Colombo public transportation forced the Ministry for Transport, Environment and Women's Affairs to schedule special buses for women only.

When domestic violence occurs, there may be little support. "Women are always seen as being at fault," notes a former WIN counsellor. "A man's indulgences are always excused, even by his own mother and mother-in-law." Daughters-in-law and daughters may receive little more than exhortations to be patient and tolerant. Nor is this surprising, given studies world-wide indicating that abuse, and submission to abuse, is often learned at home.

Pressure is put on women to accept the status quo. "Women are still conditioned in Sri Lanka to be property – first someone's daughter, then someone's wife," says a former WIN counsellor who asked not to be named. A woman's husband is her 'passport to society' to whom she owes obedience.

Shame and social stigma play an important psychological role in keeping women from seeking help – or from receiving help when it is sought. The shame factor is especially acute among higher-income groups. Economic resources, education and social position do not automatically increase a woman's recourse to counselling or legal protection. Women from lower-income groups "may, at least sometimes, go to their mothers for a couple of weeks, walk around with their bruises and let everybody see that they've been beaten, or even go to the police", says Abeyesekera. But among upper and middle-class women, the burden of cultural conditioning and keeping up appearances is heavy. "So even if you're desperately unhappy, desperately brutalised, you'll still smile, entertain and put make-up on your bruises."

Sensitivity to social stigma is not limited to the well-to-do. Poor families also cite fear of disgrace in refusing to receive a battered daughter. Says a 40-year-old Sinhalese woman and mother of three, separated after 15 years: "At first, I would come to my parents' home, before I had children. But each time, my mother would tell me that this would have a negative effect on their social position, and would talk to my husband and send me back. After that, I left him and came to my parents' home with my children, but my brothers and sisters disapproved, saying that my being at home is a source of shame for them. So I hope to go abroad for work [as a domestic worker], though I will leave my children behind."

Women may blame themselves for a husband's attacks. Of 40 village women interviewed in Remunagoda, a village in Kalutara District, at least seven attributed battery to their own lack of patience. [20] In the event of bodily harm, 25 of the women said they would seek advice from relatives or friends. Twelve said they would not divulge the incident to anyone. Not a single woman said she would go to the police. [21]

In the WIN study of 200 women in Colombo, roughly a third left their homes after battery, but only for a brief period. [22] "Most of my cases went back to their abusive husbands," a former counsellor noted, "and not just because of poverty, but for reasons of social stigma, family reputation and children. It is always the women who compromise their own safety."

Divorce is a difficult option. Lawyer Ramini Muthetuwegame believes it is becoming more acceptable for an economically independent woman to seek a divorce, but notes that many clients ask her to keep initial proceedings hidden from their husbands, for fear of violent repercussions. In the absence of a protracted period of separation, major grounds for divorce remain limited to impotence at the time of marriage, adultery and malicious desertion.

Once a woman is alone, she faces a new set of problems. In Sri Lanka, single women who have been married are considered sexually available and promiscuous, so that leaving an abusive man may actually increase a woman's vulnerability to unwanted advances from others.

The lack of choices for women, coupled with social attitudes towards divorced women, affect even the minimal support available to abused wives. Only two non-governmental shelters, one in Kandy – the Women's Development Centre (WDC) - and one in Colombo – Women in Need (WIN) - provide temporary refuge as well as counselling and legal aid to Sri Lankan women. Both have faced criticism for upholding society's traditional views of men and women's sexual roles. "We explain reality to them," says a WIN counsellor, referring to attempts to reconcile couples. Despite its limitations, WIN counsellors say the shelter "fills a void, gives support. Men are aware of WIN's existence. This in itself is empowering."

Society 'keeps the peace'

Like the rest of society, most health care providers turn a blind eye to domestic violence, despite the first-hand contact they have with its victims. A gynaecologist at a private nursing home says he and the other staff sometimes see complications due to battering. When they do, they "try to comfort the women and treat their symptoms". Occasionally, a woman may want to make a judicial report, in which case she is directed to the appropriate authorities.

The nursing home does not report the man but may try to reconcile the couple. "But if we feel that his temper is too much, we try not to get involved. We don't want to be the target of the husband's anger, nor do we want to get involved in the judicial inquiry. We try to play it safe."

Where women do seek police intervention and legal recourse against domestic violence, they often run into a wall of indifference and insensitivity and misplaced motives. Police of both sexes usually try to persuade a battered wife to return to her husband. According to Shalani Premachandra, Chief Inspector of Police, Crimes Division, Children and Women Unit, of an average of 4,000 crimes reported against women every month, nearly 80 percent were "settled" when the wife was persuaded, after counselling by the police, to drop charges. [23] Of the nearly 50,000 cases of domestic violence reported in 1996, nearly five percent were reconciled before the Mediation Board – a judicial body empowered to try to secure out-of-court settlements before criminal proceedings are embarked on. Just over two percent of cases went to court.

Says Rani, who endured 17 years of battering: "In those days, when I used to go and tell the police they would come and advise the two of us and that was all. That was a hell of a thing. Finally, I went and blasted the police, saying that what was the justice in it for me? Why couldn't they beat him up for beating me – they go and beat up the other thieves and all those they take into custody? Every day, I get beaten up and that was all. He gets away scot-free. Then one day the police actually did beat him up, thoroughly. After that, he was somewhat scared." [24]

In 1993, a network of Women's Police Desks was established nationwide. The idea had been well received. Grace Poore, a lawyer working on domestic violence issues and a member of the Task Force on Domestic Violence, believes that "when word goes out that women are staffing those units, women will go to seek help."

In reality the desks have been plagued with problems. They are restricted to office hours and closed when women most often need help. Nor do female police travel to the scene of violence when a complaint is made. This task is assigned to male officers.

The presence of women officers in the stations does not automatically guarantee help. In Kandy, policewomen felt strongly that the law should not govern intimate relationships. "If [a woman] goes to the police and they dismiss her, or trivialise her complaint or compel her to patch it up, she's less likely to go to them for help the next time," says Poore. "One of the main criticisms by the Task Force of...police officers [of both sexes is] the tendency not to enforce the law but to act as 'counsellors'. The point is, police officers are not counsellors.... [They] are supposed to enforce the law."

Coomaraswamy concurs. "The criminal justice system and the social support system all seem to be geared toward reconciliation, all under the guise of 'protection' of the marital relationship and the family."

Only if a woman sustains serious physical injury or is killed are police likely to make an arrest, says S.P Pramila Divakara, of the Women and Children's Bureau. When this occurs, offenders are prosecuted for grievous assault under normal criminal law as part of the Penal Code. Even then, resistance runs high.

"By involving the courts in these affairs," states Karuna Karunaratne, an officer in the Women and Children's Bureau of Colombo suburb Mount Lavinia, "we might even tear the family further apart."

Frustrated initiatives

In 1993, the Sri Lanka government approved a Women's Charter with general guidelines aimed at ensuring equality and justice for women. It states that "gender-based violence is a violation of human rights and fundamental freedoms" and that it "impairs or negates women's enjoyment of [other] recognised rights and freedoms".

A National Committee on Women was formed to oversee the implementation of the Charter, but unless the Committee's powers are augmented, the Women's Charter will remain a reform on paper only. At present, the Ministry responsible for Women's Affairs is in the process of strengthening the Committee by raising its status to that of a Commission – an independent, quasi-judicial body able to receive petitions from the public, conduct research and facilitate conflict resolution. The legislation to establish the Commission has been drafted but has yet to be approved by Parliament.

In 1996, the Ministry for Transport, Environment and Women's Affairs convened a Task Force on Domestic Violence to submit recommendations to modernise Sri Lankan law. Inclusion of guidelines for health professionals faced with cases of abuse were not part of its remit. Draft legislation was to have been prepared by the end of 1997. As of early 2000, this legislation was still in the pipeline.

According to Coomaraswamy, also a Task Force member: "A decision has not been made about whether there should be a separate law on domestic violence, or whether the existing Penal Code and civil law should be amended." Separate domestic violence legislation might carry less weight, whereas the Penal Code is effective with the police: it "moves" them, says Coomaraswamy.

The uphill struggle to bring in laws defending women's reproductive rights is well illustrated by the unsuccessful outcome of a 1995 parliamentary debate to amend the Penal Code. This was the same bill that proposed the inclusion of marital rape as a criminal offence. The original draft legislation also contained a section decriminalising abortion in cases of rape, incest and foetal malformation.

The abortion reform proposal was stymied even prior to its presentation to Parliament by then Justice Minister G.L Peiris, who decided to delete the abortion section in its entirety because of its 'controversial' nature. "We have tried to accommodate different points of view, different religious convictions and different cultural and moral traditions," Peiris said. [25] "It is difficult to conceive of absolute norms or principles which cut across cultural distinctions. It sometimes becomes necessary to recognise different standards and values applicable to different sections of the community. This is part and parcel of life in Sri Lanka." [26]

Despite Peiris' attempt to pre-empt discussion on the issue of abortion reform, the topic dominated the debate. The majority of MPs opposed the reform. Some for religious reasons, while others claimed that access to safe abortion would encourage female promiscuity and give unscrupulous women a weapon against men. One MP justified denying abortion to a raped woman by saying: "We know half these stories [of rape] are made up." [27]

In withdrawing the amendment to liberalise abortion, the Minister of Justice expressed his personal commitment to decriminalising abortion. "Decriminalisation of abortion is a feature of evolving legal systems in many parts of the world and I do not see any reason why Sri Lanka should be out of step with that general development." [28] Although he promised to introduce health legislation to address the issue of unsafe abortion, it has not materialised, and abortion continues to be a criminal offence in Sri Lanka.

And so, in the end, cultural traditions that favour men took precedence over women's human rights.

For Abeyesekera, it is not a question of different points of view but rather "the anomaly of different legal standards which apply to public and private life". In the public sphere, "murder is murder", she argues. But "legal norms...relegate the private sphere 'beyond justice'", treating women as "unequal and lesser beings". [29]

According to Abeyesekera, the 1995 debate, which exemplified the convergence of "conservative religious and political opinions against women's right to control their sexuality and reproduction...is of grave concern for women in Sri Lanka". [30]

Beyond services

De facto policies to 'settle' disputes and 'reconcile' couples override justice in the guise of 'protecting' marriage and the family, taking Sri Lankan women further from a position of enjoying their human rights. These attitudes trivialise spousal battery as a mere 'family tiff' rather than recognising it as a violation of an individual's physical and mental integrity.

Similarly, a strictly family-planning approach to women's reproductive health minimises issues of women's rights. Women may know how many children they want, and even how to achieve this through contraceptive use, but technology alone does not ensure that women's choices will be respected as the rights of individuals with preferences and needs.

Transforming legal treatment of domestic violence from protection to prohibition and eventually prevention "is an enormous task", Coomaraswamy admits. She sees mandatory charging or arrest of aggressors as a clear signal that would at least obligate police to enforce the law. But Coomaraswamy also realises that real-life scenarios can be complex. As a defender of human rights, she wants to criminalise domestic violence and "get those men in jail". But another part of her "listens to these women who have been abused and [sees their] children" and understands that "they don't want their husbands in jail – they want them rehabilitated. And that part of me says, if there's a possibility of rehabilitation, perhaps that's the option." [31]

Kanthi, a lawyer and co-founder of a battered women's shelter, suggests an approach that moves away from penalties and sanctions toward a "more positive attitude" of standards and dignity. [32] She calls for society to "make perpetrators aspire to a sense of social acceptance by adhering to certain standards".

Situating the fight against domestic violence within the quest to protect the human rights of all citizens makes strategic sense. "There has to be...awareness that this is not a way to treat human beings," affirms Abeysekera.

For Coomaraswamy, the campaign to eliminate gender violence remains "both encouraging and depressing". [33] While change is taking place to improve women's lives, she believes, the accounts of those who have suffered act as a gruelling reminder of "how horrible the world can be". [34]

Less than Human Treatment
Maternity protection in Kenya

*Dorothy Munyakho**

Susan Wamai went into labour at 4.30 pm while chairing a meeting at her local government offices. "I walked out and asked my boss to replace me. I caught a public bus to the hospital and delivered."

Like most working women in Kenya, Wamai defied her employer's requirement to go on leave at least one month before her expected date of delivery (EDD). Entitled by law to only two months' paid maternity leave, she needed it all after delivery, especially if she had a late birth or post-natal complications. "I knew I wanted to work until the end rather than stop one month before, otherwise my child would suffer.... Can you imagine leaving your baby after only two weeks?" she asks.

Wamai breastfed for just a few weeks. "I arrive at work at 7.30 am and I don't get home before 6.00 pm. Sometimes I feel so tired, I have to force myself to play with the baby." She thinks women should be entitled to at least six months' paid maternity leave.

Njuguna Gichuki, a lecturer at the Kenya Institute of Mass Communication (KIMC) agreed with his wife, Susan Mumbi, an advertising consultant, that she would take seven months' leave – five of them unpaid. But their story is the exception rather than the rule. No statutory provision grants

---

* And the IRIS (Interlink Rural Information Service) research team: Evaline Were, research coordinator; researchers: Alex Diang'a, Oscar Obonyo, Jane Naitore, Andrea Useem, Sheri Bird.

a woman job security when she takes unpaid leave over and above stipulated company leave, although some employers grant an additional one or two months' leave on medical grounds. Owing to the employment crisis, women lucky enough to get jobs fear to demand their rights. Limited economic growth and rapid population growth have led to rising unemployment and poverty, with inadequate employment opportunities in both the formal and informal sectors.

The lack of job security makes women wary of the Gichuki type of arrangement. Rachel Wambui (not her real name) says: "I have a husband who also works. He meets all our financial needs." But Rachel has never considered staying at home for more than a few weeks after delivery. "If you leave your job to take care of your children and your husband abandons you – these men are unpredictable – what would be your fate?"

Traditionally, most Kenyan communities confined a mother to the home for about three months after giving birth so that she could nurture her child. She would be largely excused from household chores, which other female relatives would perform. Such traditional societies supported maternal child care, but this support has been eroded by urbanisation and requirements to fit into the rules and regulations of modern employment systems.

For some, tradition persists – in modified form. Monet, a 45-year-old from Machakos District, works as a cook and caretaker in a coffee cooperative that fails to implement a maternity leave policy. Monet stopped working one month before each of her babies was due and took three to four months away from work. "To secure my job, I would ask my mother to replace me, or I would 'hire' another person to stand in for me while I was on leave and we would split the wage."

Monet's mother helped with the younger children, while her elder daughters and relatives fetched water. Back at work she says: "My mother baby-sits my children, and...I take care of her needs."

Agonising choices

The situation is grim for casual employees who do not qualify for paid maternity leave. Jennifer from Machakos District, who withheld her surname because her employer does not allow her to talk to strangers, has worked on a sisal plantation for six years. "I am not a professional. I am only paid for the goods that I deliver. I stayed at home for only four weeks after delivery because I needed money," says the 28-year-old mother of two. Her salary was discontinued during her maternity leave.

Jennifer's employer does not allow children on the plantation. Upon resuming work, her younger sister cared for her child and she could breastfeed only early in the morning and late in the evening after work. "It is painful to stay away from such a little kid.... I had no option but to resume my poorly paid casual job," she said. Her work as a cutter entails bending down in the sun all day. "While I always felt like going straight to bed after work, the fact that I had been away from the baby all day did not allow me to."

Esther Wairimu, a labourer on a coffee plantation and a single mother of two, worked until the eve of the birth of her second child. "Having to solve your problems spurs you on to continue working even when you feel defeated," she says. Dependent on a fortnightly wage, Wairimu returned to work three weeks after delivery. "I don't have a husband and there is no one to help me," she says. She carried the baby on her back and could feed and comfort her – a situation better, she felt, than that of many urban women.

"Mothers carrying children to work is the norm in plantations, although it is officially prohibited," says Ms Kathini Maloba-Caines, acting regional secretary for Africa of IUF (the International Union of Food, Agricultural,

Hotel, Restaurant, Catering, Tobacco and Allied Workers' Associations). "The problem is that the farms are not the same ones our mothers carried us to. These ones are full of pesticides and other chemicals, which pose a great danger to the child, even more than to the mother," she says. Physiologically, infants are much more vulnerable to the effects of pollutants than adults. In the case of pesticide residues, effects may not show up until years later. [1]

Women who depend on casual or low-paid jobs make agonising choices. In order to keep her job, Evaline (not her real name), who works as a hospital cleaner, took only the two months of unpaid maternity leave entitled to her. As soon as she felt strong enough to resume work, she left her baby at home, unattended. Her home in the hospital quarters was just a five-minute walk away. "I would sneak out during the day to feed my child. The supervisors wouldn't give me permission."

"I was very scared, but what could I do? I got used to it.... Later, when he grew big enough to walk, I would tie him to the bed with a rope around the hand so that he could not walk around and hurt himself."

Urban living appears to pre-empt or, at least, significantly limit the role of the extended family – traditionally perceived as a pillar of African society – in infant and young child care. The declining role of extended family and community involvement in child upbringing is a matter of concern vis-à-vis women's increasing involvement in the employment sector. Poverty forces women not entitled to paid maternity leave back to work as soon as they are able, while existing labour arrangements give mothers too little time with their infants.

That a mother has little choice but to leave an eight-week-old baby indoors, alone and virtually imprisoned, is an indictment of laws that accord a certain category of workers less than human treatment.

Employers first, mothers and children last

Kenya has not ratified either of the International Labour Organization (ILO) Maternity Protection Conventions, which spell out minimum standards of 12 weeks' maternity leave with cash benefits of between two-thirds and 100 per cent of previous earnings and entitlement to medical care to be paid for by compulsory social insurance or public funds.[2] Subsequent ILO standards recommend extending the period of maternity leave to 14 weeks [3] and granting a period of parental leave immediately following maternity leave.[4] Recently, the Committee on Maternity Protection has proposed that ILO member states further extend the maternity leave to 16 weeks, a recommendation that will be considered at the next ILO Conference in 2000.

Kenya is one of only a handful of sub-Saharan African countries whose national provision falls below even minimum ILO standards. Moreover, the provisions that do exist apply only to the minority of women in longstanding, formal employment.

Kenyan law provides for just two months' paid maternity leave with forfeiture of annual leave. This, in effect, means that mothers are entitled to only one month's maternity leave, the second month being their annual leave.

The Employment Act Chapter 226 (revised 1984), paragraph 7 (2), states that "a woman employee shall be entitled to two months' maternity leave with full pay: provided that a woman who has taken two months' maternity leave shall forfeit her annual leave in that year". The Act is silent on who pays for the maternity leave and the burden has fallen on employers, although the ILO explicitly states that in no case should the employer be individually liable for the cost of benefits.[5] Employers' contracts stipulate how long a woman must work before qualifying for leave, usually at least the probation period.

The Regulation of Wages (General Order) of the

Regulation of Wages and Conditions of Employment Act (revised 1989) also grants two months' maternity leave with forfeiture of annual leave. Ambiguity arises over whether 'two months' is made up of calendar (consecutive) days or working days. Interpretation is left to the employer or, in some cases, to the woman's supervisor.

In most local small privately-owned firms, women suffer discrimination in employment. The 1989 Act states that childbirth is not sickness and the employer is not required to meet medical costs incurred.

Most employers with medical schemes do not cover pregnancy-related health costs. Employees are entitled to all medical services except cosmetic (beauty-related), dental and optical services. Employers do not consider any maternity-related conditions. The cost of financing a complicated delivery such as a caesarian section, forceps delivery or vacuum extraction, becomes a woman's responsibility, says Ms Margaret Mugo, Women's Affairs Coordinator of the Central Organization of Trade Unions-Kenya (COTU-K). "A few employers have now agreed to include maternity. Others, however, believe maternity is a self-inflicted injury, whose costs must be borne by the employee. Some will cover normal delivery, but if it is a caesarian, the employee pays for it."

Atsango Chesoni, a researcher with the Women's Rights Monitoring and Report Writing Project of the International Federation of Women Lawyers (FIDA) Kenya Chapter, notes that although reproductive disorders are covered on many employers' health insurance policies, pregnancy is not. "Some employers take a health package and end up discriminating against their female staff. These are some of the invisible ways to condone sexism," she says.

The 1989 Act further states that a woman who takes maternity leave shall not incur any loss of privileges during that period. "Some employers don't treat maternity leave like any other leave," says Mugo, "and deny you travelling allowance or other benefits you may get when you go on annual leave."

"We have other employers whose collective bargaining agreements read: 'A married woman shall be entitled to two months' maternity leave.' Does that mean that the one who is not married is not entitled to any rights? You...have to prove whether you are married or not. Yet your marital status should not deny you this maternity protection."

Employment stipulations on maternity leave have led to knock-on discrimination against all women. "In some companies, before a woman can take annual leave, she must undergo a pregnancy test, which must be negative for her leave to be approved," says Mugo. "If the test result is positive, she loses her leave and waits for maternity leave." If the result is negative, the woman has still suffered the indignity of being obliged to undergo a test.

Breastfeeding: a birthright, a mother's right

Tabitha Oduori, Family Health Officer at the World Health Organization (WHO) office in Nairobi, interprets maternity rights through breastfeeding policies. The WHO guidelines on breastfeeding are clear: exclusive breastfeeding for the first four to six months of the baby's life gives infants the best chance of survival. The baby should be put on the breast immediately after birth, and be able to stay with the mother to be able to feed on demand.

For a mother to breastfeed exclusively for up to six months, she needs support. According to Mrs Pamela Malebe, national breastfeeding coordinator in the Division of Primary Health Care, Ministry of Health, out of 350 hospitals with maternity facilities surveyed nationwide in 1994, 232 were adequately implementing the '14 Steps to Successful Breastfeeding', a brainchild of Unicef and WHO. The initiative calls for post-natal rooming-in, which allows mothers and infants to remain together 24 hours a day. Mothers are shown how to breastfeed and maintain milk supply and are encouraged to breastfeed on demand.

For the 55 percent of births that occur at home, the Ministry of Health is mobilising community support groups for mothers, which give advice on breastfeeding, usually under the supervision of a trained Traditional Birth Attendant (TBA). In four districts, these groups are succeeding in sustaining breastfeeding, Malebe says.

Kenya's adoption in 1983 of the Kenya Standard Code for Marketing of Breastmilk Substitutes, adapted from the 1981 WHO/Unicef International Code, has aided the breastfeeding campaign. A ministerial directive places restrictions on the marketing of substitutes and imposes a compulsory label on any substitute products, which states: "Breastmilk is the best food for feeding a baby."

But although 97 percent of children in Kenya are initially breastfed, only 27 percent of infants under two months are exclusively breastfed. By two-to-three months, 82 percent of infants are already receiving supplements. At 20-24 months, 54 percent are still partially breastfeeding. The infant mortality rate, although one of the lowest in sub-Saharan Africa, remains high. Approximately six percent of children will die before their first birthday, though there are wide regional disparities.[6]

Breastfeeding in Kenya is on the rise and there is a slow but increasing awareness of the health benefits of breastfeeding to mothers themselves – including speedy contraction of the uterus after childbirth to its pre-pregnancy size and a reduced risk of breast and ovarian cancer. Meanwhile, the costs of infant formulae and fuel to boil water to prepare the formulae and sterilise bottles are increasing.

During the 1960s to 1980s there was a proliferation of infant-feeding substitute formulae. Breastfeeding was perceived as 'backward', 'uncivilised' and 'embarrassing'. 'Baby bottles' became a typical advertising image of modernity. The legacy lingers. Says Bernard Nyawanda, a Value Added Tax (VAT) inspector: "Women who breastfeed for more than three months lack manners."

Tabitha Oduori, WHO family health officer dismisses such views. "Before, you would see mothers hiding as they breastfed," she says, "but these days...nobody is looking at them." Officially, WHO does not make links between maternity leave and exclusive breastfeeding. But to enable mothers to breastfeed, Oduori urges employers to make working conditions flexible.

Maternity: penalty or protection?

When Lucy Ndung'u, a pioneer lobbyist for a better lot for nursing mothers, joined KUDHEIHA (Kenya Union of Domestic, Hotels, Educational Institutions, Hospitals and Allied Workers) as an industrial relations officer in 1985, maternity leave days were counted consecutively. Although ordinary employees were entitled by law to one day off in every seven – and many employers observe a five-day working week – when it came to maternity leave, even these mandatory days were lost within the consecutive count, as were public holidays.

Ndung'u challenged the status quo: "I started asking these men 'Why?' Why should a woman be penalised? Because if she did not give birth, she would have got her annual leave. And here is a case where the woman needs even more rest, because she has given birth, and this is when she is being denied her leave! What mistake has she made? - because this was like a penalty. And why do you include the public holiday in the leave? Why do you include even the day off, which you are ready to give to a man who may not even need it? Yet here is a mother, who has got a kid, and desperately needs this leave."

KUDHEIHA started negotiating and got maternity leave days treated as working days. The result was an automatic eight days extra leave for women members of KUDHEIHA. Moreover, KUDHEIHA members no longer lose public holidays coinciding with the maternity leave. In agreements

KUDHEIHA has negotiated with some employers, there is now a provision that the woman does not forfeit her annual leave. In others, her annual leave is protected in particular circumstances.

Ndung'u traces Kenya's harsh maternity policies to the history of the labour movement in the country. "It is men who started trade unions. In most cases, they did not include issues affecting women. They made their own kingdoms and the structures surrounding them, which are very difficult to penetrate," she says.

"We need to educate women [about] their rights and what they should expect when they join the union," she says. "They need to be...active in the unions by seeking electoral positions." Only from the top can women lobby and convince employers of the need for change, she argues.

Mugo of COTU-K has seen a steady move of women into trade union leadership, boosted by the momentum generated by the 1995 Fourth World Conference on Women held in Beijing, China. "We made the right to maternity protection our theme. We held a series of workshops about integrating gender issues into the trade union," she says. From that start, the Women's Department began training CBA (collective bargaining agreement) negotiators within the 30 trade unions affiliated with COTU-K.

Says Ms Anne Karume, Women's Affairs Coordinator of the Railway Workers Union (RWU) affiliated to COTU: "Before we go to negotiate workers' issues with management, we prepare a memorandum covering all terms and conditions of workers, including salaries, breastfeeding, maternity leave, sick days, etcetera."

Karume is careful to integrate women's concerns within the main agenda. "If we separate them, they will be looked at as unimportant. I want them seen as workers' issues that are specific to women," she says. When they were previously negotiated as simply women's issues, women were invariably discriminated against. For example, married women, unlike their male counterparts, were not entitled to medical coverage for their families, or house or travel allowances.

RWU convinced management to grant women 60 calendar days of leave plus their annual leave calculated at 30 working days per year. "This arrangement usually enables women to stay at home for four to five months with their babies," Karume says. Women are also entitled to breastfeeding breaks of one hour per day for three months after resuming work. The women negotiate with their supervisors whether to come in late, leave early, or take a long lunch break to go and breastfeed. RWU is presently negotiating for daycare centres at the workplace.

"[It is] an uphill task," says Karume. "When we push for better rights such as those in the [ILO] Convention, employers keep referring us back to the Kenyan law of two months."

The Kenya Union of Journalists (KUJ), like the RWU, has succeeded in securing better provisions by considering interlinkages in employment conditions. Its members were among the first Kenyans to get three months' fully paid maternity leave in addition to one month's annual leave and sick leave entitlements.

Mr Kihu Irimu, KUJ secretary-general, laments, however, that these standards cover only a minority of journalists – they do not apply to freelancers or affect employers who have not negotiated CBAs.

"We are trying to get government and employers to take into account that an employee is a social being. She or he belongs to a family and is a member of a community. The employer should be sensitive to his or her needs in that context," he says.

Nursing breaks and hour cuts

Lobbying in 1995, says Mugo of COTU-K, led some companies to begin implementing nursing breaks that ease the transition back to work. KUDHEIHA has also begun a campaign for paid breastfeeding breaks. "We feel mothers need breastfeeding time of maybe two hours every day for six months or one year," says Ndung'u. ILO recommends at least one and a half hours during the working day and the establishment of nursing and day care facilities.[7]

A major hindrance to nursing breaks is their duration. Most mothers entitled to 30-minute nursing breaks find the time too short to be of any practical use. KUDHEIHA is negotiating for a situation where mothers could opt to report at 9.00 am rather than 8.00 am, when buses are congested. This would enable them to stay a little longer with their babies until the rush hour ends. And in the evenings, instead of knocking off at 5.00 pm, they could leave at 4.00 pm, before the evening rush hour starts. That way, they would get home earlier and attend to their babies.

This arrangement also eliminates additional transport costs, which may impede a mother from making the extra trip home in the middle of the day.

Nairobi's rush hours, characterised by frequent traffic jams, are an ordeal for most commuters. The city's population has grown to 28.7 million, according to the latest census in August 1999. Economic liberalisation has fuelled the influx of cheaply imported cars, yet these changes have not been matched by road expansion. Most workers leave home one-and-a-half to two hours before reporting time, and take as long to get home in the evening. Those using public transport must, on most routes, queue for long periods to board municipal buses or *matatus* - the unofficial transport minibuses.

Says Mrs Elizabeth Timba, assistant personnel manager at the Kenya Railways Corporation: "Some [employers] interpret the hours we give for breastfeeding breaks as 'hours lost'. But what I have found in working with women is that because they feel the employer is taking care of them, they are ready to put in extra hours of work when it is needed. I've also found that they care more for their jobs because they see a caring employer. So, very few of them leave their jobs because they've had a baby," she says.

"As a woman manager, I see no conflict whatsoever between assisting our employees' welfare in this way, and our interests as employers."

Malebe, the Ministry of Health's national breastfeeding coordinator, says the Ministry promotes milk expression at the workplace – to enable mothers to empty their breasts, prevent engorgement and thereby sustain milk production. "We rarely ask them to store expressed milk for reasons of hygiene," she adds.

Unions advocate time off for breastfeeding, instead. Says Karume: "Mothers don't want to store their babies' milk in common places used by many people, some of whom they do not know, in case someone has ill intentions towards them. They want to feed their babies, not empty their breasts at a distance."

Changing national law

How are the employers responding to these requests? Most oppose changes, Ndung'u of KUDHEIHA says. They fear demands for maternity protection may reduce their profits.

"Trade unions don't lobby Parliament aggressively. And few women's organisations lobby on labour issues," says Mugo of COTU-K, who sees the solution as lying with changes at the legislative level. "Every women's organisation in this country, not just workers' organisations, must...lobby for a complete review of the labour law. This law is outdated and does not relate to the current world of work because it was enacted during the colonial era."

"If our unions were strong...we could lobby, especially against those laws that require mothers to forfeit their annual leave," Ndung'u says. If the law is changed, "then employers will have to comply, whether or not they like it".

Nationally, the effort to lobby for maternity rights is disjointed. Health and nutrition advocates liaise with each other on breastfeeding issues. Trade unionists work together on maternity leave and nursing breaks. Although collaboration would make for a stronger lobby, trade unions and other groups rarely work together. "Nobody has really mooted the idea," says Karume of RWU.

Progress on breastfeeding breaks and maternity leave has been slow. "When the Task Force for the Review of Laws Relating to Women was formed, we were hopeful it would be a push factor," says Mugo. "But they seem to have gone underground."

Tripartite collective bargaining negotiations at national level between the Federation of Kenya Employers (FKE), COTU-K and the Ministry of Labour yielded a proposal to amend the law so that women do not forfeit their annual leave when they take maternity leave. "Breastfeeding breaks," says Mr A.O Ambenge, assistant labour commissioner in the Ministry of Labour, "have not featured in the discussions. As a Ministry, our role is to enforce legislation and advise. Unless the trade unions propose the issue of breastfeeding breaks, or any other issue, we as a Ministry have no mandate to take it up since any labour law amendments must be tripartite." [8]

Some officials argue a 'lesser evil' position. In a stance that appears to condone the punitive measures mothers face, Mrs B.W Mwai, another assistant labour commissioner in the Ministry of Labour and Manpower Development, worries that "if we push for three months, we may be doing women a disservice. Employers may choose to hire men instead of women."

A matter of representation

"The main problem is that the issue is not being taken up as it should," says Mugo. "Parliamentarians who can make a difference don't."

The leadership crisis in Kenya's trade union movement is mirrored by the lack of women in Parliament. Numerical weakness means that when motions that concern women come to Parliament, they are thrown out.

In November 1996, one week after the Beijing Platform for Action (BPA) was tabled in Parliament, a bill to criminalise female genital mutilation (FGM) was defeated, even though the Platform calls for elimination of the practice. "One of the biggest problems is awareness," says Millie Odhiambo of the Kenyan chapter of the International Commission of Jurists. "A lot of male parliamentarians ...mocked [the bill] and said things like, 'Cut them, cut them.' It highlighted that the problem is not just with [communities] but with policy formulators and legislators.... You have to educate the policy-makers." [9]

To date, there are no legal sanctions against FGM, apart from Presidential statements against the practice. "We would like to see some legal sanctions," says Mrs Leah Muya, an official of *Maendeleo ya Wanawake*, the oldest grassroots women's organisation in Kenya. A national plan of action to eliminate FGM was launched in November 1999, using public education to fight the practice.

The BPA stipulates that 33 percent of national administrative and legislative seats be reserved for women. Some African countries have introduced affirmative action to transform this aspect of the Beijing document into law but attempts to do so in Kenya have so far been defeated.

As regards maternity protection, the issue becomes difficult in that the Members of Parliament who are supposed to ameliorate the situation of women are also the employers. "They are the people who own these hotels. They are the people who own the tea estates and the coffee estates. They are the people who own these factories. So they are very sensitive to any suggestions concerning the workers," Ndung'u says.

She accuses people with 'big money' of going into politics

to protect their wealth. She does not spare the government, which she describes as "the biggest single employer".

Unlike in many countries where civil servants have better provisions than other sectors, in Kenya, they are entitled only to the statutory provision of two months' maternity leave, forfeiting annual leave.

New initiatives

The women who have made a difference in companies are all members of the Kenya Women Workers Organisation (KEWWO), who were trained by KEWWO to lobby for change within their companies – Nzoia Sugar Company, Kenya Power & Lighting Company and Kenya Railways. KEWWO began in 1993 as a loose network of female trade unionists but has since broadened its membership to women in all sectors.

Says Maloba-Caines of the IUF union, which is also affiliated to KEWWO: "We are asking for more maternity leave – for sufficient maternity leave, that is, a minimum of four months. We would be comfortable with six months, without women losing their annual leave. This is because the WHO recommendations, which the government of Kenya has endorsed, state that for a child to develop sufficient immunity against diseases, she or he needs four-to-six months of exclusive breastfeeding. There is also the need for a weaning period of about two months, under the mother's close supervision. After those six months, you can go back to the office comfortably."

"The length of maternity leave we are calling for guarantees breastfeeding. Since there would be improved health among children, it would reduce the cost of medicine and...save foreign exchange used to import medicines," says Maloba-Caines.

She recognises that calls for additional maternity leave must identify who will pay for it: "The main reason an employer will not want you away for a long period is that you must be paid, and the person they may have to get to do your work in the office must also be paid, so that the employer faces a double cost." In her view, that is basically transferring the responsibility from the state to the employer.

In countries with long maternity leaves such as South Africa, where many women are entitled to six months' leave, it is not the employer who foots the bill 100 percent. The social security fund pays a certain percentage in order to transfer the costs from individuals and employers to the nation. "It is a duty for the nation to make sure its children are taken care of," says Maloba-Caines. "I know that if all the Kenyan women didn't have children for three years, they would bribe us to have them to ensure they maintain a future workforce! If the National Social Security Fund invested some of its money in child care rather than lending it to companies, the employer's business would just be to ask when the employee was planning to take her leave."

On 8 March 1997, International Women's Day, KEWWO launched a new campaign to improve maternity protection and also to link maternity leave to day care centres. As a result, Parliament on 8 November 1998 passed a motion increasing maternity leave from the current two months (with forfeiture of annual leave) to three months. It remains for the Attorney General to table a bill to legalise three months' maternity leave. The motion tabled before Parliament was silent on annual leave. As of now, the operational law, yet to be changed, grants two months' leave with forfeiture of annual leave. The motion, it is believed, equally implies three months with forfeiture, a duration still short of minimum ILO recommendations. Employers will still foot the entire bill. Likewise, there has been no shift towards covering maternity-related costs in medical insurance schemes provided by employers.

"We have known our Parliament to pass a motion and stay for even three years before enactment.... The process is long.... The bill has to be read three times before presidential assent," says Benedicta Kilonzo, a nurse at the Pumwani Maternity Hospital and a KEWWO worker. "But it is our intention to influence the A-G's [Attorney General's] Office to get the Bill through Parliament through whatever means," she adds. "We have been struggling for 15 years. When we started the struggle [for maternity protection], the trade unions were deaf to it," says Maloba-Caines. "We have not arrived yet because we think it should be four months, in line with ILO recommendations."

"We are seeking broader improvements.... Our frontline concerns are going to focus around day-care centres and nursing breaks, which really go hand in hand," she says. Support services to ensure child welfare when a woman reports back to her job are lacking. "We depend on people from rural areas who are untrained in child care, and whom we don't have time to train, so they remain untrained. These people are not just baby-minders. They mind the house and do everything else as well. So there are cases of injuries to children because of neglect," she points out.

KEWWO wants to keep track of pitfalls and progress and plans to continue to make maternity protection a priority issue, including in the countdown to the 2002 general elections.

Adds Maloba-Caines: "With pluralism, we now have leeway as women and room to breathe and give our views. Women have to know that begging men will not help. We have our strengths – we are the majority of voters and we must remind ourselves of that."

'Business Orphans'
Maternity rights and child care in the Philippines

Roselle Leah K. Rivera

Her eyes welling with tears, Malou explains why her six-month-old son Ogie was in and out of hospital for almost three weeks. Desperate to earn a paltry 22 pesos (83 US cents) per hour in overtime, she was forced to remove her child from the factory nursery – which closed at 5pm – and arrange a rota of well-meaning but inadequate childminders to look after him at home during her long working day. Taking Ogie out of the nursery – where she could breastfeed him during nursing breaks from the shop floor – meant she also had to abandon breastfeeding. Although neighbours and older children of relatives tried to take care of him, they did not sterilise water for his infant formula. Ogie – often left propped up in his cot with a bottle – developed a life-threatening bout of diarrhoea.

Malou lost the income from her factory job while looking after him and spent more than a week's earnings on medicines alone. Her monthly salary is only 4,200 pesos (US$140), which she earns sewing fashionable Nike and Reebok jackets for Western consumers at the Sun-Moon Subcontractors in Teresa, Rizal, 20 km from Quezon City, the capital of the Philippines.

Lorna works at another garment firm in the Matcan Export Processing Zone (MEPZ) in Cebu City, a provincial centre in the Visayas, a group of islands in the central Philippines. She lives in a poor, urban community near the South Bus Terminal. Lorna has three children aged eight, seven and three. Her workday begins well before dawn when she rises to cook her children rice and leftover vegetables for their lunch. After she leaves for work, the eight-year-old tries to look after his younger siblings.

"I ask my neighbours to help me out. They are busy, too, but they are also the only help available," Lorna says. She knows that the children often stray into the streets to play with their friends, which is a source of concern. Her eldest sons cannot attend school since she lacks money to buy supplies and books, but Lorna is hoping to claw back some of her earnings so that she can educate her children. Her husband has been incapacitated with a liver ailment for the past three years, and her average monthly income of US$123 is barely enough to feed the family, pay her transportation to the Zone, purchase medicines for her husband and repay money she owes to friends.

Tragically, Lorna's attempt to walk the tightrope between the conflicting demands of economic survival and motherhood failed when she returned to work after the birth of her youngest child. The seven-month-old was left at home with her older siblings who tried to bottle-feed her. The baby died from complications of diarrhoea.

The MEPZ ranks second in terms of numbers of foreign firms operating and workforce size among the six major export processing zones (EPZs) in the Philippines, and 72 percent of the workers in the MEPZ are women.[1] According to the non-government organisation (NGO), Cebu Labor Education Advocacy and Research Center (CLEAR), the main problem for women in the MEPZ is how to care for their children. Ruth Restauro, CLEAR's education officer for women's concerns explains that children have to be left on an erratic basis with friends or older sisters or brothers. Relatives rarely live close by and working women's pay "is not enough to cover the salary of a [trained] caregiver", she says. Another Cebu-based NGO, the Fellowship for Organizing Endeavors (FORGE), runs a community mobilisation programme for women and men that raises issues of shared parenting and domestic work. But this requires a departure from the norm. "Shared parenting is not widespread in many communities," says Gwen Ngolabdan, executive director of FORGE.

It is not only female factory workers who make hard choices. Rural poverty forces many women to migrate to the urban centres of the Philippines for work as domestics. Gina, 26, is a domestic helper for a family with two young children. Her second son Jason was only 18 months old when she left Bicol, a southern Luzon province 400 km and a 17-hour bus ride from Quezon City, where she works. She is separated, and receives no support from her estranged husband. "Sometimes I go home. The last time was for two weeks at Christmas. My child calls me Mama Gina. He also calls his grandmother who cares for him Mama." Sadly, her small son hides from her when she visits. When she returns home to bring something for him he cries and says he doesn't want to go to her. "One or two weeks when I am on vacation is not enough [time] for him to be close to me, his mother. Still, I am more at ease knowing my mother is caring for my child. She does everything for him."

"Motherhood is not simply the joy of welcoming babies," says Ines Fernandez of *Arugaan* (Nurture), a women's support group which set up the Sun-Moon daycare nursery in cooperation with company personnel and a trade union in 1996. She believes that pregnant women and working mothers have special needs and should have legal protection, not only to cover pregnancy and childbirth, but also afterwards.

The Philippines has – on paper – maternity laws, albeit weak ones: provision for paternity leave and even a law supporting the establishment of workplace nurseries with trained personnel. All are routinely flouted by employers who do not wish to pay out benefits and ignored by a government anxious to promote foreign investment.

Unfortunately women's groups like *Arugaan* are not active in Cebu City. There are no childcare facilities at the MEPZ and no unions to fight for them. Employer hostility to attempts to establish collective bargaining agreements (CBAs) has kept the MEPZ non-unionised despite efforts of organisations such as the Federation of Free Workers and the National Federation of Labor.

Without enforced legal and social protection of working mothers and their children, "our babies become 'business orphans'", Fernandez laments.

Persistent poverty

Like women all over the world, most Filipino women must work as a matter of economic necessity, combining motherhood and childcare with labour in the fields, or working as household domestics, market traders, or, in recent years, as cogs on assembly lines in purpose-built, foreign-owned factories in the EPZs. In 1986-90 women comprised 48 percent of the country's total workforce [2] - although in reality the female workforce may be considerably larger as the government does not recognise the large number of urban poor women who eke out a living in the 'informal' sector as part-time market traders or providers of personal services, such as cleaners and cooks for middle and upper-class families.

In 1990, the Philippines had one of the lowest per capita GNPs (US$760) in the East Asia and Pacific region and was one of the most heavily indebted countries in the world. [3] Although per capita income has now reached US$1,000, poverty – both urban and rural – is widespread and profound even though the government has calculated the per capita 'poverty threshold' at only 8,969 pesos (US$234).

Therefore, someone who earns as little as 24 pesos (63 US cents) per day should – by official calculations – meet his or her food requirements and other basic needs.

The Philippines remains predominantly agricultural, and about 44 percent of family breadwinners work on the land, with little security. Many families combine agricultural work with other jobs to augment their limited income. [4] Because ownership of land is concentrated in the hands of a few families, well over half of the farms in the country are still tenanted and in general remain non-mechanised.[5] Displacement – and the hope of finding a better standard of living in the cities and factories – has led to an exodus of small farmers and agricultural labourers and their families from rural to urban areas. Of the country's 15 regions, 10 have lost a significant segment of their population due to rural out-migration. [6] Most of these families end up in urban shantytowns. Joining the ranks of their urban counterparts, they now make up 70 percent of what is generally known as the urban poor. [7]

Dr Tess Umipig of *Kababayen Andam Pag-undong sa Kaangayan Para sa Samar* (KAPPAS – Women Working for the Development of Samar) works with poor communities in Calbayog and Villareal in the poverty-stricken province of Samar in Western Visayas, an island south of Luzon island where Metro Manila is. According to Umipig: "Many of the women we work with come from large families of five to nine members. There are those with 13 children. Few are able to reach secondary school. Due to poverty, many women marry young and end up in Manila to work as domestic helpers."

According to the World Bank, in 1990 Metro Manila, where the country's employment and resources are concentrated, contained 14 percent of the national population and 32 percent of the urban population. Half the citizenry of the megalopolis were classified as poor and at least one third were squatters. [8]

Approximately 80 percent of EPZ workers are women. They are recruited for their supposed manual dexterity and patience for repetitive tasks, and because managers assume they are also more docile and so desperate for employment they will accept lower wages than men doing comparable work.

Women's wages in the EPZs are low. CLEAR cites a Department of Labor and Employment (DOLE) inspection report of 56 MEPZ companies in 1995 which revealed that 41 percent were paying workers below the minimum rate of 3,501-4,500 pesos (US$109-140) per month. DOLE findings also showed that 46 out of 56 companies violated health and safety standards.

Maternity leave...for some

Maternity leave provisions in the Philippines have been in a state of flux during the last five decades. In 1952, when the International Labour Organization (ILO) revised its Maternity Protection Convention [9] and supplemented it to recommend a minimum of 14 weeks' maternity leave with cash benefits at 100 percent of past earnings, [10] the Philippines was in step on some counts. Its employers were mandated to grant employees 14 weeks' maternity leave on 60 percent of regular or average pay.

These benefits were slashed in 1973 when the military dictator President Ferdinand Marcos issued a presidential decree that reduced maternity leave to just six weeks – two weeks before the birth and four after – albeit on full pay.

By 1977, maternity benefits were integrated into the Social Security System (SSS) - but only for women in formal, full-time employment. Conditions gradually improved again with private sector employees being granted nine weeks' leave on full pay, though this still fell far short of ILO minimum recommendations.

Not until 1992 was maternity leave extended to 12 weeks,

[11] although for government employees it remains at just six weeks. [12] Finally in 1996, fathers, in both the public and private sectors, were granted seven days' paternity leave on full pay. [13]

Despite these modest improvements, many women remain unprotected by maternity laws; neither agricultural workers nor urban poor women working in the 'informal sector' are covered.

To be eligible for maternity provision, workers must be signed up for social security benefits, and all businesses are required to enlist their employees for SSS membership. Not all companies comply with the law; some "do not uphold their commitments, either by not paying their own contribution to the fund or by retaining that of their employees". [14]

"Non-compliance with the SSS law is rampant in the entire country," admits Lydia Galas, head of the legal division of the SSS in Davao City, which has been working closely with local government in the renewal of business permits. [15]

Childcare...on paper

In the wake of Cory Aquino's electoral victory over the corrupt Marcos regime in February 1986, proclamations of gender equality were written into the 1987 Philippine Constitution, addressing women's maternal and economic role. This was in acknowledgement of the organised and visible presence of women in the 'People's Power' movement that ousted Marcos. Article 13, Section 14, of the new Constitution mandates the state to "protect working women by providing safe and healthful working conditions, taking into account their maternal functions, and such facilities and opportunities that will enhance their welfare and enable them to realise their full potential in the service of the nation".

Article 132 of the Philippine Labor Code, which refers to childcare facilities for workers, appears, at first glance, to give the Constitution 'teeth' as far as nursery provision for working women is concerned. But a closer reading of the text shows that the provision of workplace childcare is, in fact, discretionary. One reason is that the provision of nursery facilities is – despite the lofty language of the Constitution - "a somewhat grey area in the eyes of the law", according to researchers.[16] The Article states, equivocally, that "in appropriate cases he [the Secretary of Labor and Employment] shall by regulations require any employer to establish a nursery for the benefit of the women employees therein".

Because Article 132 fails to spell out the precise conditions under which employers must provide childcare, it is unlikely that the government – in pursuit of foreign investment, particularly in the EPZs – will enforce more than the bare minimum of restrictions on foreign companies.

Another reason there are so few childcare facilities in the EPZs is management's well-documented preference for hiring young, single women, whom they assume will be more productive and reliable than married women with children and households to manage. [17] Although women can return to work in the EPZs after childbirth, if they want a factory nursery, the onus, it seems, is on vulnerable women workers to press for it. In 1995, the Department of Labor and Employment set aside a modest 6 million pesos (US$20,000) for a Pilot Action Project on the Implementation of Child Care Facilities in Selected Regions. According to Au Sabilano, the former director of DOLE's Bureau of Women and Young Workers, "No one was submitting proposals. Women themselves are not actively pressing for this demand. Many are afraid that they would be laid off if they do so."

The childcare situation is so desperate that many

working women in the EPZs, particularly rural migrants, must resort to the emotionally painful solution of fostering out their children with relatives in their home villages. Fortunately, in rural areas like Bicol and Samar, two provinces in the Visayas which are among the most poverty-stricken regions of the country, there is a long tradition of "sharing of childcare", according to Dr Tess Umipig of KAPPAS. Grandparents and older children take care of younger ones, especially the children of those forced to migrate to the cities for work. "People in the community borrow each other's cooking pots.... If a mother is not there to breastfeed, her neighbours will wet-nurse," she says.

In cities and urban slums, where women are without the help of the extended family and village traditions, NGOs like *Arugaan* have stepped in to help working mothers by setting up a few workplace nurseries. Established in 1996 – in cooperation with management and a trade union – its nursery at Sun-Moon was originally intended to give women a choice of childcare that would enable them to continue breastfeeding babies while working. The NGO soon discovered a more widespread need. Of the 22 workers (approximately 10 percent of the workforce) who were then pregnant or had children under three years of age, only eight had relatives they felt were reliable enough to care for their young children while they worked.

Although employers are mandated by Philippine law to provide two 30-minute breastfeeding breaks for working women who need them, many women feel the provision is little more than "comical", according to Carol Añonuevo, who works as a women's educator with UNESCO. Proud that she breastfed all four of her daughters, she believes a woman cannot simply rush off from a sewing machine or assembly line and breastfeed – all within 30 minutes. She must have more time to relax and emotionally switch gears to allow for the "let down" reflex of breastfeeding.

"We are not cows that can be milked mechanically," Añonuevo says indignantly.

A bottle-feeding culture

With a scarcity of childcare facilities – and not just in factories – many women find it difficult, if not impossible, to continue breastfeeding their children once their short maternity leaves have ended.

Cely Rochas is a young corporate lawyer with a medium-sized law firm in Makati, the financial district of the Philippines. Half its staff are women. Rochas' first child, now six years old, was born before she started working, and she was able to breastfeed for 12 months. After the birth of her second child by caesarian delivery at the Capitol Medical Center, a private hospital, she took two and a half months' leave. She is also breastfeeding her second baby, but since going back to work she has used a combination of breast- and bottle-feeding. "It is so difficult to be apart from your baby. It hurts if your breasts are full and you have to express your milk." She admits that bottle-feeding has its appeal, since if you are away from your baby, "when you are bottle-feeding, there is not much physical discomfort".

Economics and career constraints of a modern lifestyle forced Rochas to return quickly to her firm: "It's no joke sending your children to school. The costs are exorbitant and we need to save." Although she works long hours, leaving for work at 6.30 am and often returning home after 10 pm, like most middle- and upper-class women, Rochas has a live-in domestic worker to cook, clean and provide childcare.

Typically, women who work in Makati's modern, air-conditioned offices only manage to breastfeed for a month, or even less, before their maternity leave is up,

Rochas says. "Women believe that breastfeeding is next to impossible if you go back to work."

Even before they give birth, pregnant women receive a plethora of positive messages about bottle-feeding. Typical gifts a pregnant women will receive at a baby shower (a party where gifts are given in anticipation of the birth) or a baptismal party usually include attractive feeding bottles and the latest in steriliser technology (one that utilises a microwave).

Many women are unlikely to sustain breastfeeding for another reason: they are bombarded with advertising for breastmilk substitutes, despite the 1986 Philippine Code of Marketing Breastmilk Substitutes and Related Products. The Code – derived from the WHO/Unicef International Code of Marketing Breastmilk Substitutes – technically controls infant formula advertising by seeking to "protect and promote breastfeeding". It requires advertisers of breastmilk substitutes to include the message that "breastmilk is still best for baby", bans advertising that idealises the use of infant formula, as well as forbidding manufacturers from distributing free samples to hospital maternity wards.

Although violators may face imprisonment of two months to one year and/or a token fine of between 1,000 and 30,000 pesos (US$40-1,100), few advertisements have been withdrawn or financial penalties imposed on companies that flout the law. The not-so-subtle messages of the multinational baby-milk producers – which imply that bottle-feeding is easier, more convenient and as safe as breastfeeding – directly counter scientific evidence which has conclusively demonstrated the nutritional superiority of breastmilk over substitutes.

The World Health Organization (WHO) recommends exclusive breastfeeding for six months to reduce the incidence of infant death or ill health. Breastfed babies have fewer incidences of diarrhoeal diseases, unlike babies fed with substitutes which may be mixed with unsterilised water. In 1991 only 15 percent of Filipino households had sewerage facilities, and only 60 percent had access to piped water. [18] Mixing infant formula with dirty water can be life-threatening for infants and babies. Diarrhoea is not the only threat. Research in several countries including the Philippines, published by WHO in 2000, showed breastfed babies are six times less likely to die of infectious diseases in the first few months of life than babies who are not breastfed. [19]

While the advantages of breast over bottle for child survival are well known, breastfeeding also imparts health advantages for women, including reduced risk of breast or ovarian cancer, reduced risk of osteoporosis (brittle bone disease) and improved post-partum recovery. Exclusive breastfeeding under optimal conditions also provides women with at least 98 percent protection from pregnancy. [20]

Several studies show a decreasing trend in breastfeeding in the Philippines. [21] In a WHO report based on information gathered from 30 member nations in the Western Pacific, the Philippines is one of 16 nations found by the report to have less than 75 percent of mothers who "exclusively" breastfeed their four-month-old babies.

Another survey of 3,000 mothers with infants under the age of one from 16 areas in the Philippines, conducted by the Maternal and Child Health Service of the Department of Health in 1994, showed that only 41 percent of babies were exclusively breastfed at any given period within 0-5 months. The same year, researchers interviewed 1,256 women in poor urban communities in Davao City, the largest city on the island of Mindanao, about why they stopped breastfeeding early on. The most common reason, cited by 21 percent of the women, was the belief that they had "no milk", although in fact this is a medically rare phenomenon.[22] Fourteen percent found breastfeeding was "a bother", while 10 percent said they were too sick. The women also raised concerns about the taste and consistency of breastmilk (it is normal for breastmilk often to look thinner than formula milk); others suffered from cracked nipples or inflammation of the breast.[23]

Infant milk advertising helps whip up women's fear that they cannot breastfeed their babies. While bound to throw in a line about "breast is best for babies", commercials console worried women who fear they have no milk – or those who have returned to work – that infant formula in a colourful tin decorated with a photograph of a serene and smiling infant is just "a few scoops away".

Despite the Code, as well as the 1992 government-inititiated Breastfeeding and Rooming-in Act – designed to comply with Unicef's '10 Steps to Successful Breastfeeding' under its 'Baby-Friendly Hospital Initiative' - hospital workers, including obstetricians and paediatricians, are often keen proponents of infant formula and reinforce prejudices against breastfeeding.

Merle, a 23-year-old farm worker, gave birth to her first child at the Regional Hospital, 50 km outside Davao city centre. "My doctor had my milk pumped. She told me that my milk was not fit for my baby to consume," Merle recounts. "For two years, I spent 280 pesos (US$7.30) for each can of milk I bought. I could have saved so much with the money I spent to buy milk."

For families earning a minimum wage, the cost of artificial feeding for a three-month-old baby, for instance, can easily consume one-quarter of household income.[24]

Although the free distribution of infant formula in hospitals is officially banned, manufacturers continue to undermine government efforts to implement the artificial milk Code by playing on the Filipino cultural imperative of *utang na loob* (debt of gratitude) among the medical profession by ingratiating themselves by means of outright gifts to medical staff and their families at birthdays and holidays. Baby-milk producers now promote their products by hiring recent nursing graduates to go directly to homes and clinics in rural communities where they entice poorly paid health workers with incentives of gifts if they sign up a quota of mothers to use infant formula. Because of the milk Code, infant formula manufacturers are also targeting the *hilots* (traditional birth attendants), as 70 percent of births in the Philippines take place at home and about three-quarters of these are assisted by traditional attendants. [25]

Given the aggressive tactics of baby-milk manufacturers, coupled with less than progressive attitudes on the part of some members of the medical profession, it is not surprising that in 1998 Unicef determined that out of 456 Filipino hospitals or maternity clinics surveyed, only 21 met its minimum criteria in support of breastfeeding and could be officially designated 'baby-friendly'. [26]

Many health advocates argue that controls on marketing of breastmilk substitutes should also be extended to marketing of weaning foods.

Paediatrician Sister Leonore Barrion, a pioneer in community-based primary health care, attends to a long line of mothers at her clinic at the Divine Word Hospital in the capital city of Tacloban, a province near Samar in the Visayas. One of her clients is Edith, 29 years old and the mother of three children. Sr Leonore asks what her daughter Claire eats and Edith tells her it is Cerelac (a packaged baby cereal of processed rice or rice and powdered banana). "Why don't you feed her *lugaw* [cooked softened rice]?" asks Leonore. "It's healthier." Over a dozen varieties of fresh, native-grown banana and other fruits are easily – and more cheaply – available at any fruit and vegetable shop. She advises Edith to feed the children fish and fruits and not to give them soft drinks but instead to squeeze *dalanghita* (native oranges) which are much cheaper and more nutritious.

Many poor women are susceptible to radio or TV advertisements for packaged foods, which denigrate nutritious traditional foods like *lugaw* for babies. Edith's husband is a fish vendor who may earn 100 pesos (US$3) on a good day and 80 pesos (US$2.50) if sales are low. Edith ekes this out to buy half a kilo of *galunggong* fish (poor man's fish) at 25 pesos and 2 kilos of rice for 40 pesos for the family's daily meal. She spends 15 pesos on cooking oil and 7 pesos on kerosene that she uses as cooking fuel. Laundry soap sells for 5 pesos for a quarter of a bar for the week's family laundry which she hand-washes. Cerelac is a very expensive extra.

Organising for change

Trade union activity represents one means, though underutilised, of pushing for working women's maternity and childcare rights; however, industries in the EPZs are notoriously hostile to unionism. Although Article 211 of the Philippine Labor Code recognises free trade unionism as "an instrument for the enhancement of democracy and the promotion of social justice", [27] the process of gaining union recognition is arduous and by no means automatic. At least 20 percent of a given workforce must vote for union representation in a certification election which must first be approved by the DOLE and company managers. Officials in federal labour centres confirm that many women workers – often the sole wage earners – are reluctant to vote for union recognition, fearing they will be identified as troublemakers by managers and fired. [28]

Trade union activism is also time-consuming for women who are already putting in long working days. As

Restauro from CLEAR explains: "Women choose not to join trade unions. [Given their limited]...time, they would rather spend it with the family."

Many women also believe that union activities are men's activities, according to Restauro. Figures for union membership in 1994 indicate that women are far less organised (36.7 percent) relative to men (63.3 percent). Men dominate the leadership of labour organisations – 98 percent of federation heads and 84 percent of local presidents are men. [29]

In 1996 CLEAR initiated a Labor Unity Forum, which has proved to be an effective lobby group of major federations of workers in Cebu province. According to CLEAR executive director Pepe Gasapo: "There is no labour organisation with a clear and definite intervention for women. If we want such a programme, it must be mainstreamed."

According to Tess Borgonos, an active organiser for MAKALAYA (*Manggagawang Kababaihang Mithi ay Paglaya* or Women Workers Fight For Freedom), the most common gender-related issues included in collective bargaining agreements (CBAs) are related to family planning. According to Article 134 of the Philippine Labor Code, a company with at least 200 employees must maintain a clinic to provide free family-planning services including contraceptive pills and intrauterine devices (IUDs) for women workers. However, enforcement of Article 134 is not routinely monitored and trade union leaders have had to insist on it in CBAs. Other benefits include light duty assignments for pregnant workers, maternity leave, including financial assistance during leave, and paternity leave.

"We push for the inclusion of gender-specific provisions in the CBAs. We make use of a grievance machinery and I think the breakthrough is that now, in CBA negotiation sessions, women are there to serve as panellists. Because of seminars and discussions on women's needs, committees have been created to reflect their interests during CBAs," Borgoños says.

LEARN (Labor Education and Research Network), an NGO based in Manila, works with labour organisations, particularly with the National Union of Workers in Hotel, Restaurant and Allied Industries (NUWHRAIN), the Caucus of Independent Unions (CIU), composed of government employees, and KAMAO (*Kapatiran Makabayang Obrero*, meaning brother/sisterhood of workers who care for their country), composed of factory-based workers. Since 1989 it has conducted a gender programme as part of its educational activities. LEARN's partner unions have been able to negotiate more entitlements than the law stipulates. These include initiatives on the relief of pregnant women from physically strenuous jobs, extended maternity leave and financial benefits.

Many believe that the single channel of trade union activism to gain working women's reproductive rights is too narrow. Gasapo of CLEAR feels the issue of women's practical needs should be raised to the level of policy advocacy. His colleague Restauro also sees the need to prioritise differently and widen the efforts to push for women's issues among working women whose daily survival concerns make union participation difficult.

"It is next to impossible to expect young women to join trade unions," she believes. "They need to be reached through their communities." Therefore, CLEAR has ventured into community-based organising of women workers.

Haley Atienza, a young, male organiser who coordinates FORGE's community childcare programme in Cebu, concurs. "We cannot only be involved in 'hard' politics.... We also have to address practical needs." FORGE – which advocates for urban land reform – uses childcare as an entry point in organising and mobilising communities.

FORGE community organisers, who are mostly men like Atienza, have benefited from gender sensitivity training – initiated in the 1980s by women trade union leaders – offered by Quezon City development NGOs. Atienza and his colleagues, in turn, hope to sensitise husbands and partners of overworked women who, researchers estimate, spend 45 hours each week on domestic activities compared with 12 hours spent by men. [30]

A contributing reason why men may shun childcare and other domestic chores is that those who are perceived as doing too much to help their wives may acquire the label of being *ander di saya* (under their wives' skirts). In a 1984 study of women workers in multinational plants in the Bataan, Luzon, EPZ, researchers found that only three percent of married women interviewed were able to delegate childcare to husbands; in the majority of cases, older siblings looked after younger children while their mothers worked. [31]

Men do attend FORGE meetings, which raise issues such as the need for gender-sensitive shared parenting and shared domestic work, but there is resistance to change. Mang Rommel, a rickshaw driver whose slum organisation is assisted by FORGE, expresses confusion. "I cannot understand why we should allow boys to play with dolls," he frowns.

Dayday, leader of a mother's association which works with FORGE, believes men's actions speak louder than any words. "The little children are all out on the streets, while their mothers are inside washing piles of clothes. Why are the men hanging out with their friends at the corner store instead of helping their wives?" she asks.

Ngolaban agrees that even men who attend FORGE gender sensitisation seminars do not always put theory into practice. "They see themselves as open, but in reality they just want to control...women." Sighing deeply, she notes that for men, "internalisation is a long, slow process".

Given many men's reluctance to involve themselves in the duties of family life, it is not surprising that the push for paternity leave in CBAs emanated from female trade union leaders rather than their male colleagues. [32]

"How can women's interests realistically be 'mainstreamed' if most of the decision- makers are men?" asks Dr Junice Demeterio-Melgar, executive director of Likhaan, an NGO that runs advice clinics for women in factories, and at picket lines and demonstrations, in urban and rural poor communities. Policy advocacy without parallel power-building among women could be futile, she warns.

A mother's right to work, a worker's right to mother

Currently maternity rights laws in the Philippines impose a heavy weight of conflicting demands on the individual and provide little support for the mother. In 1952, on paper, employed women enjoyed 14 weeks maternity leave. Now maternity leave is significantly shorter (12 weeks) with an inadequate increase in cash benefits – and only for those in the 'formal' sector.

Dr Mel Ben of the Local Government Assistance and Monitoring Services (LGAMS) of the Department of Health highlights the need to support breastfeeding by tackling inadequate maternity leave provisions, as well as the virtually non-existent childcare facilities at places of work while also creating a stronger policy on marketing breastmilk substitutes. The promotional activities of companies selling infant formula must be monitored and enforced, and the poor training and lack of political will in the medical sector addressed, Ben believes.

Community support groups for breastfeeding mothers should also be encouraged.

While supporting specific initiatives such as Ben's, many women's health and rights activists believe that larger social attitudes and prejudices toward women must change. According to Ines Fernandez of *Arugaan*, Filipino society simultaneously idealises motherhood and ignores the conditions in which women must mother.

"Our society is completely unsympathetic towards motherhood," she challenges.

"There is a tendency to romanticise motherhood," she adds, particularly by those ignorant of the obstacles that women face in their homes, communities and workplaces in caring for the very young.

All women, Fernandez believes, "must be assured of support systems that will allow them to successfully combine their multiple roles".

As researcher and women's health activist Dr Sylvia Estrado-Claudio points out: "Government programmes and labour sector initiatives that unquestioningly accept the productive/reproductive and public/private divisions of standard political and economic frameworks do not work for women."

No Mother's Day for Women Workers
Sex discrimination in Mexico

Guadalupe Hernández Espinosa

Seen from afar, the Antonio Bermudez Industrial Park presents a vision both compelling and contradictory, like a set by film-maker Luis Buñuel for a movie about the plight of the forsaken. In plant after plant, well-tended buildings house sophisticated manufacturing operations that produce high-tech items for consumption abroad. Behind these monuments to modernity lie shantytowns with names like Rebirth and Hope. These are the homes of a labour force of migrant women. This is the land of the *maquiladora*, the export-processing plants that are today's global sweatshops and a mainstay of Mexican-US economic relations.

The *maquiladora* industry began in the mid-1960s after the termination of the Braceros Program which channelled migrant labour to the United States. US industrialists, eager to exploit the huge pool of displaced and jobless deported back to Mexico, established a 'free-trade zone'. Originally a 12-mile strip of land, the zone spread explosively along the Mexico-US northern border in the early 1980s. [1]

Since the signing of the North American Free Trade Agreement (NAFTA) between Mexico, the US and Canada in 1994, *maquiladoras* have mushroomed, spreading south to '*maquila-ise*' the whole country. The majority are US-owned, but Japanese and Korean manufacturers are increasingly common. Economic incentives of tax exemptions and cheap labour, coupled with a lack of enforcement of labour and environmental laws, have made Mexico an attractive location for production. In 1995, the *maquiladora* sector generated more export earnings for Mexico than oil or tourism. [2]

Evidence continues to be gathered on the environmental nightmare of the *maquiladora* zone, of children playing alongside toxic dumps, of contaminated soil and water poisoning entire communities. But little attention has been paid to the specific impacts of NAFTA and the *maquiladora* boom on women workers. Concern for the reproductive health of factory women is largely limited to foetal health. Systematic violations of women's right to have children and keep their jobs are only beginning to come to light.

Women testify

In January 1998, a coalition of women's, labour and legal groups launched a campaign against pregnancy testing and the dismissal of pregnant women. Among the campaign's principal demands were that the Mexican government ratify and implement Convention 158 of the International Labour Organization (ILO), which states that pregnancy is not a justifiable cause for terminating workers' contracts. It also called for the amendment of federal labour law in order to ban the practice of pregnancy screening by employers, on pain of sanctions.

The campaign's first major initiative was a Tribunal to Reconcile Motherhood and Work which took place in October 1998. Before an audience of representatives from labour unions, human rights organisations, the legal profession and government officials, including the labour ombudsman of Mexico City, women gave stark testimonies of their experience of discrimination in the workplace.

No Mother's Day for Women Workers

Teresa Hernández Caballero, a worker in a car assembly plant in Matamoros in the northern state of Tamaulipas, presented eight documented cases of dismissal of pregnant women and 183 cases of workers required to supply a urine sample every month - "practically in front of the firm's doctors" - to prove they were not pregnant. "We have evidence that at least 56 manufacturing firms in Tamaulipas are guilty of firing women who become pregnant," she said.

It is not only *maquiladoras* that are indicted. Employer hostility toward pregnant women affects blue, pink and white-collar women – from assembly line workers and office secretaries to university lecturers and civil servants. Some are harassed until they quit. Other who resist bullying or cannot afford to lose their statutory three-month paid maternity leave are often subject to unfair working conditions that recklessly endanger their own – and their unborn babies' - health. Culprits include certain government departments and public institutions as well as foreign firms with marketing arms in Mexico.

"My pregnancy was a high-risk one but my boss said to me 'Forget all the sentimentality and choose between the baby and your work'," reported Maria Angélica Juárez Garcia, a sales manager with Avon Cosmetics. Her doctor advised complete bed rest on several occasions but she was pressurised into working 12 hours a day. "My baby died a week after it was born," she told the tribunal.

Maria del Rosario Franco, a cashier at the Sonora Hotel International in Hermosillo, also testified that she was ousted from her job when her pregnancy became obvious. Before being fired she was made to work night shifts and subjected to insults and provocative remarks from supervisors. "The personnel boss kept going on at me for being pregnant. I'd had five years of fertility treatment, but the ensuing arguments were so distressing that I nearly miscarried."

Women wanted...

"The employment of women with acute economic needs by the *maquiladora* industry represents...the use of the most vulnerable sector of the population to achieve greater productivity and larger profits," writes anthropologist María Patricia Fernandez-Kelly. [3]

Thirty years ago, it was a novel experience to watch the dirt roads of Nogales fill up with women workers. Employers seeking female applicants attracted migrants from the interior, and Nogales, like other border towns, became a "city of women", says Susana Vidales, a journalist and human rights activist from northern Mexico. "They lived in groups, crowding into small quarters and paying dearly. They worked long shifts in noisy buildings with no ventilation, surrounded by unsafe machinery and exposed to toxic substances, and took nameless pills distributed by foremen to increase productivity. Their only entertainment was to dance all night in the enormous barracks that came to be called discotheques." [4]

From the beginning, *maquiladora* industries have targeted women as the ideal assembly-line workers – nimble-fingered, diligent, docile and obedient. Beyond these gender stereotypes lie more significant economic factors. Women are paid low wages because their incomes are considered supplementary, not essential to supporting their families, and they are less likely to be unionised or informed about their rights.

During the *maquiladora* boom of the early 1980s, women made up 80 percent of the workforce. More men have been hired in recent years but the labour force remains overwhelmingly female. Companies such as Zenith, TRW and Delnosa (owned by General Motors) send trucks into residential neighbourhoods, advertising assembly-line jobs for "women only" over loudspeakers. [5]

As assemblers and line workers, women solder television circuit boards, assemble car radios, arrange medical kits, pack cables, sew garments and perform a thousand similar tasks. They may never see the finished product or even know precisely what they are assembling. Typically, they work eight-hour or longer shifts, performing monotonous, repetitive movements at high speeds in conditions of intense noise, noxious fumes and suffocating heat.

...but not the childbearing kind

Women's massive presence in the border workforce has led to the institutionalisation of discriminatory employment practices. Pregnancy testing as a condition of employment is routine; forced resignation if the worker becomes pregnant is commonplace.

"In this respect," writes Cecilia Soto, former presidential candidate and legislator, "employers have proved to be faithful believers in the Holy Spirit, since no one has yet to hear of a man being required, on asking for a job, to show proof of not having got anyone pregnant." [6]

Pregnancy testing is a form of sex discrimination unique to women because it targets a condition that only women experience. In 1995, a Human Rights Watch (HRW) team spent three weeks in five Mexican cities (Tijuana, Chihuahua, Matamoros, Reynoso, Rio Bravo) interviewing women employed in 43 *maquiladora* plants. Its report was published in August 1996. [7] Dissatisfied at the Mexican government's failure to take adequate action, HRW carried out further investigations between May and November 1997, extending its research to towns not visited before, including Ciudad Juárez. Its second report was published in December 1998. [8]

Isabel applied for a job at TRW (headquarters in Cleveland, Ohio) in Reynoso, Tamaulipas state, in 1992. "There were about 40 of us there [at the interview], all women," she told HRW. "We were all asked by a doctor there when we had had our last periods... [and] if we had active sexual lives.... My period was overdue, so they did not let me stay. They told me to come back when I had my period." Several days later, when Isabel returned and proved she was menstruating, she was hired. [9]

HRW's further research revealed a particularly shocking and humiliating form of post-hire pregnancy-based discrimination – workers being compelled to show used sanitary towels or tampons as a condition of their continued employment. [10]

While the procedure differs from factory to factory, the information sought is the same. Female applicants are asked, in job application forms or interviews, or both, if they are pregnant, if they are sexually active, if they have regular menstrual cycles, if they use birth control. Many plants employ on-site nurses or physicians to administer pregnancy tests. Others send applicants to private clinics for testing. Sometimes, only a pregnancy test is required. At other times, it is administered in conjunction with testing for blood pressure, anaemia or diabetes. Such examinations are often a pretext to test for pregnancy.

"When I first started working at Matsushita, the director of personnel told me to make sure that I tested every single female applicant...because pregnant women were too costly to the company," Dr Adela Moreno of Tijuana told HRW. "It seemed that was all I did. I was appalled, but I did the pregnancy exams. At times, I would be so angry...with how they were exploiting these very young girls that I would tell them [the supervisors] that girls were not pregnant when they were." [11]

Companies claim that pregnancy screening protects women from dangerous jobs, in line with Mexican labour law, [12] but keeping pregnant women out of factory jobs is a policy designed to minimise costs, not prenatal complications. The federal labour code, formulated in the wake of the Mexican Revolution and a new Constitution in 1917, contains explicit maternity provisions, including 12 weeks' paid maternity leave and breastfeeding breaks. Cash benefits are paid by the state if a woman has been in a particular job for 30 weeks. If not, her employer is required to foot the bill.

The president of Zenith responded to HRW by stating that Mexico's labour codes "contain no provision explicitly precluding companies from inquiring about the pregnancy status of women applicants". [13] His defence of pregnancy screening was that pregnant women not eligible for social security "took advantage of company-funded maternity benefits [and]...were not true job applicants". [14]

"As nasty as it sounds, the companies are within their rights," says lawyer Nestor de Buen, a member of Mexico's negotiating team before the signing of NAFTA. "The concept of social justice is not part of the NAFTA document." According to Cecilia Soto, pregnancy tests are standard hiring practice even among Mexican government agencies. [15]

But legal interpretations vary. Mexican legislation also states that no discrimination may be made between workers on the grounds of sex. The ILO's Convention 111 on Discrimination in Respect of Employment and Occupation, ratified by Mexico, does not refer to pregnancy testing *per se* but categorises pregnancy discrimination as impermissible sex discrimination. [16]

Maria Luisa Sánchez of GIRE (*Grupo de Información en Reproducción Elegida* – Information Group on Reproductive Choice) says that one problem is the lack of statistics on pregnant women seeking employment. GIRE believes the numbers are low. "If we can document the number and show that it is low, we can work on building trust and thereby diminish the employers' feeling that...women are out to 'cheat'," says Sánchez. "Women, too, should not abuse, and consciousness of the problem should be raised."

Says Matamoros labour inspector Gustavo Belmares, "In many cases, the woman who is pregnant does not even bother looking for work. She waits. And this is very hard for a woman who has few resources." [17] Factory worker Noemi, aged 20 and soon to be married, objects to waiting for a different reason. A supervisor's warning that "anyone thinking of having kids soon should start looking for a job elsewhere" has cast a shadow over her dream of having children "right away and watching them grow".

Punishments for pregnancy

No pregnant worker can be sure she will keep her job. "The supervisors aren't going to change the machinery for a woman to be comfortable in her seventh month," says Mary, a former factory worker. "And since she's uncomfortable, she may as well quit, since her productivity's gone down anyway."

Patricia became pregnant after four years at Zenith, in Reynoso. At first she hid her pregnancy. After a threatened miscarriage she took a day off work. On her return, her supervisor refused to let her work. "I went to other managers...and told them I had been at the Social Security Office and was at risk of having a miscarriage. I asked them to change me to another line.... [They] told me that if I did not want to return to my position under that supervisor, I could resign.... Then the other supervisor began to say that this was not the first time I had missed a day without alerting her. I felt very pressured and resigned that same day." [18]

Workers interviewed by HRW reported that when they were pregnant, punitive working conditions – heavier physical labour, jobs requiring long hours of standing, obligatory overtime – were used to pressurise them into resigning.

Women who continue working may hide their pregnancy. In a widely reported case, a supervisor's refusal to allow a pregnant woman to leave the assembly line in a Tijuana plastics factory ended in her having a miscarriage. She later underwent a tubal ligation, explaining that she wanted to avoid future problems on the job. [19]

Women *maquiladora* workers "can't opt for motherhood and can't opt for abortion", says Reyna Montero, a former assembly-line worker who now coordinates the health programme for *Grupo Factor X* (Factor X Group) of the Women's Centre in Tijuana. [20] Abortion is severely restricted in Mexico. Women with access to a passport, a visa and US$250 – not many among the ranks of *maquiladora* workers – fill the beds of abortion clinics across the US border. [21]

Maquiladora work and women's reproductive health

Since the large majority of *maquiladora* workers are of reproductive age, understanding the health impacts of *maquiladora* work should be a research priority, but few studies have been conducted. Those there are confirm the existence of a broad spectrum of reproductive health complaints – menstrual disorders, miscarriage, infertility – but fail to pinpoint specific causes from among multiple risk factors.

Underlying many workers' health problems – reproductive and otherwise – are automated technologies, intensive work pace, stressful and repressive working conditions, and chemically-polluting industries.

Automated technology keeps workers in one position doing monotonous, repetitive work for hours on end. Supervision is constant, quite often repressive. Even the amount of time spent using the bathroom or drinking water is recorded. "Supervisors kept lists of who needed to use the bathroom, and you couldn't go a second time if you'd already gone once," recalls Gloria Padilla Favela of her eight-year stint in a Coahuila factory.

High levels of stress in the *maquiladora* plants have been associated with gastric and menstrual disorders, 'hysteria' and depression. Ailments vary by industry. In one study, electronic assembly workers complained of eye irritations, headaches, nervousness, allergies and a high rate of miscarriage. [22]

According to a 1996 study, a "disproportionately large number" of chemically dirty industries shifted from the US to Mexico after NAFTA came into effect. [23] Women interviewed by Human Rights Watch told of "assembling medical kits without the benefit of mouth and nose covering to protect them from noxious fumes; [being] given protective gloves for the soldering work only when managers visited from the US; lacking protective eye-wear when oiling car parts, so that oil habitually fell into their eyes; being dizzy with fumes but not allowed to take breaks". [24]

Far from being resolved, health and safety violations endemic to the *maquiladora* sector have been reproduced on a wider scale following NAFTA. "Industry has grown but protective measures have not, nor have the policies operating in Mexico," says Bertha Luján of the Mexican Action Network on Free Trade.

Stress and unstable working conditions interact with and aggravate health ills related to activities performed on the job. Nor is it easy to distinguish between harmful environmental factors on the job and those at home. Polluting *maquiladora* industries that violate regulations for use, transport and disposal of toxic substances poison not only factory workers but entire communities.

Foetal impacts: low birth weight and malformation

Researcher Catalina Denman of the Colegio de Sonora in Hermosillo, capital city of the border state of Sonora, studied 169 mothers who worked in the *maquiladoras* and 131 mothers who worked in the commercial and service sectors in the city of Nogales. [25] Sixty-five percent of the *maquiladora* workers reported being exposed to toxic substances, and of these, 67 percent were in contact with toxins for the entire working day. Service industry workers, in contrast, had no contact with toxins.

Denman found that 14 percent of the children born to *maquiladora* workers were underweight at birth, compared to 5 percent among service industry mothers. A high percentage of the low-birth-weight children were also born prematurely. Other researchers found that *maquiladora* mothers were more likely to have taken more than a year trying to conceive, but that it was not possible to determine the causes. [26]

One such report, produced by the Coalition for Justice in the *Maquiladoras*, revealed that in 1992 some 42 families of ex-workers of the PR Mallory electronics plant in Matamoros successfully sued the company for malformation and mental retardation of their children. [27] The high number of cases of anencephaly (partial or complete absence of the cerebral hemispheres of the brain) and spina bifida (exposed spinal cord) found in some border cities has added to concern about industrial pollution. Along the Brownsville, Texas-Matamoros border, the number of infants born with anencephaly between 1989 and 1991 was four times the national average. [28]

In August 1992, some 81 cases of anencephaly were reported among the children of Tamaulipas *maquiladora* workers. [29] Nonetheless, researchers Sylvia Gundelman and Monica Jasis Silberg say that many studies "do not consider multiple risk factors, including factors inherent in living conditions in the poor neighbourhoods where the majority of female workers reside". [30] Once again, there is no consensus among researchers about the causes.

An industrial spill in October 1996 in a Nogales plant intoxicated 20 workers, including four pregnant women. [31] The solvent was identified by a confusing variety of names, and estimates of its toxicity ranged from "highly dangerous" and "highly toxic" to "minimal". Newspapers reported that some workers experienced difficulty breathing and that others had to be evacuated on stretchers.

The plant manager was quoted as saying that the pregnant workers were "in no danger". The public hospital director noted that this was the first report of intoxication from that particular solvent and that the pregnant workers would be monitored "to determine any subsequent effects on mothers or children".

Canadian researcher Karen Messing points to a larger problem: women's occupational health problems are nearly invisible because the wrong methods are employed to study them. "Most concepts and methods in use in the field have developed in relation to jobs usually held by men, to male physiology and to male-pattern lifestyles. Given this bias, it is not surprising that health problems related to women's bodies, jobs and family responsibilities are misunderstood and underestimated." [32]

A study of work-related accidents and illnesses in Nogales showed that most physicians working in *maquiladora* plants lack training in occupational medicine. [33] Research into epidemiological and toxicological aspects of environmental and occupational health presents special challenges, including the difficulty of isolating and measuring levels of toxicity, long latency periods, variable relationships between exposures and responses, exposure to multiple toxins and determining who has or has not been exposed.

New jobs, old attitudes

Cultural factors combined with economic pressures also put the health and welfare of women workers at risk. Female *maquiladora* workers are mostly young - 50 percent under the age of 25 - who have migrated from other parts of Mexico. [34] Most have finished primary school, and more than half have had at least some secondary education. Nearly 40 percent are single. [35] Of those who have partners, about 45 percent are not formally married. Just under one-third have children. [36] Those with higher levels of education tend to remain single longer, have more knowledge of family planning and use contraceptive methods more frequently.

Despite a certain economic independence, says Rebeca Berner of *Servicio, Desarrollo y Paz* (SEDEPAC – Service, Development and Peace), a national non-government organisation (NGO) with one of the longest-running programmes on rights issues in the border zone, in a young woman's emotions "cultural factors are stronger than labour or economic dynamics". Modern in their working lives, young women remain traditional in their romantic expectations. Although data are unavailable, unintended pregnancy is a common occurrence among female employees, according to women trade union leaders. Yet no matter how difficult the circumstances, motherhood is held in high esteem. Babies are received as life companions to love and care for – with or without a father's support. Single motherhood is a fact of life for young women along the border. That men are likely to move on, to a new job or another woman, is taken for granted.

"Women are left behind and care for children," says Sara, a worker in Nogales. "That's how it's always been." Even when there is a man around, housework, cooking and childcare await the woman after her factory shift, no matter how much overtime she has put in to meet the day's production quota.

Rafaela Carrizales, 34 and mother of five, remembers the struggle of coping single-handedly: "When I found myself on my own, the children were small.... I would come home after work, do the housework, feed the children, have some food myself. Often I went to bed at midnight and got up at 5 am."

Many *maquiladora* workers migrating to the north find themselves stripped of the strong family and community networks of their home villages. Housing is scarce, with two or three families sharing quarters that may lack drinking water, sewerage and electricity, in neighbourhoods without schools, transportation or street lights.

Childcare is a source of constant anxiety for working women, as Sara explains. "In the evening, when I would come back from the plant, I would find that my daughter and niece hadn't touched the beans or potatoes I cooked before leaving. And they would skip school. I used to take Brenda to my mother's house, but since my mother died there's been no one to watch her." The government has promised more childcare provision – but this has yet to materialise. In Tijuana, women have resorted to leaving their children in orphanages as a substitute for day care centres. [37]

In providing for themselves and their families, women workers, especially those working night shifts, may be dangerously vulnerable to attack and rape. Since 1993 nearly 200 women, most of them *maquiladora* workers, have been raped and murdered in Juarez, a manufacturing town of 1 million residents and 400 assembly plants. [38]

Women's groups have accused local authorities of indifference; they believe the attacks reflect male anger over women's independence. The Mexican *macho* – the ruthless male who forces women into submission – was born in these northern deserts and *machismo* is strongly rooted in popular culture.

"Women have not become liberated, they just have a double workload," says Esther Chavez Cano, an activist monitoring police investigations on behalf of victims' families. "But some men resent what they perceive as women's newly independent lifestyles. A patriarchal backlash has accompanied these murders." [39]

The establishment of the city's first crisis centre for women, opened in June 1999, and the introduction of measures to prevent violence against female workers in the *maquiladoras* are due largely to increased political activism by women across the country. But for Patricia Olamendi, of the opposition Party of the Democratic Revolution's national executive committee, these measures are still too little, too late. "The problems facing poor working women in Mexico remain a marginalised theme," she believes. [40]

NAFTA, *maquiladoras* and the defence of workers' rights

Maquiladora work has many advocates. "Women with jobs in the *maquiladora* sector enjoy favourable conditions," says Mariano Carrillo, a regional coordinator of the Mexican Social Security Institute. "They are participating in the possibilities for development that Mexico offers and they have access to social security. The woman with a job enjoys all of her rights as a Mexican [citizen] and can provide basic support to her family."

A different perspective is provided by Reyna Montero, of the Factor X Group. "Mexican women are making a significant contribution to the national economy," she says, "but their quality of life has not enjoyed a corresponding improvement."

Economic necessity makes women willing to endure long hours and bad conditions to keep *maquiladora* jobs. Women without skills prefer *maquiladora* work over domestic service, the other likely alternative for employment in these borderlands, for its social security benefits. In reality, even these supposed benefits are far from dependable.

Moreover, workers are reluctant to complain about mistreatment for fear of losing their jobs or finding themselves blacklisted. The likelihood of redress is minimal.

Domestic and international protection

Tolerance of pregnancy-based sex discrimination violates Mexican laws that guarantee equality between the sexes, prohibit discrimination on the basis of sex, protect the health of pregnant workers and guarantee the right of women and men to decide freely the number and spacing of children.

Three government-run mechanisms investigate cases of private-sector labour dispute: the Office of the Inspector of Labour, the Office of the Labour Rights Ombudsman, and the Conciliation and Arbitration Board (CAB).

Eduardo Chávez Uresti, inspector of labour for Reynoso and Río Bravo, describes the inspectorate as "...an authority without a body and without hands. We have a head only. Only for show". If companies refuse to be investigated when complaints are filed, no help can be expected from his superiors. "*Maquiladoras*...are a source of employment and hard currency to be left alone.... The state inspector tells me this is a federal issue and is none of my business." [41]

Government failure to remedy this form of discrimination calls into question Mexico's commitment to such international obligations as the Convention to Eliminate all forms of Discrimination against Women, the Inter-American Human Rights Convention and NAFTA's own North American Agreement on Labour Cooperation. [42]

Article 1114 of NAFTA states that parties "should not" encourage investment by relaxing domestic health, safety or environmental measures, but lacks enforcement mechanisms. "The labour agreement is a means to promote trade, not protect workers," says lawyer Nestor de Buen, of Mexico's NAFTA negotiating team.

Labour unions and women's organisations

With few exceptions, unions take a hands-off attitude.

When Patricia was forced out of her job at Zenith for pregnancy-related absence, she complained to the union delegate. "He said he could not really help...but that maybe he could do something to help me keep my insurance. In the end, he did not even manage that." [43]

"The experience I have," says Susana Vidales, "is that in the majority of cases women workers begin their battles on their own...and then the established trade unions step in...and stop the conflict, and that's that." Where labour action has been successful, however, women *maquiladora* workers have defended their rights using work stoppages and surveillance of plants that might otherwise pack up overnight rather than resolve labour disputes – a tendency that has led the *maquiladoras* to be referred to as 'rape-and-run' industries. [44]

Trade, labour and women's rights groups in all three NAFTA countries have created networks to monitor accords, coordinate protests and share expertise. This scrutiny has been important in putting pressure on the Mexican government to uphold its own regulations.

Groups can be found in all the major border towns. Factor X runs three programmes: on women's labour, health and safety, and violence against women, each of which help raise workers' awareness of their rights and what they can do when these are abused. It is also creating a women's medical centre to deal with occupational and reproductive health. [45]

Some women's groups – Factor X is one – help fired workers to fight back, by providing advice and legal aid. One successful case was the suit filed by 118 women fired from a Tijuana plant after denouncing sexual harassment, when, during a visit by the company president, they were made to put on a bikini fashion show at a picnic and subsequently propositioned. The settlement in 1995 marked the first time Mexican workers had sued a transnational corporation in US courts for violations of Mexican labour law. [46]

In Baja California, Chihuahua and Coahuila, the *Red por la Dignificación de las Trabajadoras de la Maquila* (Network for the Dignity of Women *Maquiladora* Workers) works with grassroots groups on campaigns to inform workers about toxins. Other NGOs are developing a Risk Assessment Map that uses surveys and observation techniques to identify toxic hazards in the workplace.

Responses like these, based on the workers' own experiences, have received support from both sides of the border and beyond. Networks like Women Working Worldwide have identified common demands among *maquiladora* workers in Latin America, Asia and elsewhere. Its 1996 manifesto on trade liberalisation notes two priority areas identified by women – reproductive rights and the right to bodily integrity – that are rarely mentioned in mainstream debates on workers' rights and have led to women organising their own campaigns. [47]

Prospects for change

High-profile initiatives such as the Tribunal to Reconcile Motherhood and Work may have begun to turn the tide. The organisers were hopeful that the Mexican Congress, reconvening a month after the tribunal, would consider legislation to clarify the law and ban the practice of pregnancy tests in the workplace. Although a bill to reform the federal labour law was introduced in the Chamber of Deputies in 1998, it 'died' in committee, and a subsequent bill introduced has not been acted on.

Some companies may be slowly adapting because of the continuing expansion of the *maquiladora* zone and the unquenchable demand for labour. Deltrónicos, a car-radio manufacturer in Matamoros, claims that some 95 percent of women return to work after giving birth. The plant has even made provision for nursing mothers, according to its managing director Steve Irwin. [48] "It's important for us to maintain stability and keep our trained work force," he says.

Negative publicity in the wake of the 1996 Human Rights Watch report prompted certain firms to declare that they were abandoning pregnancy screening. However, the second (1998) HRW report states: "Even in instances where corporations pledged to change their discriminatory practices, evidence abounds of apparent violations of that policy."

In the nearby Central American country of Nicaragua, *maquiladora* workers scored a victory recently by enlisting the government into their fight for better conditions. One of the last countries in the region to introduce *maquiladora* plants, Nicaragua is the first to draw up a Code of Ethics. On 1 February 1998, the Labour Minister signed guidelines regulating working conditions in free-trade zones and recognising the demands of women *maquiladora* workers for equal pay, freedom from pregnancy-based discrimination, and protection against abuse by factory owners. [49]

Whether the Mexican government will take action remains to be seen. In 1996, Reyna Montero was pessimistic: "Underlying causes go unexamined. The government continues to promote foreign investment at the expense of women workers' health." [50]

There are signs of hope. In March 1997, US car manufacturer General Motors, one of the largest private employers in the country, announced it was ending its pre-hire pregnancy tests. And in June 1999 the federal Education Ministry pledged that teachers would no longer be asked to undergo pregnancy tests. [51]

In October 1999, Mexico City's first female mayor, Rosario Robles, was elected. In one of her first official acts, she signed an amendment to the city's penal code such that businesses that require pregnancy tests or fire a woman because she becomes pregnant will be fined. The new law also mandates that those who violate the anti-pregnancy discrimination code will face 100 hours or more of community service; serious offenders may face three-year jail sentences. [52]

On hearing a report presented by the Mexican government in November 1999, the United Nations Committee on Economic, Social and Cultural Rights revealed its concern about a multitude of social ills, including domestic violence, the growing number of street children and pregnancy exams for women job applicants. [53]

Although heartened by these partial victories, tribunal organisers and women's and human rights organisations are holding out for nothing less than reforming national labour law to include prohibition of pregnancy tests and dismissal due to pregnancy. They are determined to overturn the country's double standard where Mothers' Day is a national holiday yet bosses routinely deny pregnant women the right to work.

Notes

Introduction

1. Violence Against Women, World Health Organization, Fact Sheet WHO/FRH/WHD/97.8, 1997
2. Genital mutilation involves cutting the genitals of girls and women, ranging from cutting the tip of the clitoris to removing the entire clitoris and the outer folds of the vagina. The practice is carried out in the belief that it will assure a woman's marriageability. Approximately 130 million women worldwide have undergone FGM
3. Seventeen nations expressed reservations to specific chapters or paragraphs in the final text, while still endorsing the document
4. For an examination of selected issues of reproductive health raised by the policy agenda set out at ICPD – including safe motherhood, unnecessary caesarian sections, prenatal sex selection, female genital mutilation and sexually transmitted infections, see the award-winning Panos book, Private Decisions, Public Debate: Women, Reproduction and Population
5. Programme of Action, Report of the International Conference on Population and Development, Cairo, 5–13 September 1994, A/CONF.171/13, 18 October 1994 (preliminary version)
6. Para 7.2, Programme of Action, Cairo.
7. Para 7.3, Programme of Action, Cairo.
8. Although the Convention has been widely ratified, many countries have lodged substantive reservations to it. For

example, several states have lodged reservations against Article 16, a core provision that guarantees equality between men and women in family life.

9. Para 69, report of the International Forum for the Operational Review and Appraisal of the Implementation of the Programme of Action of the International Conference on Population and Development, which was held at The Hague from 8 to 12 February 1999, note by the Secretary-General, 7 February 1999, E/CN.9/1999/PC/3. One of two documents before the March preparatory committee for the ICPD+5 review for information.

10. Para 95, Report of the Ad Hoc Committee of the Whole of the 21st Special Session of the General Assembly, Addendum, Key actions for the further implementation of the Programme of Action of the International Conference on Population and Development, 1 July 1999, A/S-21/5/Add.1

11. Para 40, Report of the Ad Hoc Committee of the Whole of the 21st Special Session of the General Assembly, Addendum, Key actions for the further implementation of the Programme of Action of the International Conference on Population and Development, 1 July 1999, A/S-21/5/Add.1

12. These rights remain elusive for women in at least two countries with a national legislature (Kuwait and the United Arab Emirates), women's rights to vote and to stand for election are not yet recognised, Women's Suffrage Chronology, Inter-Parliamentary Union (IPU), the World Organisation of Parliaments of Sovereign States. http://www.ipu.org/wmn-e/suffrage.htm

13. Women in National Parliaments, situation as of 15 April 2000, IPU, http://www.ipu.org/wmn-e/world.htm

Sexuality under Wraps

1. 'Adolescent Sexual and Reproductive Behavior: A Review of the Evidence From India', Shireen J Jejeebhoy, *Social Science and Medicine*, London, vol 46, no 10, 1998, pp1275–1290
2. Figures quoted in *India Today*, 21 September 1998
3. ibid
4. 'Adolescent Sexual and Reproductive Behavior' op cit [note 1]
5. 'Sex Education and Adolescent Sexuality', Module 4 for Primary Health Centre Medical Officers, Modified District Project for Integrated Delivery of Reproductive Health Care Services at District Level, 1996
6. 'Adolescent Sexual and Reproductive Behavior', op cit [note 1]
7. ibid
8. UNAIDS, June 1998
9. 'Adolescent Sexual and Reproductive Behavior', op cit [note 1]
10. ibid
11. ibid
12. 'Defining a Reproductive Health Package for India: A Proposed Framework', S Pachauri, South and East Asia Regional Working Papers no 4, Population Council, New Delhi, 1995
13. 'Watering the Neighbour's Garden: Investing in Adolescent Girls in India', Margaret E Greene, South and East Asia Regional Working Papers no 7, Population Council, New Delhi, 1997
14. 'Adolescent Sexual and Reproductive Behavior' op cit [note 1]
15. ibid
16. ibid
17. ibid
18. ibid

19. 'Premarital sexual behaviour of urban educated youth in India', M.C Watsa, Paper presented at the Workshop on Sexual Aspects of AIDS/STD Prevention in India, Bombay, 23–27 November 1993
20. 'Watering the Neighbour's Garden', op cit [note 13]
21. 'Adolescent Sexual and Reproductive Behavior' op cit [note 1]
22. International Conference on Population and Development Programme of Action, para 7. Fourth World Conference on Women Platform for Action, para 95
23. 'Adolescent Sexual and Reproductive Behavior' op cit [note 1]
24. CHETNA Publication no 35, Madhya Pradesh SCERT, Bhopal (undated)
25. 'Watering the Neighbour's Garden', op cit [note 13]
26. 'No more hesitation of sex education: let's open the main door', Swati Bhattacharjee, *Ananda Bazar Patrika*, Calcutta, India, 26 November 1998

Tested to their Limit

1. 'Sexual harassment in employment: Recent judicial and arbitral trends', Jane Aeberhard-Hodges, *International Labour Review*, vol 135, no 5, 1996
2. 'Educating Girls: Gender Gaps and Gains', Population Action International, Washington DC, October 1998
3. 'Adolescent Sexuality and Fertility in Kenya: A Survey of Knowledge, Perceptions, and Practices', Ayo Ajayi et al, *Studies in Family Planning*, vol 22, no 4, July/August 1991
4. 'Family Planning Needs in Colleges of Education', A Ferguson et al, report of a study of 20 colleges in Kenya, Ministry of Health, Division of Family Health, Nairobi, 1988
5. 'Schoolgirl Pregnancy in Kenya', report of a study of discontinuation rates and associated factors, Division of

Family Health, Nairobi 1988
6. 'Sexual Initiation and Premarital Childbearing in Sub-Saharan Africa', D Meekers, *Population Studies*, vol 48, 1994, pp47–64
7. 'Kenya: Women Face Rising Threat of Rape, Violence', UN Wire, 19 October 1999

Sacred Knots and Unholy Deals

1. 'Medical aspects of FGM', Els Leye et al, in *Proceedings of the Expert Meeting on Female Genital Mutilation, Ghent-Belgium, November 5-7, 1998*, International Centre for Reproductive Health, Ghent, 1998, pp45–48
2. *The Silent Endurance: Social conditions of women's reproductive health in rural Egypt*, Hind Khattab, Unicef/Population Council, Cairo, 1992
3. ibid
4. 'Post-ICPD: The Decline of Female Circumcision in Egypt', Population Council News Release, Cairo, Egypt, 22 February 1999
5. *Proceedings of the Expert Meeting on Female Genital Mutilation*, op cit [note 1], p77
6. *Transitions to Adulthood. A National Survey of Adolescents in Egypt*, Sahar El-Tawila et al, Population Council, Regional Office for West Africa and North Africa, Cairo, Egypt, 1999
7. 'Egypt: Women's Rights Bill Wins Preliminary Approval', UN Wire Service, 20 January 2000
8. 'Marriage is an ever-changing game', Nawal El-Sadawi, in *Rose El-Youssef*, Cairo, November 1998

No Paradise Yet

1. *Bangladesh Demographic and Health Survey 1993–1994* (Summary report), National Institute of Population Research and Training (NIPORT) and the Ministry of

Health and Family Welfare, Dhaka, Bangladesh, 1995
2. ibid
3. 'Areal Variations in Use of Modern Contraceptives in Rural Bangladesh', N Kamal, PhD thesis, University of London, 1995
4. 'A Fork in the Path: Human Development Choices for Bangladesh', UNDP, 1994
5. Human Development Report 1998, UNDP
6. *Bangladesh Demographic and Health Survey*, op cit [note 1]
7. *Ours by Right*, ed Joanna Kerr, Zed Books, 1993, cited in 'The Tension Between Women's Rights and Religious Rights: Reservations to CEDAW by Egypt, Bangladesh and Tunisia', Michele Brandt and Jeffrey A. Kaplan, footnote 78, *Journal of Law and Religion*, vol 12, 1995–96
8. Bangladesh Constitution, articles 27, 28 and 30
9. 'Equality in the Home', Sara Hossain, in *Human Rights of Women, National and International Perspectives*, ed Rebecca Cook, University of Pennsylvania, Philadelphia, 1994
10. The Muslim Family Laws Ordinance 1961, Section 7(1)
11. 'Legal Status of Women in Bangladesh', Salma Sobhan, Bangladesh Institute of Law and International Affairs, Dhaka, 1978
12. *The Hedaya, Commentary on the Islamic Laws*, vol 1, translated by Charles Hamilton, Pakistan, Darul-Ishaat, 1989
13. *The Guardians and Wards Act and the Majority Act*, ed Shaukat Mahmood, Pakistan Law Times Publications, Lahore, 1969
14. *The Hedaya, Commentary on the Islamic Laws*, vol 1, op cit [note 12]
15. The Guardian and Wards Act of 1890, Section 7
16. The Guardian and Wards Act of 1890, Section 17
17. 'Legal Status of Women in Bangladesh', Salma Sobhan, Bangladesh Institute of Law and Foreign Affairs, Dhaka, 1978, p29.

18. See, among others, *Rahela Khatoon vs Ramela Khatoon*, (1970) 22 DLR 245; *Rahimullah Choudhury vs Mrs Sayeda Helali Begum* (1968) 20 DLR (SC) 1
19. See, for example, *Akhtar Ahmed vs Mrs Hazoor Begum* (1965) 17 DLR (WP) 39
20. *Sharon Laily Begum Jalil vs Abdul Jalil*, (1996) 48 DLR 460
22. Personal correspondence, 2 December 1998
21. *Bangladesh Demographic and Health Survey 1993–1994*, op cit [note 1]
22. Personal correspondence, 2 December 1998
23. 'Women and Men in Bangladesh', *Facts and Figures*, 1970–1990, Bangladesh Bureau of Statistics, April 1995
24. 'A Fork in the Path', op cit [note 4]
25. 'Impressions of Women and Children', Unicef, Dhaka, 1991
26. 'The Bangladesh Women's Health Coalition', *Quality*, The Population Council, 1991
27. 'Male involvement in family planning: Experiences from innovative projects', Directorate of Family Planning Government of Bangladesh, National Institute of Population Research and Training (NIPORT) and the Population Council, August 1997
28. 'The Advent of Family Planning as a Social Norm in Bangladesh: Women's Experiences', S Schuler et al, *Reproductive Health Matters*, no 7, May 1996
29. *Expanding Access to Safe Abortion: Strategies for Action*, A Germain and T Kim, International Women's Health Coalition, New York, 1998
30. 'The Bangladesh Women's Health Coalition', op cit [note 26]
31. ibid
32. 'The Uniform Family Code', Mahila Parishad, Dhaka, 1993.
33. 'An Experience of Religious Extremism in Bangladesh', S Kabir, *Reproductive Health Matters*, London, No. 8, November 1996

34. An NGO worker quoted in 'The Fear of the Fatwa', *India Today*, 30 June 1994
35. 'Women Demand Equality, Government Cites Religious Bar', Tabibul Islam, Inter Press Service, 14 June 1999, from <cedaw-in-action@edc-cit.org>
36. Bangladesh Report, CEDAW/C/BGD/3-4, paragraph 1.2.6, 1 April 1997
37. Bangladesh Report, CEDAW/C/BGD/3-4, paragraph 2.1.3, 1 April 1997
38. Bangladesh Report, CEDAW/C/BGD/3-4, paragraph 2.1.4, 1 April 1997
39. 'Bangladesh Prime Minister Promotes Empowerment of Women', *Daily Star* (Dhaka), 27 April 1999, on UN Wire, 28 April 1999, taken from NewsNewsNews (email service of IPPF, London, 29 April 1999)

A Field of her Own

1. *The Extent and Health Consequences of Violence Against Women in Zimbabwe*, C Watts, M Ndlovu et al, Musasa Project, Harare, 1998. Cited in C Watts, E Keogh et al, 'Withholding of Sex and Forced Sex: Dimensions of Violence against Zimbabwean Women', *Reproductive Health Matters*, vol 6, no 12, November 1998
2. 'The Magaya Judgment by Supreme Court in Zimbabwe', N Gumbonzvanda, from cedaw-in-action@edc-cit.org, 29 April 1999
3. 'Urgent Action Alert: Zimbabwe's Supreme Court Decision Denying Women's Inheritance Rights Violates International Human Rights Treaties', http://www.sigi.org/Alert, 30 June 1999, from <cedaw-in-action@edc-cit.org. 6 July 1999
4. 'Zimbabwean court decides women are junior males', Andrew Meldrum, *The Guardian* (UK), 20 May 1999
5. 'Children and Women in Zimbabwe: A Situational Analysis Update', Unicef, 1994, p47

6. *Women and Land Rights in Resettlement Areas in Zimbabwe*, booklet produced by Women and Law in Southern Africa Research Trust, Harare, undated
7. ibid
8. 1993 survey conducted by Maia Chenauwx-Repond on three Resettlement Areas in Mashonaland province
9. 'Reproductive Health Rights in Zimbabwe', R Lowenson, L Edwards and P Ndlovu-Hove, Training and Research Support Centre, Harare, and Ford Foundation, 1996
10. 'The Mediating Effects of the Attitudes of Significant Others on Women and Development in Zimbabwe', N Wekwete, draft report prepared for the Women's Studies Project 1998, cited in *Women's Voices, Women's Lives: The Impact of Family Planning*, Women's Studies Project, Family Health International, June 1998
11. 'Zimbabwe Demographic and Health Survey', Central Statistical Office and Macro International Inc., Calverton MD, US, 1994, cited in *Women's Voices, Women's Lives: The Impact of Family Planning*, op cit [note 10]
12. 'Patterns and predictors of infertility among African women: a cross-national survey of 27 nations', K Ericksen and T Brunette, *Social Science and Medicine*, vol 42 no2, 1996, pp209–20, cited in *Reproductive Health Matters*, May 1996, no 7
13. *Reproductive Tract Infections: Global Impact and Priorities for Women's Reproductive Health*, eds A Germain et al, International Women's Health Coalition, Plenum Press, New York, 1992
14. 'Withholding of Sex and Forced Sex: Dimensions of Violence against Zimbabwean Women', op cit [note 1]
15. 'Maternal Mortality Rises', *Herald* (Harare) 21 July 1995. Cited in E Njovana, and C Watts, 'Gender Violence in Zimbabwe: A Need for Collaborative Action', *Reproductive Health Matters*, May, no 7

16. 'Aids Epidemic Impacts Negatively On Economy', *Herald* (Harare), 17 March 1999
17. 'Reproductive Health Rights in Zimbabwe', op cit [note 9]
18. 'Women and Land Rights in Resettlement Areas in Zimbabwe', op cit [note 6]

Women no Cry

1. *Women in the Third World, Gender Issues in Rural and Urban Areas*, L Brydon and S Chant, Edgar Elgar Publishing Ltd, UK, 1989
2. 'Towards Equity in Development: A Report on the Status of Women in 16 Commonwealth Caribbean Countries', Alicia Mondesire and Leith Dunn, CARICOM, 1995
3. 'The Intersection of Reproduction and Production – Women in Guadeloupe', Hugutte Dagenais, in *Women and Change in the Caribbean*, ed Janet Momsen, James Curry (London), Ian Randle (Kingston) and Indiana University (Bloomington), 1993
4. 'Meeting the needs of young adults', A.P McCauley and C Salter, Population Reports, Series J, no 41, Population Information Program, John Hopkins School of Public Health, Baltimore, MD, 1995, pp14–15
5. ibid
6. 'Prospects for Young Mothers and their Children: a review of childbearing in developing countries', M Buvinic and K Kuurz, 1997, paper presented at the National Academy of Sciences Workshop on Adolescent Sexuality and Reproductive Health in Developing Countries, Washington DC, 24–25 March 1997
7. 'Survey on Sexual Decision-making Among Jamaicans', funded by Family Health International, Institute of Social & Economic Research (ISER) Library, University of the West Indies, Mona, Jamaica, 1990–1994, unpublished

8. 'The Contribution of Caribbean Men to the Family: A Jamaican Pilot Study', Janet Brown, Pat Anderson and Barry Chevannes, University of the West Indies, January 1993
9. 'Case Study of the Women's Center of Jamaica Foundation Program for Adolescent Mothers', Family Health International, 1996, p17
10. *CAFRA News*, Trinidad. January-June 1998
11. 'Violence Against Women in the Caribbean: The Case of Jamaica', Nesha Haniff, 1994, unpublished manuscript, University of Michigan, Ann Arbor, USA
12. ibid
13. 'We Kind of Family: The Women's Movement and Family in the Caribbean in the International Year of the Family', Ninth Anniversary Lecture for Women Working for Social Progress, Trinidad & Tobago, 1994, Merle Hodge, unpublished paper
14. 'Stresses and Strains: Situation Analysis of the Caribbean Family', Barry Chevannes, United Nations Economic Commission for Latin America and the Caribbean (UNECLAC), 1993
15. Dr Tirbani Jagdeo, personal communication
16. 'Man Is Not Supposed to Go There', Nesha Haniff, WAND Occasional Paper June 1995, reprinted in *Women's Health Journal*, 1997, no 1
17. *Expanding Access to Safe Abortion: Strategies for Action*, A Germain and T Kim, International Women's Health Coalition, New York, 1998, p21
18. 'Man Is Not Supposed to Go There', op cit [note 16]
19. UN Wire, 8 October 1999

Legalised Cruelty

1. *Pakistan: No progress on women's rights*, Country reports – ASA, index no 33/01/1998, Amnesty International, London. Website:http://www2.amnesty.se/wom.nsf/27b

...46191c12566a700739c19?Open Document
2. 'The Murder at AGHS', Neelam Hussain, for the Working Committee, Women's Action Forum, Lahore, 9 April 1999
3. 'Pakistan: Violence Against Women in the Name of Honour', Amnesty International USA. http://www.amnestyusa.org/countries/pakistan/reports/honour/overview.html
4. From *Dawn* (Karachi), 18 October 1999, UN Wire, 20 October 1999
5. 'A grim reminder' (editorial), *Dawn* (Karachi), 8 April 1999
6. *Gazette of Pakistan*, 1990, p145
7. This replaced the Evidence Act, 1872.
8. *Two Steps Forward, One Step Back?* Farida Shaheed and Mumtaz Khawar, Zed Books, London, 1987, p106
9. Quoted in *The Hudood Ordinances: A Divine Sanction?* Rohtas Books, Lahore, 1990
10. 'Discriminatory Laws and Practice', Nausheen Ahmed, paper presented to a pre-Beijing Seminar, 4 November 1997
11. *The Human Rights Watch Global Report on Women's Human Rights*, Human Rights Watch, 1995, p148
12. 'Pakistan: Most Jailed Women Face Long Waits for Trial', UN Wire Service, 5 November 1999
13. ibid
14. 'Report of the Commission of Inquiry for Women', Commission of Inquiry for Women, Pakistan, 1997, pp56–76
15. The Supreme Court tried to reverse this trend (PLD 1990 SC 295) by declaring "...where coeducation is permitted and the institution is not reserved for one sex alone, the fixation of numbers on the ground of sex will directly be opposed to the requirements of Article 25 (2) unless it is a justified and protective measure for women and children under Article 25 (3)..." Article 25 of the

Constitution of Pakistan declares all citizens equal before the law, forbids discrimination on the basis of sex alone, but allows the State to make special provisions for the protection of women and children.
16. Interview with journalist Nafisa Shah, Islamabad, February 1999
17. *Newsline* (Karachi), January 1993
18. *Islamic Hudood Laws in Pakistan*, Khyber Law Publishers, Lahore, 1996, p4
19. *Dawn* (Karachi), 9 March 1997
20. Established by the Zia regime in 1980 to ensure enforcement of the new Islamic laws.
21. Her petition questioning the Islamic validity of the Hudood Ordinances filed at the Federal Shariat Court was decided in 1989, with the verdict that the specific Ordinances, including *zina*, were not repugnant to the injunctions of Islam (Begum Rashida Patel v Federation of Pakistan PLD 1989 FSC 95). Other feminists, including members of WAF, are of the opinion that the petition should have been filed in the regular courts, which would have allowed the matter to be pursued on appeal to the Supreme Court.
22. *Herald* (Karachi), January 1992
23. ibid
24. Speech at Karachi meeting of the Alliance Against Discriminatory Laws, June 1997
25. Pakistan ratified the Convention in 1996 but has so far not proposed any new legislation to change its own discriminatory laws.
26. Riffat Hassan, a Pakistani feminist theologian, addressed the ICPD NGO Forum to present a progressive and Muslim perspective on reproductive rights issues.
27. *Pakistan: No progress on women's rights*, op cit [note 1]
28. Pakistan ratified the Women's Convention with the reservation that it would implement its articles only insofar as they did not contradict the Constitution of

Pakistan. Since the Constitution also stipulates that all laws in Pakistan must be in accordance with the injunctions of Islam, this reservation can be used as a loophole by the government to avoid addressing discriminatory legislation.
29. 'Report of the Commission of Inquiry for Women', op cit [note 14]
30. Article by Saba Khattack, Sustainable Development Policy Institute, published in *Dawn*, 4 August 1998, cited in *Pakistan: No progress on women's rights*, op cit [note 1]
31. 'Maternal Death Rate Too High, Panel Says', *Dawn*, Karachi, 8 December 1999, UN Wire Service, 10 December 1999
32. ibid

Democracy in the Nation, but not at Home

1. 'Amor, Sexo y Matrimonio en Chile Tradicional', Cavieras and Salinas, p122
2. In January 1997, Congressional deputies agreed to discuss the possibility of legalising divorce.
3. *Violencia Puertas Adentro: La Mujer Golpeada*, Soledad Larrian, Editorial Universitaria, Santiago, 1994
4. 'Violence Against Women: The Hidden Health Burden', Lori Heise, Jacqueline Pitanguy and Adrienne Germain, World Bank Discussion Papers, no 255, Washington DC, 1994, p4
5. 'World Development Report: Investing in Health', World Bank, Oxford University Press, New York, 1993
6. 'Modulo de Sensibilizacion en Violencia Intrafamiliar' SERNAM, Santiago, 1995, p26
7. *Ending Violence against Women*, L Heise, M Ellsberg and M Gottemoeller, Population Reports, Series L, no 11, Population Information Program, John Hopkins University School of Public Health, Baltimore, MD,

December 1999, citing A.R Morrison and M.B Orlando (ref 212)
8. 'Violence and Women: The Potential and Challenge of a Human Rights Perspective', Rhonda Copelon, p114, *The Right to Live Without Violence: Women's Proposals and Actions*, Women's Health Collection, no 1, LACWHN 1996
9. 'Violence Against Women: Global Organizing for Change', Lori Heise, *Future Interventions with Battered Women and their Families*, eds Jeffrey Edleson and Zvi Eisikovits, Sage Publications, 1996
10. 'Studying Domestic Violence: Perceptions of Women in Chiapas, Mexico', Namino Melissa Glantz and David C. Halperin, *Reproductive Health Matters*, no 7, May 1996, pp122–128
11. 'Gender-based Violence and Women's Reproductive Health', Lori Heise, *International Journal of Gynecology & Obstetrics*, no 46, 1994, p221
12. 'Domestic Violence Legislation in Chile and the United States', Katherine Culliton, unpublished manuscript, 1992, p26, citing Moltedo, 'Estudio sobre Violencia Domestica en Mujeres Pobladores en Chile', 1989
13. 'Gender-based Violence and Women's Reproductive Health', op cit [note 11], p224
14. *Women's Rights in Chile: A 'Shadow' Report*, May 1999 [submitted by Chilean NGOs to the UN Committee on the Elimination of All Forms of Discrimination Against Women]
15. 'Clandestine Abortion: A Latin American Reality', Alan Guttmacher Institute, New York. 1994, p23
16. 'Mujeres Procesadas por Aborto', Lidia Casas and Foro Abierto, Santiago, 1996, citing Guttmacher
17. Lidia Casas, unpublished manuscript, Santiago, 1996
18. ibid
19. *Violencia Puertas Adentro: La Mujer Golpeada*, op cit [note 3], p61

20. 'Gender-based Violence and Women's Reproductive Health', op cit [note 11], p225, citing J MacFarlane
21. 'Gender-based Violence and Women's Reproductive Health', op cit [note 11], p225, citing Campbell, etc
22. 'Gender-based Violence and Women's Reproductive Health', op cit [note 11], p225, citing Steward, etc
23. 'Violence Against Women: The Hidden Health Burden', op cit [note 4] p26
24. Interview with Soledad Larrian, *Women's Health Journal*, Santiago, nos 2–3, 1994, p112
25. Solange Bertrand and Ana María Harper, Santiago, unpublished thesis, 1993, p73
26. *Violencia Puertas Adentro: La Mujer Golpeada*, op cit [note 3]
27. *Violencia Puertas Adentro: La Mujer Golpeada*, op cit [note 3], p48
28. *Violencia Puertas Adentro: La Mujer Golpeada*, op cit [note 3], p49
29. *Violencia Puertas Adentro: La Mujer Golpeada*, op cit [note 3], p60
30. 'Casa de La Mujer de Valparaiso', cited in *La Nacion* (Santiago), 29 August 1996
31. *Violencia Puertas Adentro: La Mujer Golpeada*, op cit [note 3], p50
32. 'Domestic Violence Legislation in Chile and the United States', op cit [note 12], p26, citing Moltedo, 'Estudio sobre Violencia Domestica en Mujeres Pobladores en Chile', 1989
33. 'Sexual Coercion and Reproductive Health: A Focus on Research', L Heise, K Moore and N Toubia, Population Council, 1995, p22
34. 'Sexual Coercion and Reproductive Health: A Focus on Research', op cit [note 33], p22, 1994 citing Agger
35. 'Violaciones en el matrimonio', *Las Ultimas Noticias*, 16 October 1996, Santiago
36. 'Mitos y Creencias Comunes Acerca de la Violencia

Intrafamiliar', Ignacio Baloian, *Violencia Domestica: Apuntes para Capacitación. Version Preliminar*, Instituto de la Mujer de Santiago, 1994, pp12–16
37. Phone interview with Lori Heise, 19 September 1996
38. 'Estudio Descriptivo Casos de Violencia Intrafamiliar Atendidos en Programa Salud y Violencia Durante Enero-Julio de 1995', Katiuska Alveal, Cecilia Olivari, Lorena Sanhueza, manuscript, Hospital Clinico Regional de Concepcion, 1995
39. 'Nicaragua: Overcoming Machismo', *The Right to Live Without Violence: Women's Proposals and Actions*, Women's Health Collection, no 1, LACWHN, 1996, p92
40. Phone interview with Lori Heise, 19 September 1996
41. *Violencia Puertas Adentro: La Mujer Golpeada*, op cit [note 3], p52
42. ibid
43. 'Gender-based Violence and Women's Reproductive Health', op cit [note 11], p224
44. *Violencia Puertas Adentro: La Mujer Golpeada*, op cit [note 3], p62
45. *Violencia Puertas Adentro: La Mujer Golpeada*, op cit [note 3], p67
46. 'Aproximacion a una estrategia gubernmental en Violencia Intrafamiliar', Ximena Ahumada, SERNAM, 1991–1993, p15
47. Personal communication, Hernaldo Bustamente Villalobos, 26 August 1996
48. 'Estudio Seguimiento de la Ley de Violencia Intra-Familiar', Instituto de la Mujer de Santiago, enero a junio de 1995, August 1995
49. *Ending Violence Against Women*, op cit [note 7], p30

File under "Hurt"

1. 'Women in Development and Politics: The Changing Situation in Sri Lanka', Amita Shastri, *Journal of*

Developing Societies, vol 8, 1992
2. *Human Development Report*, UNDP, 1998
3. *The State of the World's Children*, Unicef, 1996
4. ibid
5. 'Sanctified Violence', Ameena Hussein-Uvais, *Options*, Women and Media Collective, Colombo, September 1995
6. 'Women and Domestic Violence: A Rural Survey', A.G Seelawathi, paper presented at an ICES (International Centre for Ethnic Studies) Seminar, Kandy, Sri Lanka, 1991
7. *Violence Against Women: Voices of Women and Activists*, Maithree Wickramasinghe, CENWOR (Centre for Research on Women) Study Series no. 12, Colombo, 1997
8. 'Violence against Women', OMCT, 11 August 1999, posted on Unifem's <end-violence@edc-cit.org>
9. 'An Investigation into the Incidence and Causes of Domestic Violence in Sri Lanka', Sonali Deraniyagala, Women in Need, Colombo, 1992.
10. 'Women and Violence: Some Field Observations', Malsiri Dias, paper presented at a CENWOR (Centre for Research on Women) convention in Colombo, 1989.
11. 'Women and Domestic Violence: A Rural Survey', op cit [note 6]
12. *Women's Rights Watch*, Women and Media Collective, Colombo, January–September 1998.
13. *Violence Against Women: Voices of Women and Activists*, op cit [note 7]
14. ibid
15. 'Sanctified Violence', op cit [note 5]
16. ibid
17. Dr Neelan Tiruchelvam, MP, quoted in Hansard, *Official report of a parliamentary debate – Penal Code (Amendment Bill)*, September 1995.
18. *Violence against Women: Voices of Women and Activists*, op cit [note 7]
19. 'The Influence of Social and Political Violence on the

Risk of Pregnancy Complications', B.C Zapata et al, *American Journal of Public Health*, vol 82, no 5, 1992, cited in *Violence Against Women: The Hidden Health Burden*, L Heise et al, World Bank Discussion Paper no 225, 1994
20. 'Women and Violence: Some Field Observations', op cit [note 10]
21. ibid
22. 'An Investigation into the Incidence and Causes of Domestic Violence in Sri Lanka', op cit [note 9]
23. 'Wife Battery Falls on Deaf Ears', *Options*, Women and Media Collective, Colombo, January 1996
24. *Violence against Women: Voices of Women and Activists*, op cit [note 7]
25. 'Abortion in Sri Lanka in the Context of Women's Human Rights', Sunila Abeyesekera, *Reproductive Health Matters*, London, May 1997
26. ibid
27. ibid
28. ibid
29. ibid
30. ibid
31. 'Profile', Radhika Coomaraswamy, *Options*, Women and Media Collective, Colombo, July 1996
32. *Violence Against Women: Voices of Women and Activists*, op cit [note 7]
33. Interview with Radhika Coomaraswamy, by Sunila Galapatti in *Law and Society Trust*, Colombo, Vol VII, No. 110, December 1996
34. ibid

Less than Human Treatment

1. When the Bough Breaks: Our Children, Our Environment, Lloyd Timberlake and Laura Thomas, Earthscan Publications Ltd, London, 1990, pp66–67

and 98–104
2. ILO Convention no 3: Maternity Protection, 1919; ILO Recommendation no 12: Maternity Protection (Agriculture), 1921; ILO Convention no 103: Maternity Protection (Revised), 1952; ILO Convention no 110 (part VII): Plantations, 1958
3. ILO Recommendation no 95: Maternity Protection, 1952
4. ILO Convention no 156: Workers with Family Responsibilities, 1981; ILO Recommendation no 165: Workers with Family Responsibilities, 1981
5. ILO Convention no 103, op cit [note 2]
6. Human Development Report, UNDP, Oxford University Press, Oxford, 1998
7. ILO Recommendation no 95, op cit [note 3]; see also ILO Convention no 3, op cit [note 2] and ILO Convention no 103, op cit [note 2]
8. In the ILO, the term 'tripartite' is used to describe equal participation and representation of governments, employers and workers' organizations. The ILO is a tripartite organisation: workers' and employers' representatives take part in its work with equal status to that of governments.
9. Quoted in 'Women's Health: Using Human Rights to Gain Reproductive Rights', Panos Briefing no 32, London, December 1998

'Business Orphans'

1. 'Strategies to Empower Women Workers in the Philippine Economic Zones', M Aganon, R del Rosario et al, research paper (unpublished), March 1997
2. 'Philippine Plan for Gender-Responsive Development 1995–2025', National Commission on the Role of Filipino Women, November 1995
3. *Women of a Lesser Cost: Female Labour, Foreign Exchange & Philippine Development,* S Chant and C McIlwaine, Pluto Press, London, 1995, p45

4. 'Family and Income Expenditure Survey', in *IBON Facts and Figures*, vol 19, no 17, 15 September 1996
5. 'Agrarian Digest', in *IBON Facts and Figures*, op cit [note 4]
6. *IBON Facts and Figures*, op cit [note 4]
7. 'Presidential Commission on Urban Poor', in *IBON Facts and Figures*, op cit [note 2]
8. *Women of a Lesser Cost*, op cit [note 3] p67
9. ILO Convention no 103 on Maternity Protection (revised), 1952
10. ILO Recommendation no 95 on Maternity Protection, 1952.
11. Republic Act (RA) 7322, 5 February 1992
12. *Conditions of work digest – maternity and work*, vol 13, International Labour Organization, Geneva, 1994
13. Republic Act (RA) 8187, 11 June 1996
14. *Women of a Lesser Cost*, op cit [note 3] p68
15. '2500 Cebu firms kept workers away from SSS', *Philippines Daily Inquirer*, 22 September 1996
16. *Women of a Lesser Cost*, op cit [note 3] p152
17. *Women of a Lesser Cost*, op cit [note 3] p149
18. *Women of a Lesser Cost*, op cit [note 3] p69
19. UN Wire, 7 February 2000
20. Lactational Amenorrhea Method (LAM) is the informed use of breast-feeding under certain conditions as a contraceptive method. LAM gives women at least 98 percent protection from pregnancy provided three criteria are met: [1] the mother fully or almost fully breastfeeds her child; [2] she has not begun to menstruate again since giving birth; and [3] the child is less than six months old.
21. 'Breastfeeding Trends and Breastfeeding Promotion Programme in the Philippines', Nancy Williamson, *Asia-Pacific Population Journal*, vol 5, no 1, March 1990
22. Marie Jansson, Nordic Work Group for International Breastfeeding Issues (NAFIA Sweden), personal

communication, 1999
23. 'Community-based Research and Advocacy on Reproductive Health among Urban Poor Women in Davao City', Rosena D Sanchez and Maribeth Juarez, Development of People's Foundation, Davao City, Philippines, 1994
24. 'Breastfeeding: The Best Investment', World Alliance for Breastfeeding Action, 1998; also personal communication, Dr Natividad Clavano, Baguio General Hospital, Baguio, Philippines.
25. Safe Motherhood Survey, Department of Health, 1993
26. Country Profiles (BFHI analysis paper), Nutrition Section, Unicef, February 1999
27. *Women of a Lesser Cost*, op cit [note 3] p135
28. ibid
29. 'Current Labor Statistics', Bureau of Labor and Employment Statistics, Department of Labor and Employment, Manila, July–August 1996.
30. *Philippine Plan for Gender-Responsive Development* 1995-2005, National Commission on the Role of Filipino Women, November 1995
31. *Women of a Lesser Cost*, op cit [note 3] p9
32. Health Action International Network (HAIN), Manila, 1991

No Mother's Day for Women Workers

1. For information on the Braceros Program and the 12-mile strip see 'Women in the Global Economy' website at http://www.utexas.edu/ftp/student/subtex/.web/Groups/crossborder/global.html
2. 'No Guarantees: Sex Discrimination in Mexico's Maquiladora Sector', Human Rights Watch Women's Rights Project Report, August 1996, vol 8, no 6, New York, p8. http://www.hrw.org.
3. 'For We Are Sold, I and My People: Women and

Industry in Mexico's Frontier', María Patricia Fernandez-Kelly, Albany, State University of New York, 1983, quoted in 'No Guarantees', op cit [note 2], p12
4. 'Women in the Maquiladoras: A History of Contrasts', Susana Vidales, in *Women at Risk: Revealing the Hidden Health Burden of Women Workers*, Women's Health Collection, no 2, Latin American and Caribbean Women's Health Network, 1997
5. 'No Guarantees', op cit [note 2], p.12
6. 'Mujeres: avancemos un trecho', Cecilia Soto, 1996, Información Selectiva. Email: csoto@rtn.uson.mx
7. 'No Guarantees', op cit [note 2]
8. 'A Job or Your Rights: Continued Sex Discrimination in Mexico's Maquiladora Sector', Human Rights Watch Report, December 1998, vol 10, no 1(B), website: http://www.hrw.org
9. 'No Guarantees', op cit [note 2], p27
10. 'A Job or Your Rights', op cit [note 8], p33
11. 'No Guarantees', op cit [note 2], p15
12. 'A Job or Your Rights', op cit [note 8], p52
13. 'No Guarantees', op cit [note 2] p49
14. ibid
15. 'Mujeres: avancemos un trecho', op cit.[note 6]
16. 'A Job or Your Rights', op cit [note 8], p48
17. 'No Guarantees', op cit [note 2], p29
18. 'No Guarantees', op cit [note 2], p26
19. ibid
20. 'No Guarantees', op cit [note 2], p36.
21. 'Women in the Maquiladoras', op cit [note 4]
22. 'The Health Consequences of Maquiladora Work: Women on the US-Mexico border', study by Sylvia Gundelman and Monica Jasis Silberg, *American Journal for Public Health* 1993, vol 83, cited in 'Women in the Maquiladoras', op cit [note 4]
23. 'No Laughter in NAFTA: Mexico and the United States Two Years After', Institute for Policy Studies,

Washington, DC, 1996
24. 'No Guarantees', op cit, [note 2], p18
25. 'Las repercusiones de la industria maquiladora de exportacion: El peso al nacer de hijos de obreras en Nogales', Catalina Denman, (master's thesis, undated), El Colegio de Sonara, cited in 'Women in the Maquiladoras', op cit [note 4]
26. 'A preliminary study of reproductive health outcomes of female maquiladora workers in Tijuana, Mexico', Brenda Eskenazi, Sylvia Gundelman and Monica Jasis Silberg, cited in 'Women in the Maquiladoras', op cit [note 4]
27. 'Women in the Maquiladoras', op cit [note 4]
28. ibid
29. 'Analizaran casos de anencefalia', *Cambio*, (Hermosillo, Sonora.) 8 April 1997, cited in 'Women in the Maquiladoras', op cit [note 4]
30. 'The Health Consequences Of Maquiladora Work: Women On The US–Mexico Border', Sylvia Gundelman and Monica Jasis Silberg, *American Journal for Public Health*, 1993, vol 83, no1, cited in 'Women in the Maquiladoras', op cit [note 4]
31. Press reports cited in 'Women in the Maquiladoras', op cit [note 4]
32. 'Tackling the Invisible: Scientific Indicators of the Health Hazards in Women's Work', Karen Messing, in *Women at Risk*, op cit [note 4]
33. 'Salud ocupacional de los trabajadores de maquila', Hector Balcazar, Catalina Denman and Francisco Lara, *The International Journal of Health Services*, 1995, vol 25, no 3, cited in 'Women in the Maquiladoras', op cit [note 4]
34. 'Women in the Maquiladoras', op cit [note 4]
35. ibid
36. ibid
37. 'The Northern Border of Mexico: Women, Health and Work in the Maquila', Reyna Elizabeth Montero, in *Women at Risk*, op cit [note 4]

38. 'Who is killing the women of Juarez?', Women CONNECT.com. http://www.womenconne...co/PoliticsDaily/pd_wedwatch_1.htm
39. 'Rape and Murder Stalk Women in Northern Mexico', Sam Dillon, *New York Times*, 18 April 1998
40. 'Grisly Murders Prompt Revolution in Women's Rights', Howard LaFranchi, *Christian Science Monitor*, 8 June 1999
41. 'No Guarantees', op cit [note 2], p39
42. 'No Guarantees', op cit [note 2], p36
43. 'No Guarantees', op cit [note 2], p29
44. 'The Northern Border of Mexico: Women, Health and Work in the Maquila', op cit [note 37]
45. 'The Factor 'X' In Organizing Women Workers: Casa De La Mujer – Women's Work in the Mexican Maquilas', Marleen van Ruyven, Report of the IRENE Roundtable workshop, May–June 1997
46. 'No Guarantees', op cit [note 2] p20
47. 'Women Working Worldwide', *Manifesto*, 1996, Manchester, UK
48. 'The Farthest Frontier', Martha Brant, *Newsweek*, 19 October 1998
49. 'Nicaragua: Women Maquila Workers Win "Code of Ethics"', Roberto Fonseca, *IPS*, 18 March 1998; and *Maquila Network Update*, March 1998, p6
50. 'The Northern Border of Mexico: Women, Health and Work in the Maquila', op cit [note 37]
51. 'Mexico: Mayor Tackles Discrimination of Pregnant Workers', UN Wire, 21 October 1999. http//:www.unfoundation.org/unwire/archives/UNWIRE991021.cfm
52. ibid
53. 'Mexico: UN Worried About Street Children, Domestic Violence', UN Wire, 20 December 1999

Contributors

Swati Bhattacharjee, a postgraduate in philosophy from Jadavpur University, chose journalism over academia. As sub-editor of the Women's Section of *The Telegraph*, a Calcutta-based English daily, she specialised in women's and adolescent health issues. In 1999, she joined *Ananda Bazar Patrika*, a Bengali daily, as a senior reporter. She has also written and published eight books of stories for children.

Suzanne Francis Brown is a Jamaican journalist, communicator and teacher at the Caribbean Institute of Media and Communication (CARIMAC), University of the West Indies. She was editor of *Media, Gender and Development: A resource book for Caribbean Journalists* (CARIMAC, 1995) and *Spitting in the Wind: Lessons in Empowerment from the Caribbean* (forthcoming from Commonwealth Foundation, 2000).

Guadalupe Hernandez Espinosa is a Mexican journalist whose professional career began in 1984. She specialises in economic, international and women's issues and has worked in television and periodicals journalism, for the Mexican government's news agency Notimex, and on the dailies *El Financiero*, *El Universal* and *El Economista*.

Dina Ezzat is a senior journalist with the Egyptian newspaper *Al Ahram*.

Lamis Hossain is a practising lawyer who studied law at the London School of Economics in the UK and Harvard Law School. She is also a freelance journalist who formerly established for the Dhaka *Daily Star* a fortnightly page dedicated to legal and human rights which she edited until 1995. She now lives in Atlanta, Georgia.

Contributors

Ayesha Khan is an independent researcher on issues relating to women and development in Pakistan. She has also worked as a freelance journalist for radio and the press, covering human rights, Afghan refugee, health and other issues. She is currently involved in a qualitative research programme to study the effect of violent conflict on women in Pakistan.

Patricia Made is a Zimbabwean-based journalist who has worked as a writer, editor and media trainer for more than 10 years. She is the Regional Director for Africa, and currently Interim Director General, of Inter Press Service global news and information agency. She has written and published articles on development and gender issues.

Judith Mirsky is founding director of the Panos Institute's Reproductive Health and Gender Programme and visiting research fellow at the London School of Hygiene and Tropical Medicine. Previously an author and editor for the Panos AIDS Programme, she has also worked for Save the Children (UK) and in India for an Oxfam/Indian government-supported NGO in Uttar Pradesh. Her background is in life sciences and social science research.

Dorothy Munyakho, a journalist by profession, is executive director and founder of the rural reporting news agency, Interlink Rural Information Services, and editor of the magazine *GendeReview*.

Juliana Omale is a journalist by training and a founding member of the African news service, African Women and Child Information Network.

Marty Radlett is co-director of the Panos Institute's Reproductive Health and Gender Programme. From 1986 to 1990 she worked with the Institute's AIDS Information Programme as a researcher and as editor of the news magazine *WorldAIDS*. She is also qualified as an existential psychotherapist, registered with the United Kingdom Counsel on Psychotherapy.

Raffat Binte Rashid is a feature writer for the Dhaka *Daily Star*.

Roselle Leah Rivera is a sociologist by training and a committed women's rights activist. She is a faculty member at the Women and Development Program of the College of Social Work and Community Development, University of the Philippines, Diliman.

Hilda Saeed is a founding member of the Pakistan women's NGO, Shirkat Gah, a freelance journalist and a member of the international network, Health, Empowerment, Rights and Accountability.

Rahal Saeed is from Pakistan, where she has worked in the fields of journalism, community development and women's rights. She recently lived in Sri Lanka where she worked with local non-government organisations, and researched the issue of violence against women. She currently lives in Washington, DC, and is pursuing graduate work in sociology.

Lezak Shallat has written extensively on women's health issues and was previously editor of *Women's Health Journal*, published by the Latin American and Caribbean Women's Health Network. Originally from California, she has lived in Central and South America for the past 20 years. She currently lives in Santiago, Chile.

The Panos Institute

The Panos Institute is an independent, non-profit information agency established in 1986 to work on information and communication for sustainable development.

Panos believes that diversity and pluralism in civil society underpin sustainable, people-centred development. It sees access to and freedom of information as leading to informed debate, which allows civil society to play a constructive role in public decision-making.

Panos works with the media, non-government and government agencies and academics to facilitate both North-South and South-South dialogue. Its aim is to stimulate debate by providing carefully researched, accessible, balanced information on neglected or poorly understood topics in fields including the environment, reproductive health and gender, HIV/AIDS and communications.

Panos commissions features, briefing papers, reports and radio programmes that are disseminated widely through both Northern and Southern media and are available on the Internet.

Panos has a decentralised structure, with offices in London, Paris and Washington DC, and in Africa, South Asia and Latin America. For more information visit http://www.panos.org.uk/

The Reproductive Health and Gender (RHG) Programme prepares briefings for media and policy-makers, commissions journalists to write for Panos Features – an international news service co-syndicated into several regional languages – and commissions media fellowships for publication in national media and in book form. Journalists are provided with a research briefing, funds to travel and editorial support. The programme runs workshops for media and policy-makers and is beginning to work with radio.

For information about RHG activities and publications contact Judith Mirsky (judym@panoslondon.org.uk) or Marty Radlett (martyr@panoslondon.org.uk).